LEGENDARY LOCALS

OF

HUNTINGTON

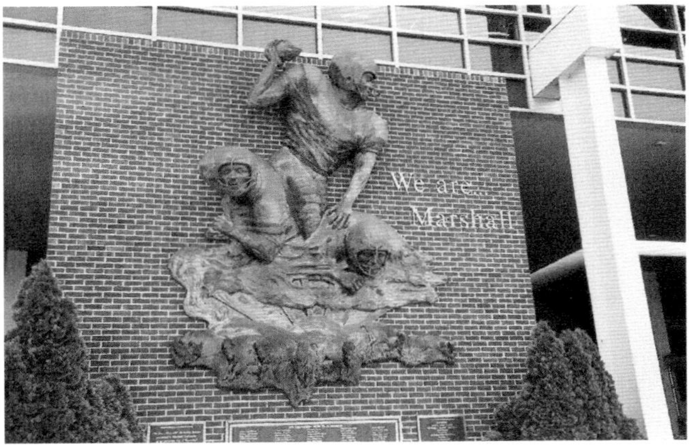

I0806115

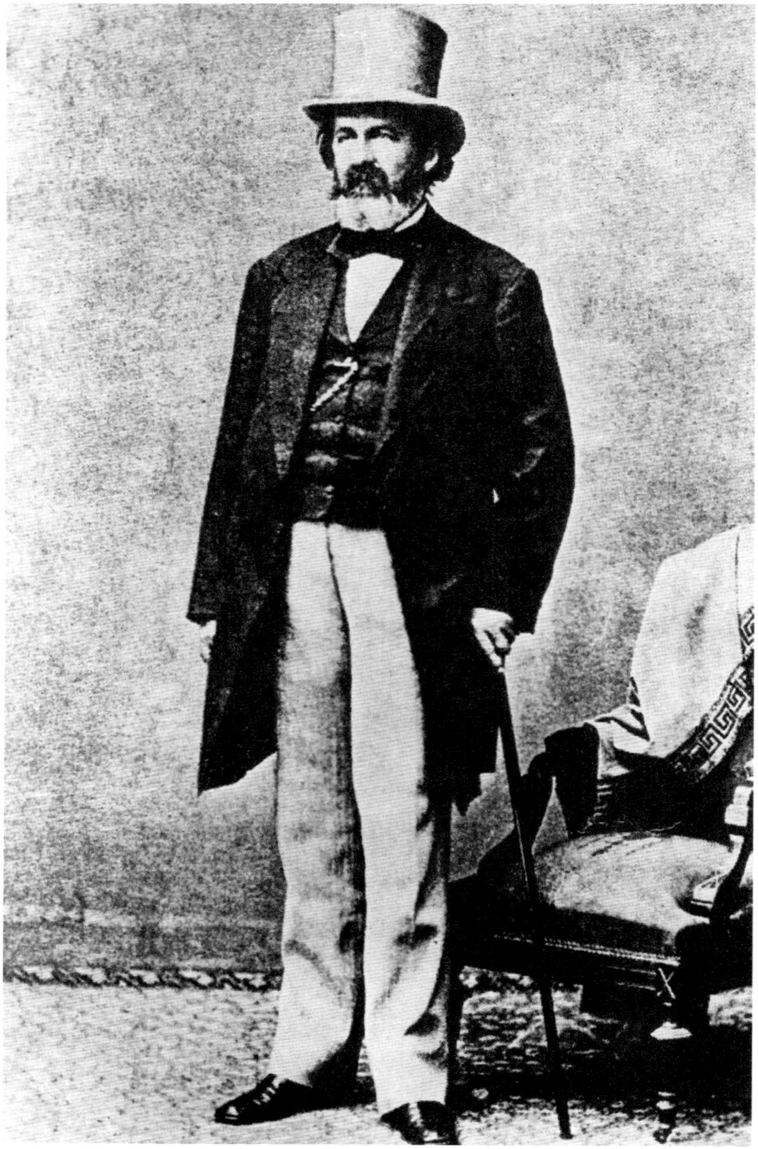

Page 1: See page 125 for information.

Page 2:
Huntington (1821–1900) never lived in Huntington, but without him the city would not exist. Born in Connecticut, he left school at age 14 and became a Yankee peddler. When gold was discovered in California in 1848, Huntington went west and became a rich man by selling supplies to miners. He and his partners built the Central Pacific Railroad, the western half of the long-dreamed-of transcontinental railroad. It was successfully linked with the rival Union Pacific Railroad by the driving of a golden spike at Promontory, Utah, on May 10, 1869. The same year, Huntington purchased the Chesapeake & Ohio Railway and set about extending its tracks across southern West Virginia to the Ohio River. There, in 1871, at a site just downstream from the mouth of the Guyandotte River, he established the city that bears his name. (*H-D.*)

LEGENDARY LOCALS

OF

HUNTINGTON

JAMES E. CASTO

LEGENDARY LOCALS

ISBN 978-1-4671-0033-5

Legendary Locals is an imprint of Arcadia Publishing
Charleston, South Carolina

Printed in the United States of America

Library of Congress Control Number: 2012938385

For all general information, please contact Arcadia Publishing:
Telephone 843-853-2070
Fax 843-853-0044
E-mail sales@arcadiapublishing.com
For customer service and orders:
Toll-Free 1-888-313-2665

Visit us on the Internet at www.arcadiapublishing.com

On the Cover: From left to right:
(TOP ROW) William C. Campbell, golfing great (*HQ*, page 72); Dagmar, early television star (*HQ*, page 100); John Hooe Russel, early banker (*H-D*, page 13); Catherine Bliss Enslow, columnist (*H-D*, page 55); and Rufus Switzer, mayor (*H-D*, page 18).

(MIDDLE ROW) Revella Hughes, musician (*H-D*, page 105); Collis P. Huntington, town founder (*H-D*, page 2); Herbert H. Henderson, African American leader (*H-D*, page 120); Soupy Sales, comedian (*H-D*, page 104); and Callie Barnett, African American icon (*H-D*, page 123).

(BOTTOM ROW) Brad Dourif, actor (*HQ*, page 108); Joan Edwards, philanthropist (*HQ*, page 125); Chuck Ripper, artist (*HQ*, page 101); Stella Fuller, settlement director (*H-D*, page 124); and John Gallagher, fire chief (*H-D*, page 30).

No book such as this one is the handiwork of just one person. My name may be on the book's cover and the title page, but *Local Legends of Huntington* would be nothing but a vague idea without the cooperation of a number of individuals who must be thanked.

Chief among those who so willingly came to my assistance are my former colleagues at the *Herald-Dispatch*. When I shared my plans for the book with editor and publisher Ed Dawson, he immediately endorsed the project and gave me a green light to rummage in the newspaper's archives for the photographs and information that I would require. "I'm sure Andrea can help you find what you need," he said, and online editor Andrea Copley did exactly that, smilingly responding to my many, many requests.

For more than 20 years, *Huntington Quarterly* magazine has helped chronicle our community's story, and there, too, I encountered quick agreement when I asked for help.

Editor Jack Houvouras immediately offered me a long list of photographs I might want to use, and art director Jenette Williams provided electronic versions of those I requested.

Thank you, Jack and Jenette.

Special Collections at the Marshall University Library is a treasure chest of vintage photographs, and curator Lisle Brown was quick to respond when I turned to him for help.

The photographs herein that are from the *Herald-Dispatch* are identified by the initials *H-D* at the end of their captions. Those from *Huntington Quarterly* are identified by the initials *HQ*. And those from Marshall are identified by the initials MU. Photographs kindly provided from other sources are individually credited.

If this book has any interest or value, it is because so many people were willing to help me with it. If there are mistakes in it, the fault is not theirs but solely mine.

It has been more than 140 years since rail tycoon Collis P. Huntington sent to Oneonta, New York, for Delos W. Emmons, his brother-in-law. Huntington wanted Emmons to accompany him on an exploratory trip westward across the then-new state of West Virginia. Their journey would take them along the route proposed for the tracks of the Chesapeake & Ohio Railway. Left all but bankrupt in the wake of the damages it had suffered during the Civil War, the C&O desperately needed capital to rebuild and expand. The railroad's board of directors turned to Huntington for help. He agreed to supply the money that was required and, in the process, installed himself as the C&O's president.

It was on this 1869 trip that Huntington first glimpsed an attractive tract of land along the Ohio River and envisioned the city that now carries his name. Huntington was seeking a convenient spot to transfer passengers and cargo between the C&O and the Ohio's riverboats. The site he selected was a stretch of farmland just downstream from the mouth of the Guyandotte River, not far upstream from where the Big Sandy River flows into the Ohio and the three states of West Virginia, Kentucky, and Ohio meet.

At Huntington's direction, Emmons purchased 21 farms totaling 5,000 acres and hired Rufus Cook, a Boston civil engineer, to design a town plan, one that featured a perfect geometric grid work of intersecting avenues and streets, each consecutively numbered so that any address would be easy to find. On February 27, 1871, the West Virginia Legislature approved an act incorporating the new city, named for its founder. On December 31 of that year, Peter Cline Buffington was elected Huntington's first mayor.

The community grew rapidly and had a population of more than 10,000 by the early 1890s. In 1887, after considerable controversy, the seat of Cabell County was moved from Barboursville to Huntington.

In selecting a site for his new city, Collis P. Huntington chose well. The community prospered as a gateway to the coalfields of southern West Virginia. Coal flowed from the mines to market via Huntington, and manufactured goods traveled the other direction, a two-way traffic that spawned thousands of jobs in the river city. In addition to its role as a transportation hub and a center of retail and wholesale trade, Huntington also attracted manufacturers who produced a broad array of products, including railcars, steel, glass, china, brick, stoves, furniture, and even church pews. The city of Huntington is known for its broad, tree-lined streets; for beautiful Ritter Park, fashioned in 1913 from land originally intended for use as a city incinerator; for the grand Keith-Albee Theater, which has welcomed moviegoers since 1928; for the imposing Cabell County Courthouse, dedicated in 1901; and for Heritage Village, with its historic buildings.

Huntington is home to Marshall University. Older than the city itself, Marshall was established in a log church at its present location in 1837. Marshall has grown steadily over the years, especially since it became a university in 1961. Today, it boasts more than 16,000 undergraduate and graduate students enrolled in a broad range of academic programs. Marshall's athletic teams are a source of community-wide pride. And its Joan C. Edwards School of Medicine, which admitted its first class in 1978, has helped make the city a regional health-care center.

Flooding was a serious problem in Huntington for many years. Serious floods occurred in 1884 and 1913, but the worst occurred on January 28, 1937, when the river inundated much of the city. The river crested at a record 69.45 feet, more than 19 feet above flood stage. Following the disaster, the US Army Corps of Engineers constructed an 11-mile flood wall to protect the city from future floods. Unfortunately, the flood wall also meant the Ohio was now hidden from view, prompting the city to forget its historic ties with the river. That was corrected in 1984, with the opening of the David W. Harris Riverfront Park.

Over the years, Huntington continued to grow and prosper. That prosperity came to an abrupt end, however, in October 1929, when the stock market crashed. Headlined the *Herald-Dispatch*: "Two Billions

Lost In Wall Street." Hundreds of people in Huntington soon found themselves without jobs as factories closed and businesses failed. Of the 11 banks operating in Huntington during the 1920s, only two survived as the Great Depression deepened. It took the outbreak of World War II to put Huntington, like the rest of America, back to work. The city's factories shifted to war production and worked 24 hours a day, seven days a week. With so many men away in uniform, female workers made their way onto the factory floors for the first time.

With the war's end, the 1950s proved a decade of remarkable growth and achievement for Huntington—the city's zenith some would argue. The decade saw the construction of Tri-State Airport, the Huntington Museum of Art, Cabell Huntington Hospital, and Veterans Memorial Field House. Sadly, in the decades following, Huntington saw many factories close, businesses slump, and jobs disappear. Part of the decline stemmed from sweeping cutbacks in coal mine employment as automation took hold in the surrounding coalfields, and part was attributable to the same "rust belt" phenomenon experienced by so many of the nation's other cities. Some saw the decision to route Interstate 64 around Huntington as a tragic mistake, and the later building of the Huntington Mall outside the city limits was clearly a body blow to downtown business.

The city's economic woes were reflected in a dramatic population decline. Huntington lost nearly 35,000 residents from 1950 to 2000, leaving a population of 51,475. In the 2010 census, the city's population was 49,138, a 4.5 percent decline from 10 years before. Some residents simply moved to growing suburban areas outside the city, but many left the region, seeking better opportunities elsewhere.

The Huntington of the 1950s is gone and is not coming back. But it would be a serious error to argue that the city's best days are behind it. There is much that today's Huntington can be proud of and encouraged by: the dramatic growth of Marshall University, the city's rise as a major medical center, the new schools that have been built, and of course the construction of Pullman Square, the retail/restaurant/entertainment complex that is breathing welcome new life into the downtown.

In 1869, Collis P. Huntington stood on the banks of the Ohio, looked out over a tract of vacant river bottomland and envisioned a busy city, one teeming with stores, factories, schools, and homes. Today, the rail tycoon's dream is alive and well and eagerly facing the 21st century.

The Early Years

Collis P. Huntington was a dreamer; not a head-in-the-clouds type of dreamer, but one who always had both his big feet solidly planted on the ground. When Congress called for construction of a great transcontinental railroad, Huntington did not just dream about that historic project, he made sure his railroad, the Central Pacific, was awarded the contract to construct the western half of the line. On May 10, 1869, a golden spike was driven at Promontory, Utah, linking the Central Pacific and the Union Pacific, which had built the line's eastern half. With the continent spanned, Huntington immediately threw himself into another project: a new railroad connecting the Tidewater section of eastern Virginia with the Ohio River, thus speeding the journey of passengers and cargo. That dream brought Huntington, in 1869, to the banks of the Ohio River, where he envisioned an entirely new town, one teeming with business and industry. And from its founding, the new town grew and prospered because it attracted men like John Hooe Russel, W.H.H. Holswade, Adolph Broh, and others who shared Huntington's dream and worked diligently to make it a reality.

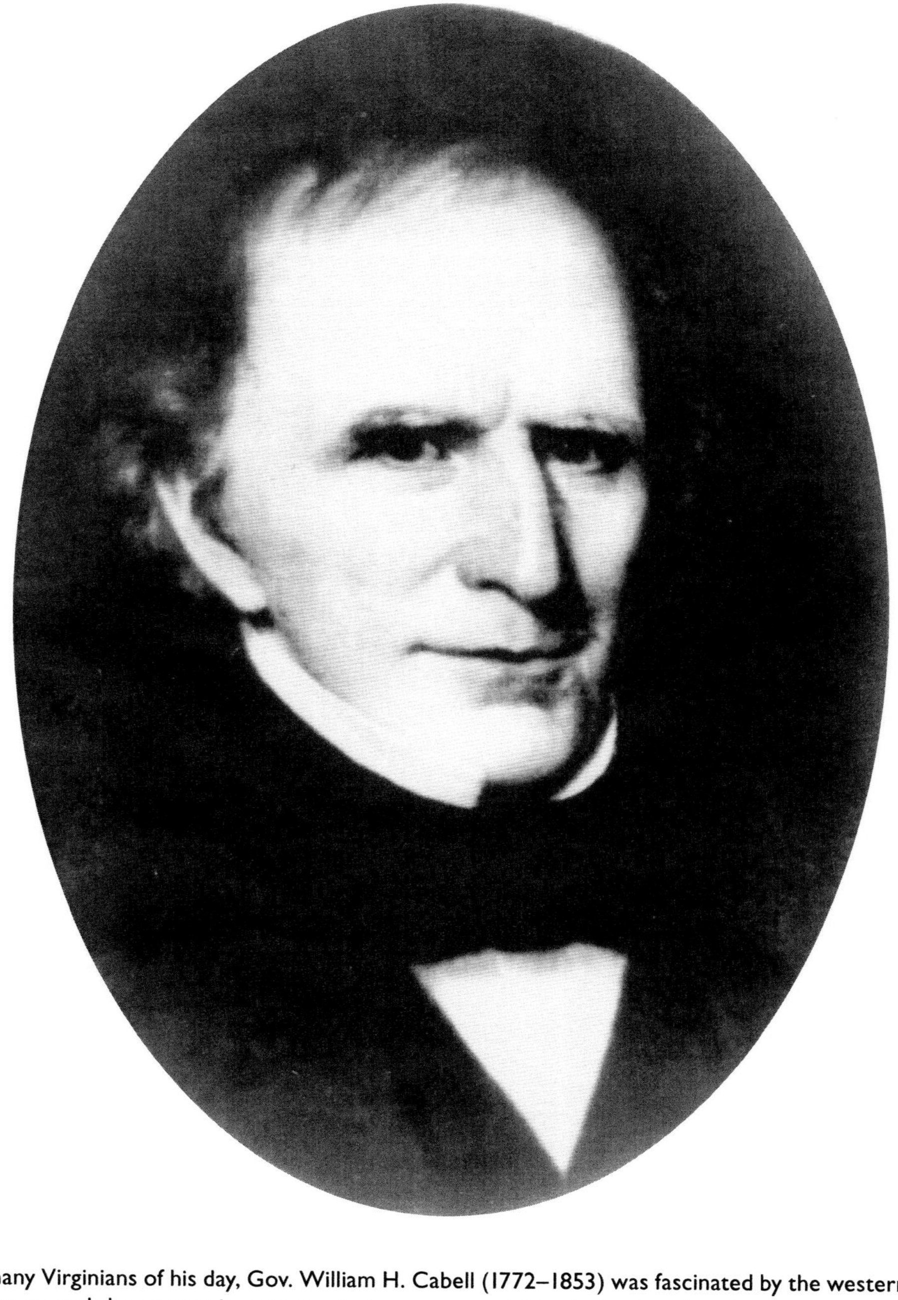

Like many Virginians of his day, Gov. William H. Cabell (1772–1853) was fascinated by the western part of the state and the economic opportunity it represented. No doubt that deep interest prompted him to attend a public auction at the Eagle Tavern in Richmond, where a promising tract of river bottom along the Ohio River was offered for sale. Cabell bid $13,000 and found himself the new owner of the 4,400-acre tract, located just up the Ohio River from the site of present-day Huntington. It was Cabell's friend Judge John Coalter who, after later buying the tract from Cabell, convinced Virginia lawmakers to create a new county and name it for Cabell. Whether Cabell ever had an opportunity to personally inspect the new county that carried his name is unknown, but it seems unlikely. (MU.)

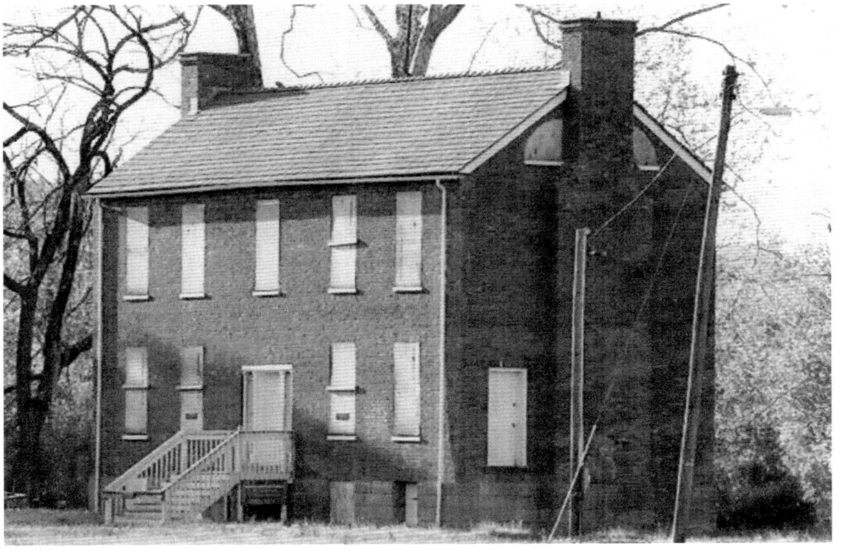

Built in 1835 by Capt. William Jenkins, father of Albert Gallatin Jenkins, this handsome brick home at Green Bottom is still standing, having survived wars, floods, wind, and weather. Constructed at least in part by slave labor, the house was a centerpiece of a 4,000-acre plantation. The tract is now owned by the US Army Corps of Engineers, which purchased it to replace wetlands lost by expansion of the nearby Robert C. Byrd Locks and Dam. Efforts to restore the house have stalled, and it faces an uncertain future. (*H-D.*)

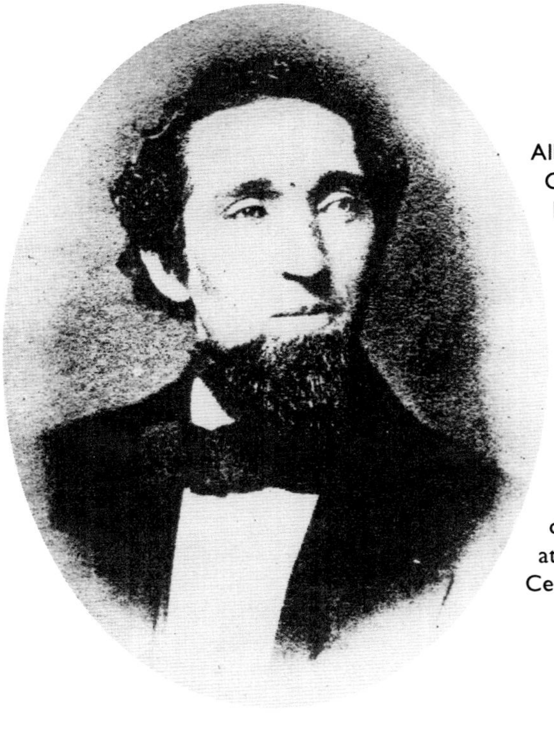

Albert Gallatin Jenkins (1830–1864) was born at Green Bottom, Cabell County, and educated at Marshall Academy (now Marshall University), Jefferson College, and Harvard Law School. He served in the US Congress from 1857 to 1861. When the Civil War came, he enlisted recruits for a Virginia unit called the Border Rangers and was elected its captain. Later, he formed the 8th Virginia Cavalry (CSA) and became its colonel. In early 1862, Jenkins was elected to the First Confederate Congress. Later that year, he was appointed brigadier general and went on to command a battalion of cavalry at the Battle of Gettysburg. He died of wounds he received at Cloyd's Mountain and is buried at Spring Hill Cemetery in Huntington. (MU.)

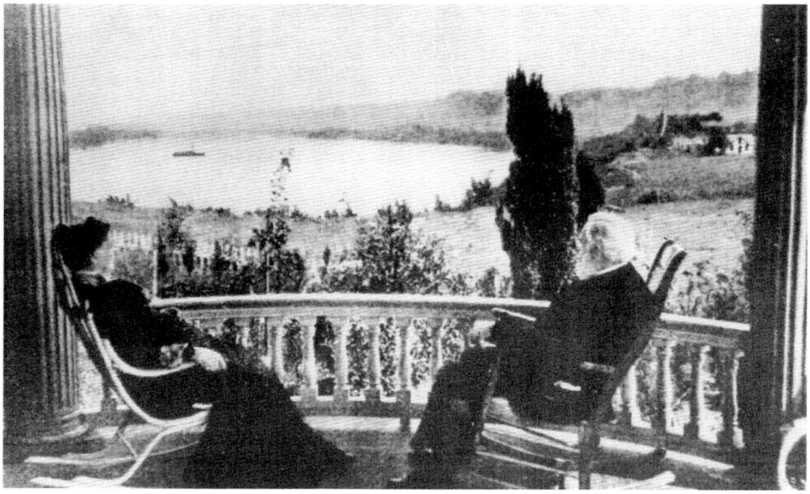

People sometimes are surprised to learn that town founder Collis P. Huntington never lived in his namesake city. The famed rail tycoon's business dealings required that he spend months at a time in California, New York, Washington, DC, and other far-flung cities. This meant he needed somebody he could leave in charge. He found that man in his brother-in-law Delos W. Emmons (1829–1905), who had married Huntington's sister Mary. The couple moved to Huntington, where Emmons oversaw the first sale of lots in the new town in 1871. This photograph shows them enjoying the river view from the porch of their Huntington home. The home was demolished in 2003. (MU.)

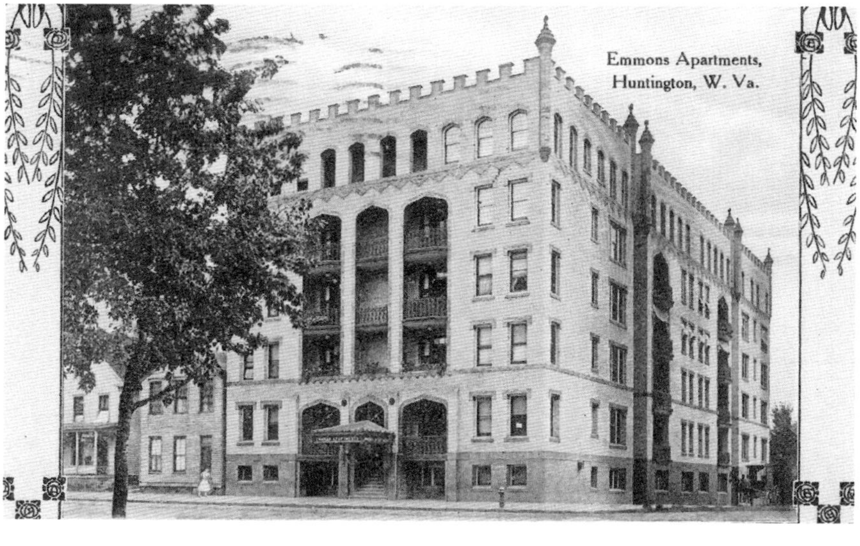

Three of Delos and Mary Emmons's children played an important role in Huntington's growth and development. Carlton D. Emmons was one of the founders of Emmons-Hawkins Hardware Company, for many years the largest wholesale hardware firm in West Virginia. J. Allen "Ollie" Emmons ran a furniture factory. Arthur S. Emmons became Huntington's first city clerk and built the Emmons Apartments in 1910. In 1924, a second apartment, the Emmons Jr., was built next door. Both buildings were demolished in 2007 after a tragic fire that claimed nine lives. (Author's.)

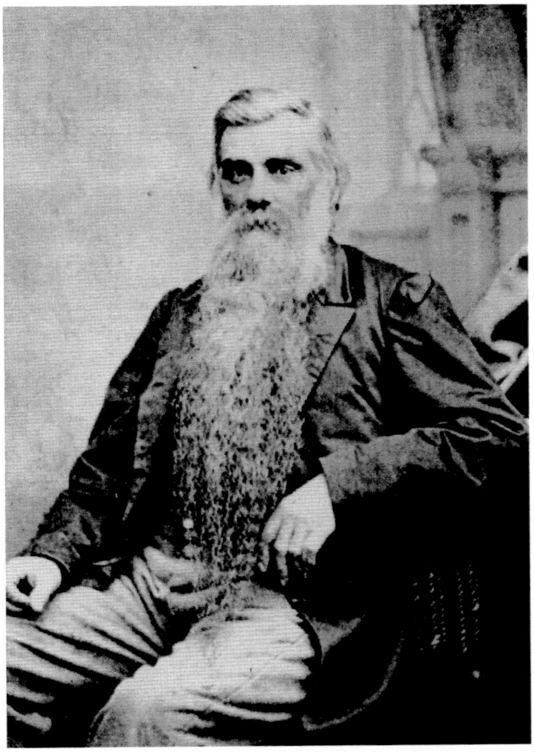

Peter Cline Buffington (1814–1875) was a surveyor, a merchant, a bridge builder, and a quartermaster in the Cabell County unit of the Virginia Militia. He represented Cabell County in the Virginia General Assembly, was the first trustee of Marshall College, and the first president of the Bank of Huntington. In 1871, when the first election was conducted in rail tycoon Huntington's new town, Buffington was elected its first mayor. He served in the post for two years and died the following year. (MU.)

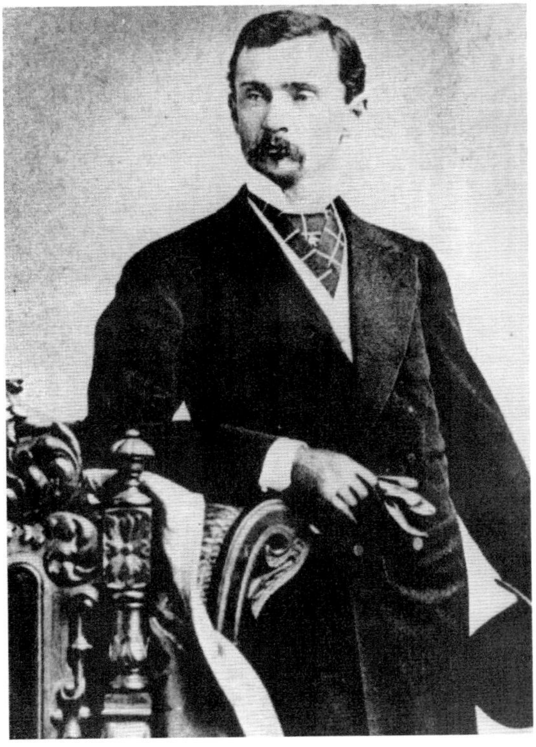

John Hooe Russel (1842–1903) was the cashier and later president of the city's first bank, the Bank of Huntington. Russel played a part in one of the new town's most exciting episodes. He was returning from lunch on September 7, 1875, when he saw four armed men (later rumored to be members of the Jesse James gang) exit the bank, moneybags in hand. Saddling his horse, he joined the posse chasing the culprits. The posse caught one robber, but the others got away. (*H-D.*)

William Henry Harrison Holswade (1845–1908) first worked as a postal clerk and then tried his hand at running a cigar stand and a bookstore before going into the furniture business. His store on the south side of Third Avenue between Ninth and Tenth Streets specialized in furniture made in its own shop. Holswade was a Mason, an Odd Fellow, president of the Huntington Chamber of Commerce, and a member of the school board. (MU.)

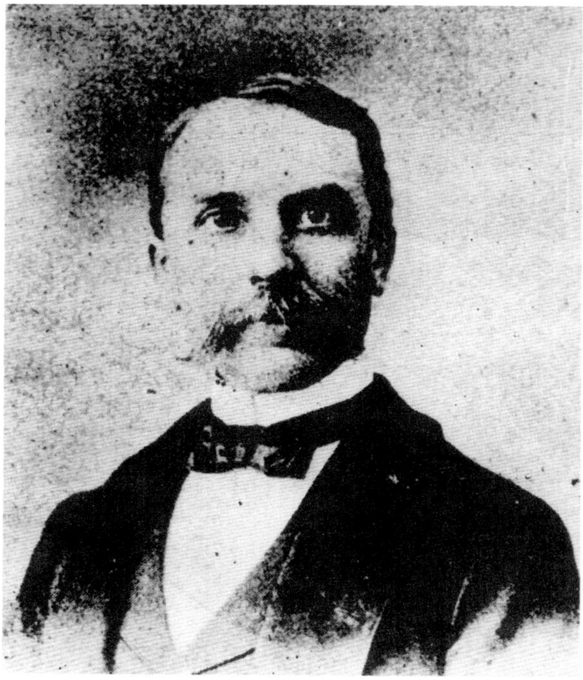

Like most furniture dealers of his era, Holswade also acted as an undertaker. In those days, it was not unusual to find coffins for sale side by side with rockers and kitchen tables. After Holswade's death, his son J.F. Holswade continued to operate the furniture store until 1915, when he sold the property to the S.S. Kresge Company, which opened a five-and-dime store, a revolutionary merchandising idea at the time. (*H-D.*)

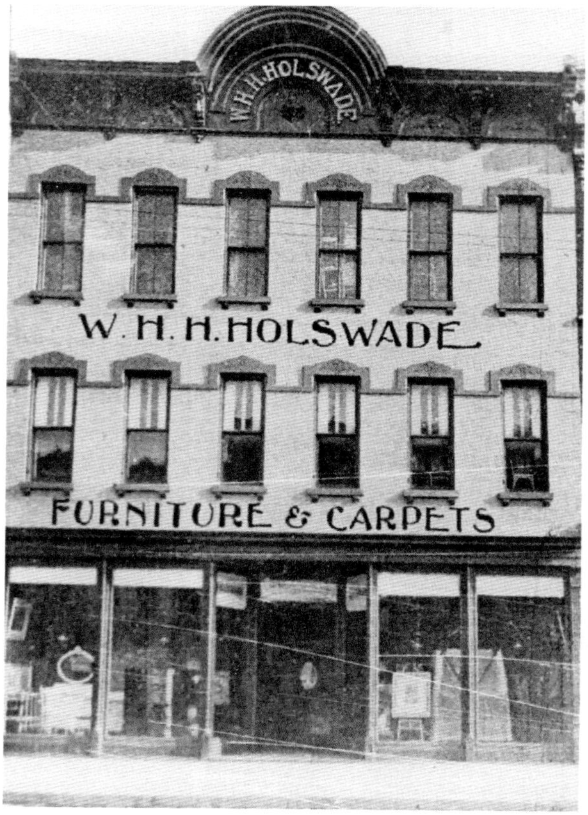

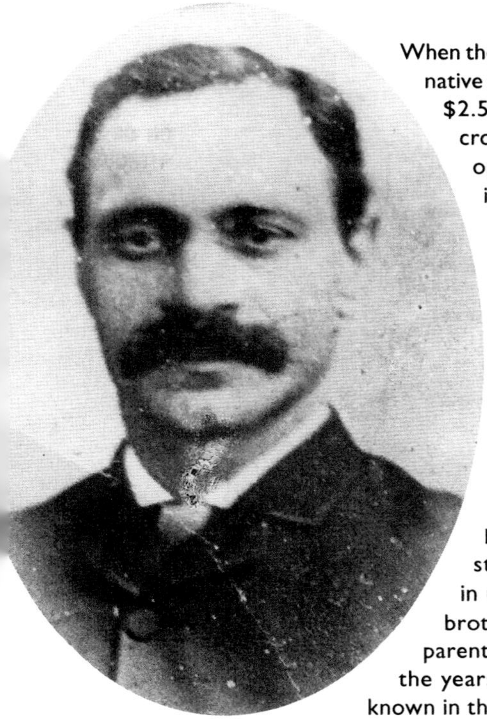

When the 17-year-old Broh (1840–1923) landed in New York from his native Germany, he was penniless. He had given all of his money—$2.50—to a sick passenger he befriended during the Atlantic crossing. A talented tailor, Broh quickly found work and later opened his own shop. When the Civil War came, he enlisted in the Confederate Army. Wounded at Shiloh, he moved to Cincinnati, where he met and married his wife, Henrietta. The couple would have 10 children. In 1887, the elder Broh dispatched two of his sons, Mike and Julius, to Huntington with instructions to open a men's clothing store. (*H-D.*)

In 1889, Adolph Broh built his sons Mike and Julius a building on the southeast corner of Third Avenue and Ninth Street, the first brick store building to be constructed in Huntington. Today, the building—one of several downtown structures recently restored by Dr. Joe Touma—remains in use, the oldest commercial building in the city. After the brothers became established in business, they brought their parents and several of their siblings to live in Huntington. Over the years, the Broh family name would become one of the best known in the community. (Author's.)

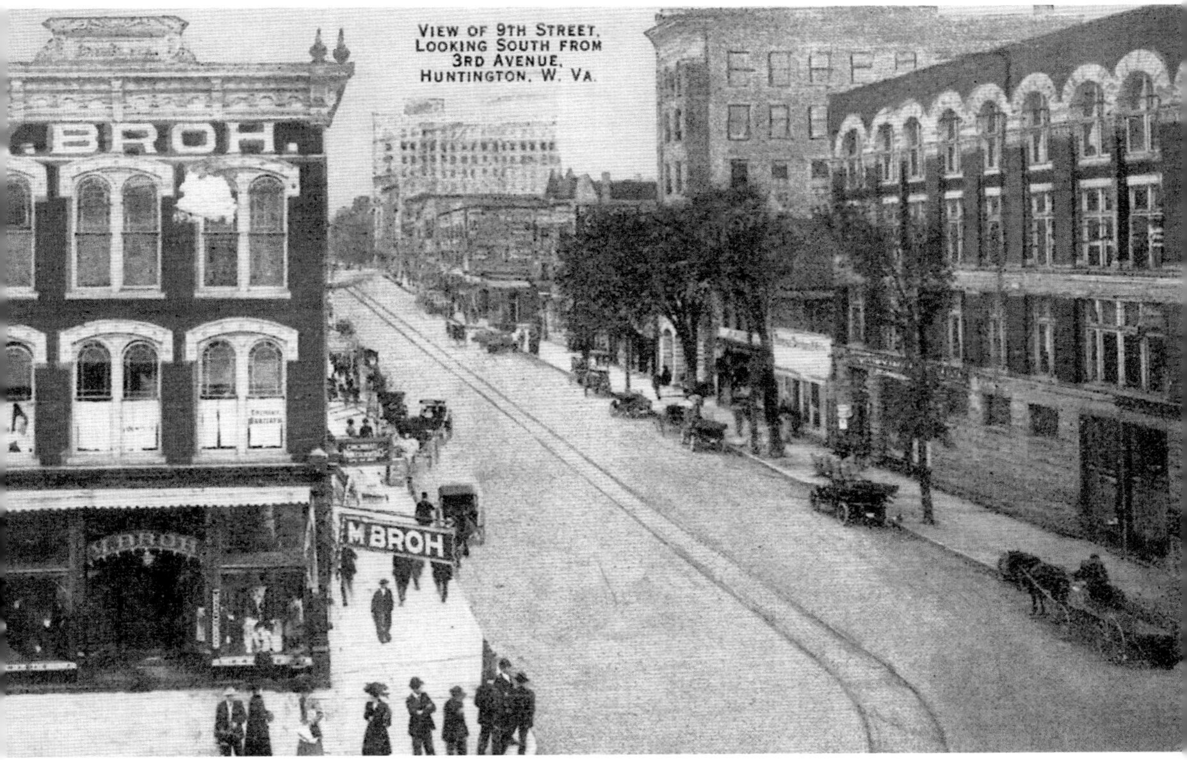

When young Darwin Eugene Abbott (1856–1942) was hired to help a family move from Vermont to Huntington, he decided to stay and cast his fortune with the new city. He attended Marshall Academy and then became interested in photography. He toured West Virginia, shooting images for *Harper's Magazine*. In 1880, he opened a successful photographic studio in Huntington on the 900 block of Fourth Avenue. (MU.)

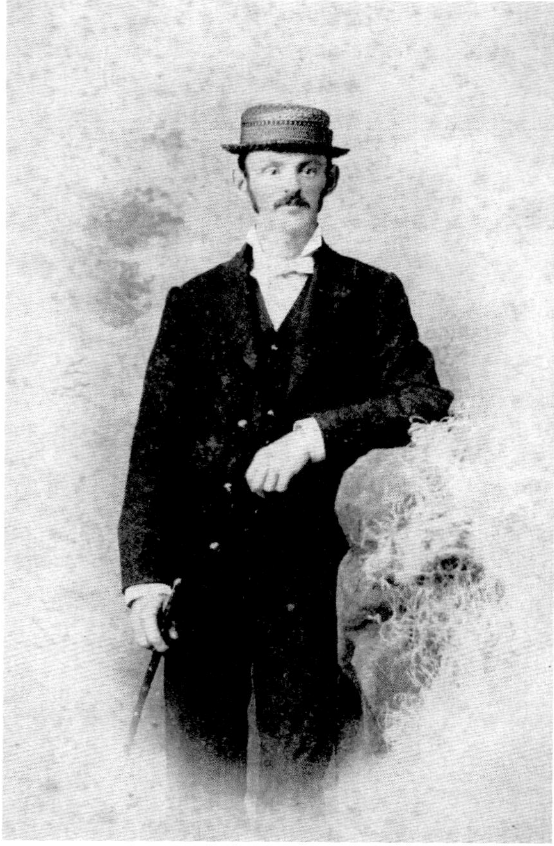

In 1898, Abbott purchased a glass plant at Washington Avenue and West Fourteenth Street. He incorporated D.E. Abbott & Company and added the manufacture of picture frames and moldings to his business. His firm proved to be one of the young city's most important manufacturing enterprises, eventually occupying five buildings. His salesmen traveled throughout 29 states, and his frames, known for their high quality, were sold throughout the United States and even exported to Europe. (MU.)

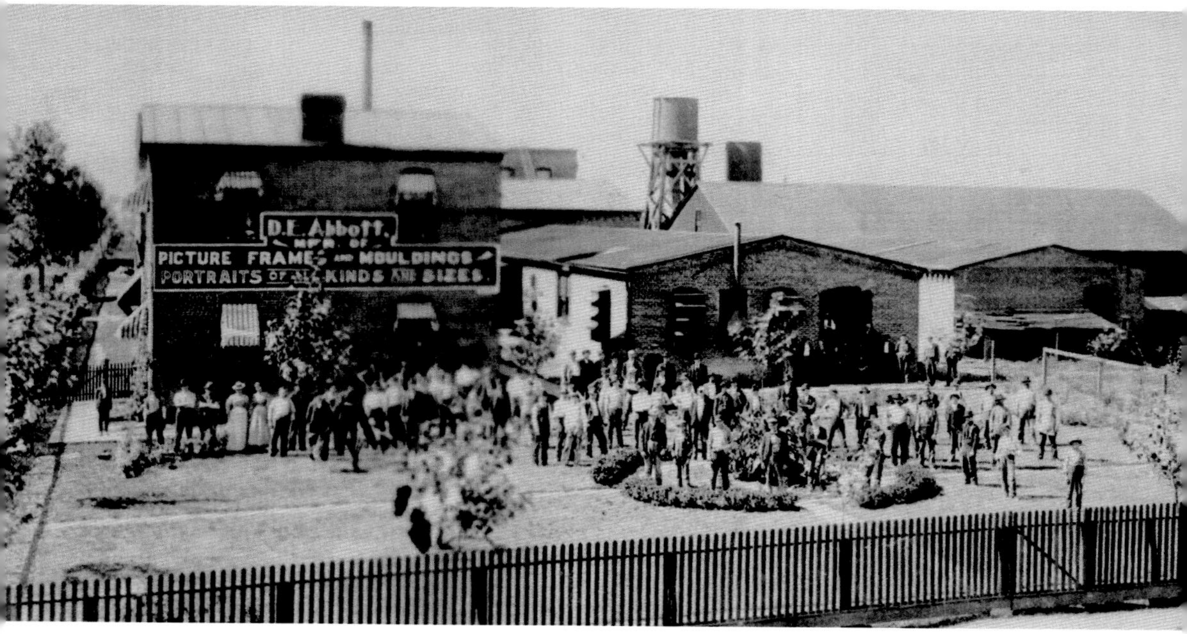

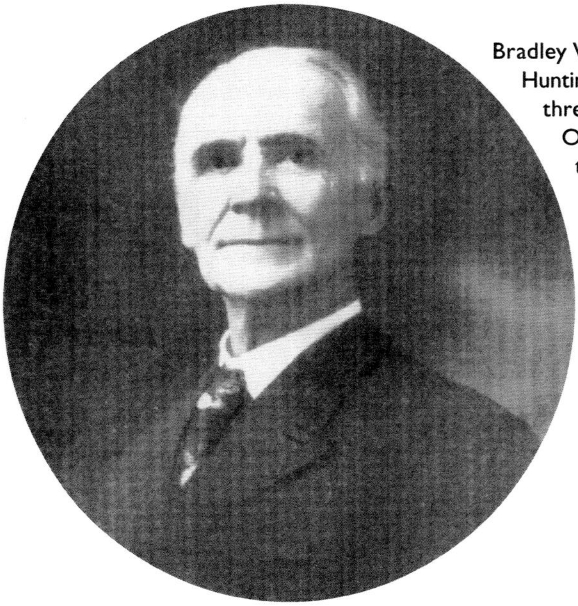

Bradley W. Foster (1834–1922) married Mary Lenora Huntington, a niece of Collis P. Huntington, in 1868 and three years later the couple moved to Huntington. On arriving, Foster built and opened one of the city's first hardware stores. The venture ultimately evolved into the Foster-Thornburg Hardware Company, a major wholesale firm. He was president of the Huntington Land Company, one of the founders of the First National Bank, a member of Huntington City Council, and one of the organizers of what today is the Huntington Regional Chamber of Commerce. (MU.)

Foster and his wife, Mary, had no children. She died first, and on his death he left $800,000 to build, maintain, and operate a home for older unmarried women and widows. Over the years, the Foster Memorial Home for Aged Women, erected on Madison Avenue in West Huntington, sheltered thousands of local women. But times change. Beginning in the 1980s, the Foster Foundation's board began talking about the growing need for adequate housing for all seniors, not just women. The result was construction of the Woodlands, a sprawling retirement community on Fifth Street Road. (Author's.)

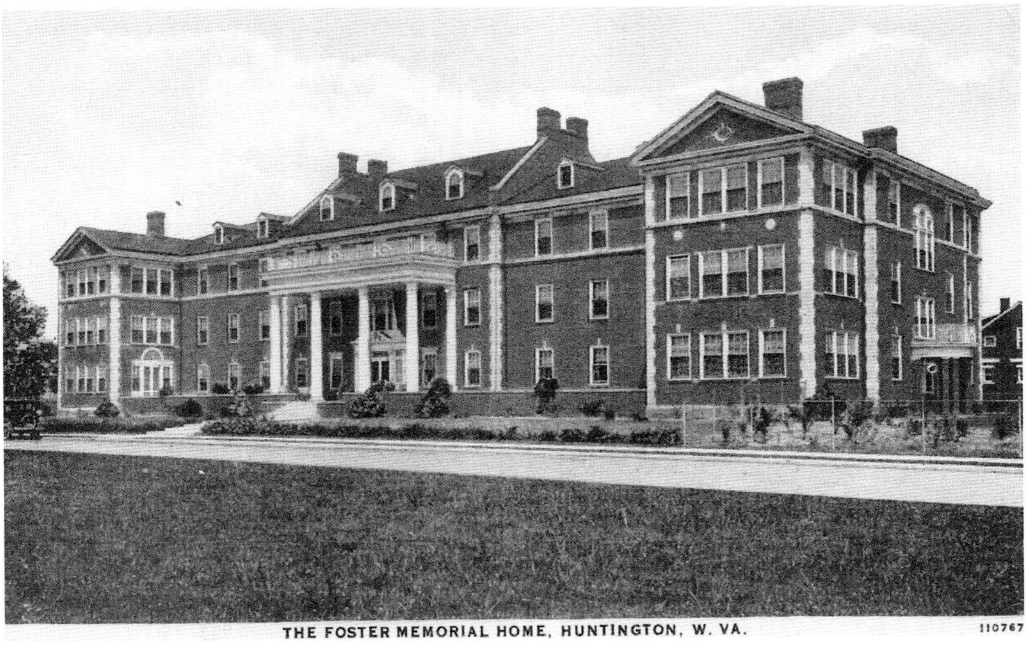

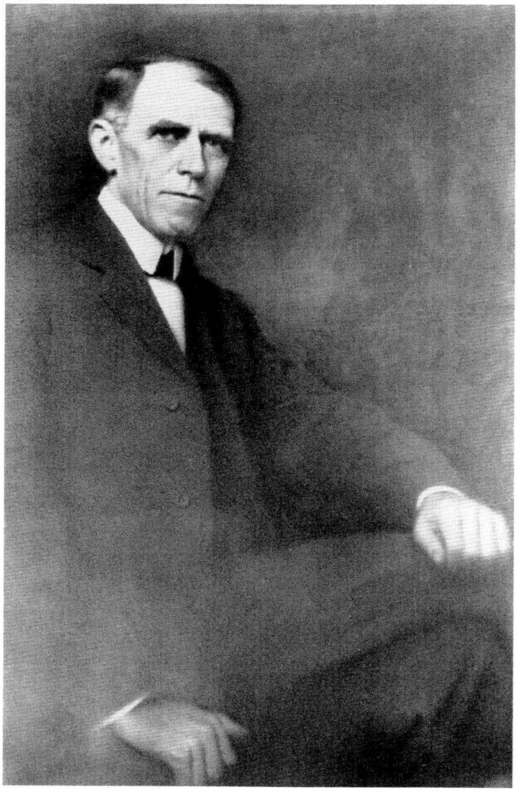

Huntington's plans for his new city made no provision for a public park. Several park proposals were offered in the city's early years, but none came to fruition until lawyer Rufus Switzer (1855–1947) was elected mayor in 1909. The city had purchased a tract along Four Pole Creek as the site for an incinerator. Not surprisingly, neighbors objected, and a donnybrook ensued. As mayor, Switzer settled the matter by declaring that the purchased property would become a park. Thus, one of the city's most popular landmarks, Ritter Park, was born. It was also under Mayor Switzer that Guyandotte and Central City were annexed into Huntington. (*H-D.*)

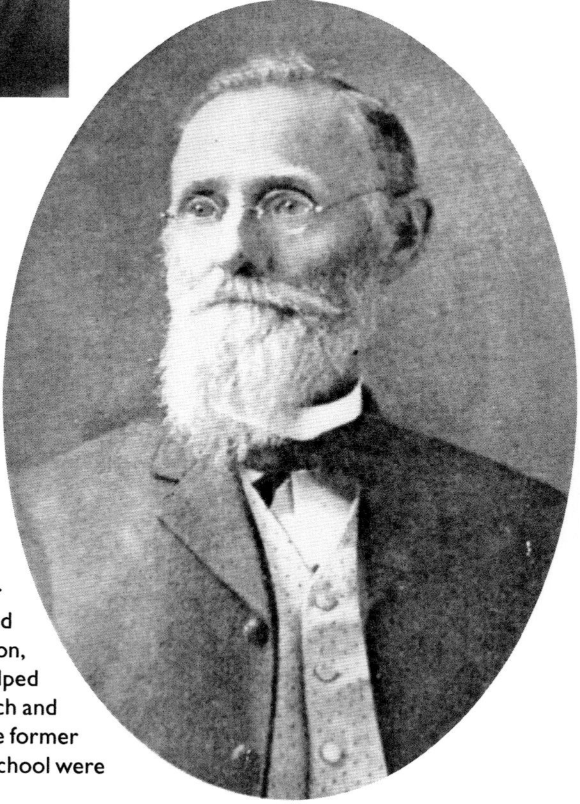

John Henry Cammack (1843–1920) was born on a farm near Dayton, Virginia. In 1859, his family moved to Harrison County, in what is now West Virginia. Entering the Confederate army at age 17, he returned to Harrison County and the family farm after the war. He later moved to Williamstown in Wood County, where he started a cigar factory. Urged by his doctor to give up cigars and find a healthier pursuit, he moved to Huntington, entering into the insurance business. He helped establish the city's Fifth Avenue Baptist Church and later the Twentieth Street Baptist Church. The former Cammack Elementary and Cammack Middle School were named in his honor. (MU.)

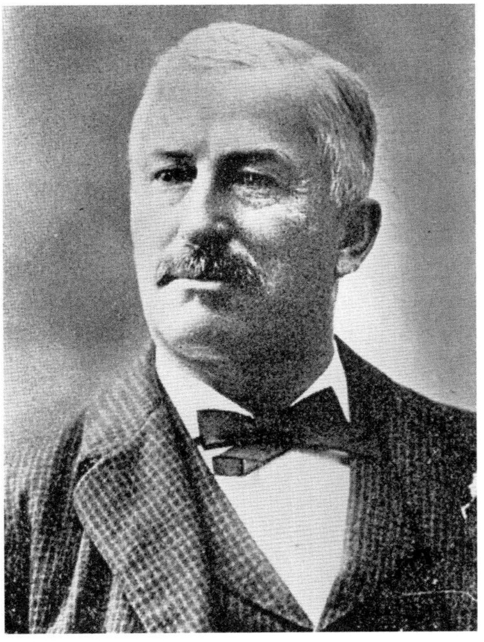

Connecticut businessman Ely Ensign (1850–1902) came to Huntington and established the Ensign Manufacturing Company in 1872. Initially, the company plant produced only railroad wheels, but in 1881 it began building wooden railcars and soon became one of the largest car-building facilities in the United States. In 1899, Ensign Manufacturing was one of 13 railcar companies that were consolidated into the American Car & Foundry Company (ACF). After the ACF consolidation, Ensign remained as general manager of the Huntington plant until his death. (MU.)

This Chesapeake & Ohio caboose, built in 1905, was typical of the wooden railcars constructed at Huntington's ACF plant in its earliest years. For decades, the plant on Third Avenue between Twenty-second and Twenty-fourth Streets was a bustling place, employing as many as 1,600 workers and producing railcars by the thousands. Today, the old plant still stands but ceased production years ago and seems to be waiting for the wreckers. (*H-D.*)

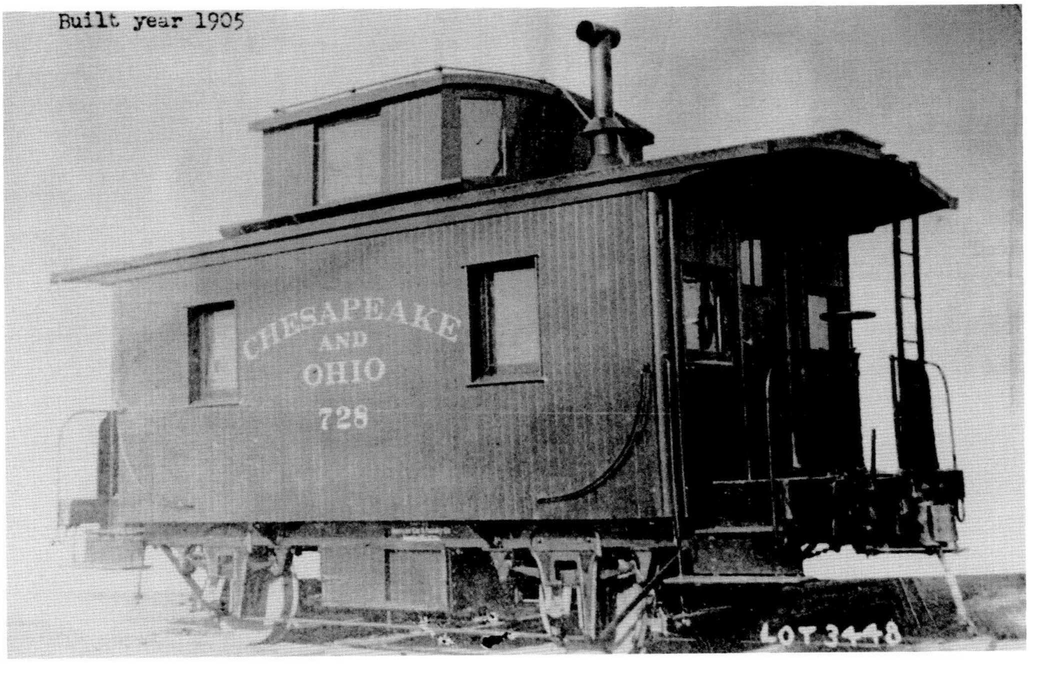

A Huntington lawyer who rose to become head of the Chesapeake & Ohio Railway, Herbert Fitzpatrick (1872–1962) is remembered today for the key role he played in establishing the Huntington Galleries (now the Huntington Museum of Art). A Virginia native, Fitzpatrick joined the C&O in 1895 as local counsel in Huntington. In 1923, he was made vice president and general counsel. He was the C&O Board chairman from 1937 to 1940. Fitzpatrick donated the land upon which the museum was built, along with his substantial collection of paintings, prints, English silver, and Islamic prayer rugs, which became the nucleus of the museum's collection. (Huntington Museum of Art.)

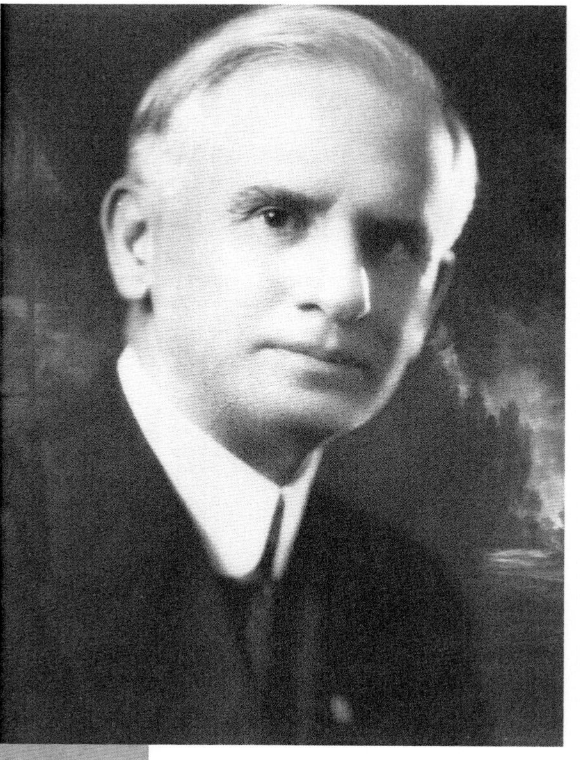

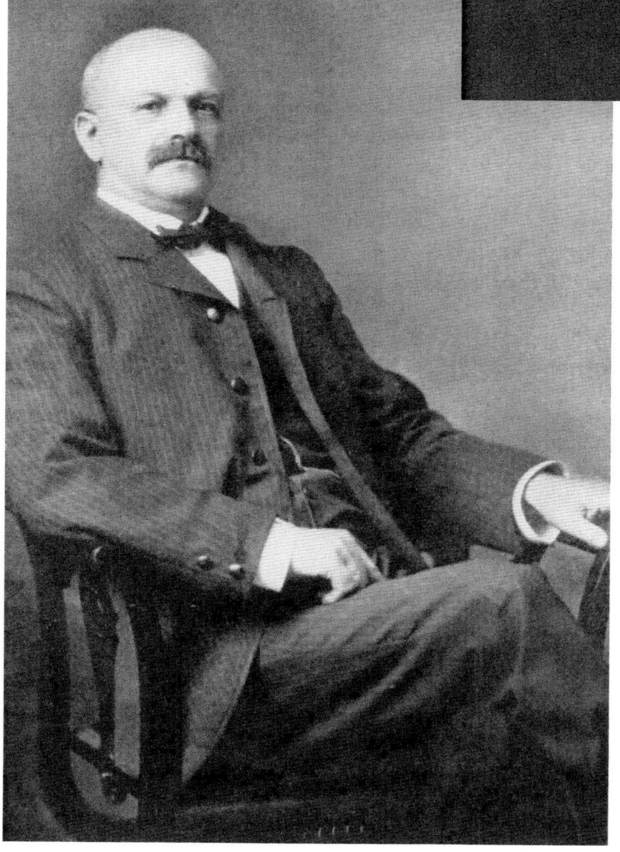

German-born Sam Gideon (1836–1923) was one of Huntington's earliest merchants and most prominent citizens. Immigrating to this country, he fought on the Union side in the Civil War. After the war, he settled in Cincinnati. He and his wife, Dora, arrived in the new city of Huntington in 1872 and opened a clothing store at 949 Third Avenue. The store was a busy part of the city's retail scene for more than 50 years. Meanwhile, Gideon also became active in politics, serving on the Huntington Board of Education for nearly 25 years and on the Cabell County Court. (*H-D.*)

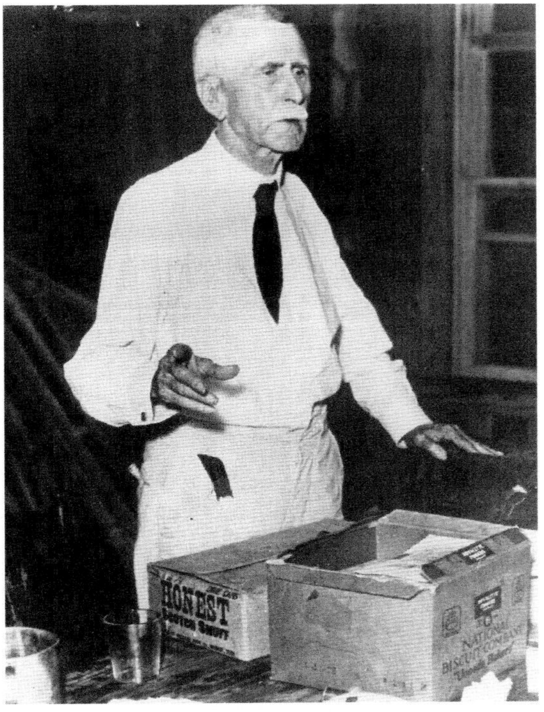

William Hope Harvey (1851–1936), better known as "Coin" Harvey, was a teacher, lawyer, silver miner, author, resort owner, and presidential candidate. Born in Putnam County, West Virginia, he read for the law and was admitted to the bar at age 19. In 1874, he briefly practiced law in Huntington. By the late 1880s, he was in Colorado, prospecting for silver. It was then he became an advocate for "free silver," a populist cause that called for the abandonment of the gold standard and a return to the free coinage of silver. When he began writing and publishing books on the subject, one of his books, *Coin's Financial School*, sold more than a million copies and earned Harvey his nickname. In 1900, he moved to Arkansas, where he built an elaborate resort and started construction of a huge pyramid to perpetuate his ideas. In 1932, the Liberty Party nominated him for president of the United States, and he received more than 50,000 votes. (*H-D.*)

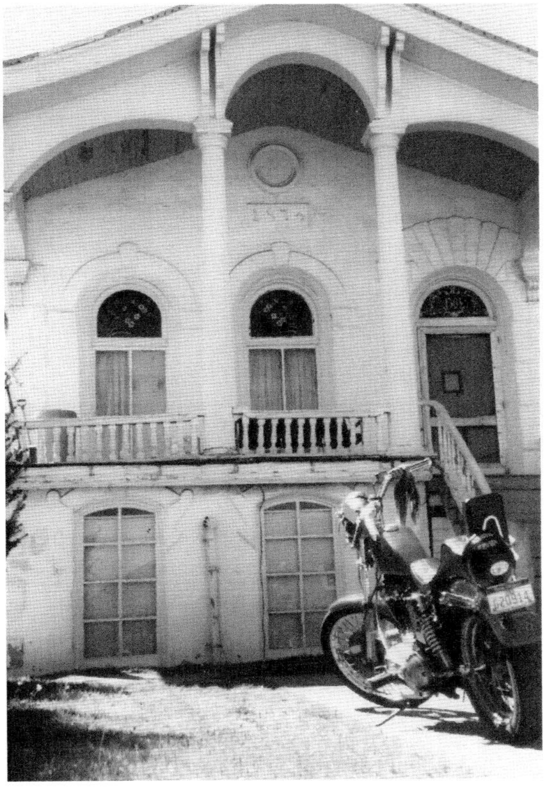

In 1874, seemingly intending to settle down in Huntington, Harvey built a handsome stucco house of his own design. He could not have lived in the house for more than a few months, as he left town the very next year. In the decades since, the house at 1305 Third Avenue has been used as a rental residence and a doctor's office and was even home to a motorcycle club. Still standing, it is now unoccupied and in disrepair. It is owned by a private foundation that would like to restore it but lacks the necessary funds. (Author's.)

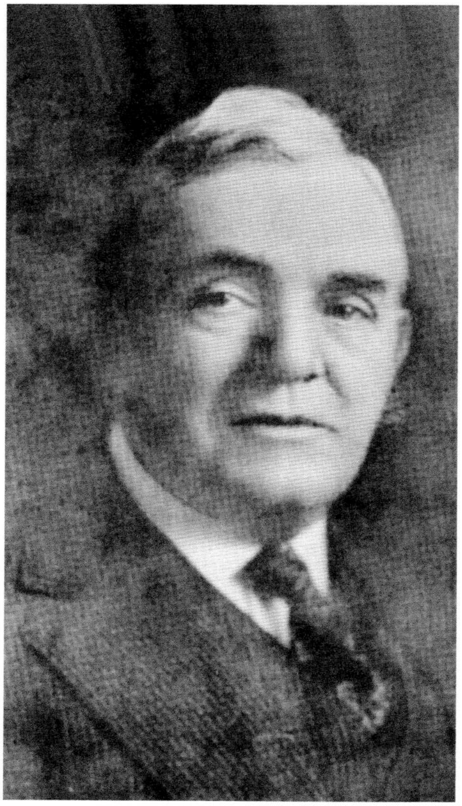

Zachary Taylor Vinson (1857–1929) was born in Wayne County, just outside Huntington, and educated at Bethany (West Virginia) College, the Law School of the University of Virginia, and Boston University Law School. He first practiced law at Ceredo in Wayne County before moving to Huntington, where he was a director and general counsel for the US Coal and Oil Company and attorney for the Ohio Valley Electric Railway Company. He was one of the founders of Huntington's Central Christian Church and taught a Sunday school class there. After his death, the class was named the Vinson Memorial Bible Class. (*H-D.*)

In early Huntington, the Chesapeake & Ohio Railway provided many jobs for the new town's African American workers. One such person was Dandridge Hill, seen here, who started out working as a porter for the C&O. After the loss of an eye in an accident, he traded jobs and opened a restaurant and grocery business on the 700 block of Ninth Street. That enterprise did not last long. In the early 1890s, he began operating the town's first taxicab. (*H-D.*)

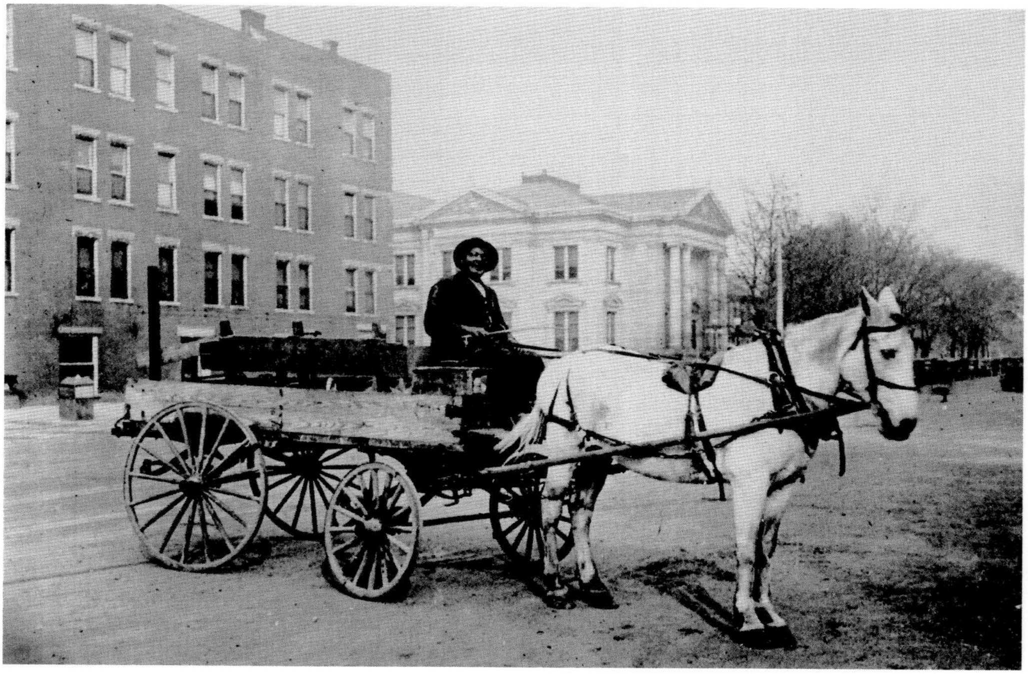

Politics and Public Service

Politics, it has been said, is the "art of the possible." Maybe that is true, maybe not. That is a question perhaps best left for debate in the political science classroom. But surely most people will agree that, labels like Democrat and Republican aside, the best breed of politicians are those who make good things possible for their constituents. Using that yardstick, Huntington and Cabell County have been blessed with many worthy political figures over the years, including two governors, Henry Hatfield and Cecil Underwood; the longest-serving speaker in the history of the West Virginia House of Delegates, Chuck Chambers; and a former congressman, Ken Hechler. The city has been well served by a number of capable mayors. It has been fortunate, too, to be served by such talented public servants as Cabell Circuit judges John W. Hereford and Dan O'Hanlon, urban renewal director David W. Harris, fire chief John Gallagher, and Tri-State Transit Authority general manager Vicki Shaffer. In their long careers of public service, they worked hard to make good things happen in Huntington, and their legacies continue to pay dividends to the community.

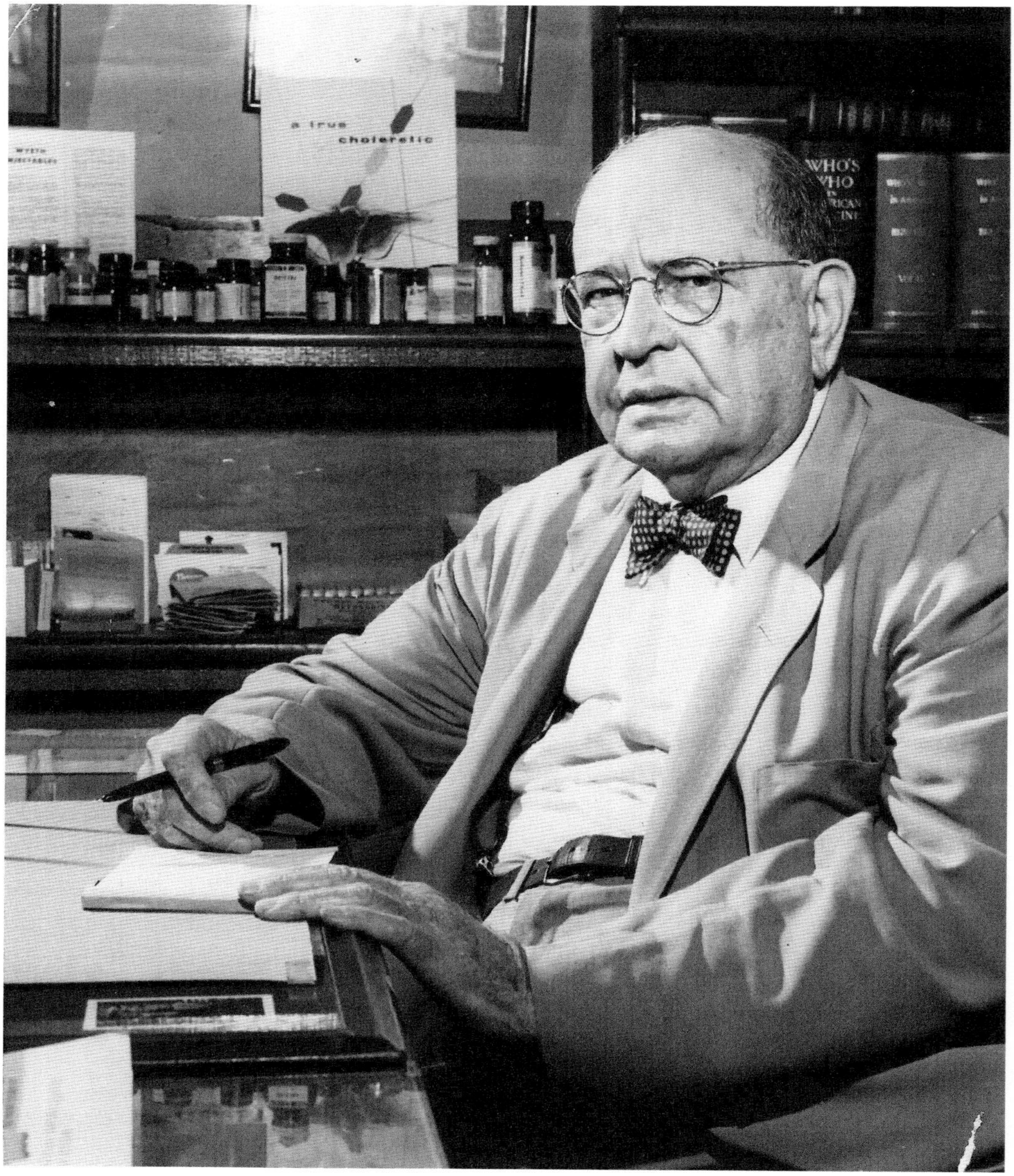

Henry D. Hatfield (1875–1962) was born on Mate Creek, near Matewan, West Virginia. A nephew of Anderson "Devil Anse" Hatfield of the famed Hatfield-McCoy feud, he earned a medical degree at the University of Louisville and returned to West Virginia as a coal-camp doctor in McDowell County. A Republican, he was elected to the McDowell County Court in 1906 and to the West Virginia Senate two years later. In 1912, Hatfield was elected governor. When he took office, the state was embroiled in a prolonged and violent coal strike, and as governor Hatfield was able to broker an uneasy truce between the striking miners and the coal operators. After his term, he practiced medicine in Huntington for the next 40 years, interrupted by a term (1928–1934) in the US Senate. During his time in the Senate, he was successful in securing a veterans hospital for Huntington. (H-D.)

As sheriff of Logan County, Don Chafin (1887–1954) was a hero to West Virginia's coal operators and a sworn enemy of the state's union miners. Born at Kermit in Logan County, he was educated at Marshall College and the Mountain State Business College in Parkersburg. He was a teacher and store clerk, then a store owner and mine operator, but he is best known as a politician and controversial lawman. In the 1921 Battle of Blair Mountain, he assembled a force of sheriff's deputies that blocked an armed band of marching miners until federal troops arrived and forced the miners to disperse. In 1924, Chafin was convicted on Prohibition charges. Released from prison, he moved to Huntington, bought the Guaranty Bank Building, renamed it the Chafin Building, and constructed himself a rooftop penthouse, where he lived out the remainder of his days. (*West Virginia Encyclopedia.*)

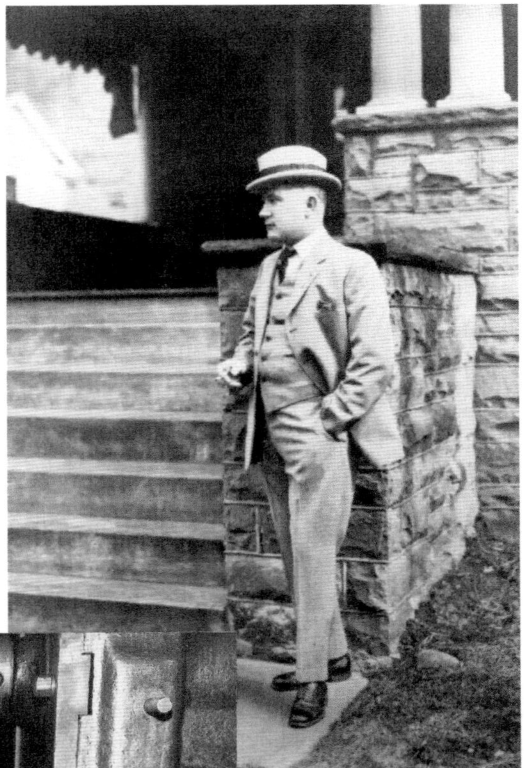

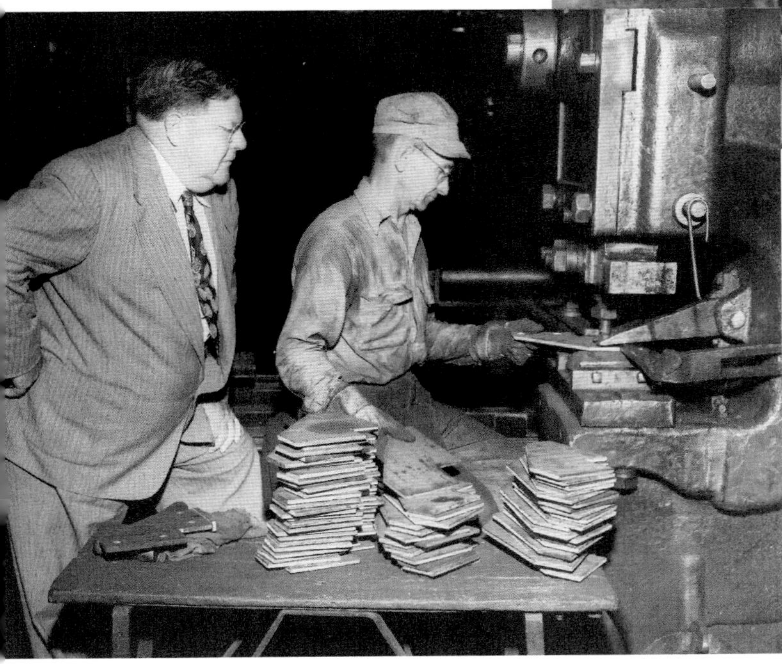

One of Huntington's most colorful mayors, Walter W. Payne (1880–1961) served from 1949 to 1952. The owner of a feed and supply store on West Fourteenth Street, Payne hated sitting behind his desk at city hall; he loved to get out of the office and move around town. Here, he is seen looking on as a machine operator punches out parts at Huntington's ACF Industries railcar plant. Payne, who always kept his fireman's coat and helmet handy, loved to don them and chase the fire trucks to the scene of a blaze. (*H-D.*)

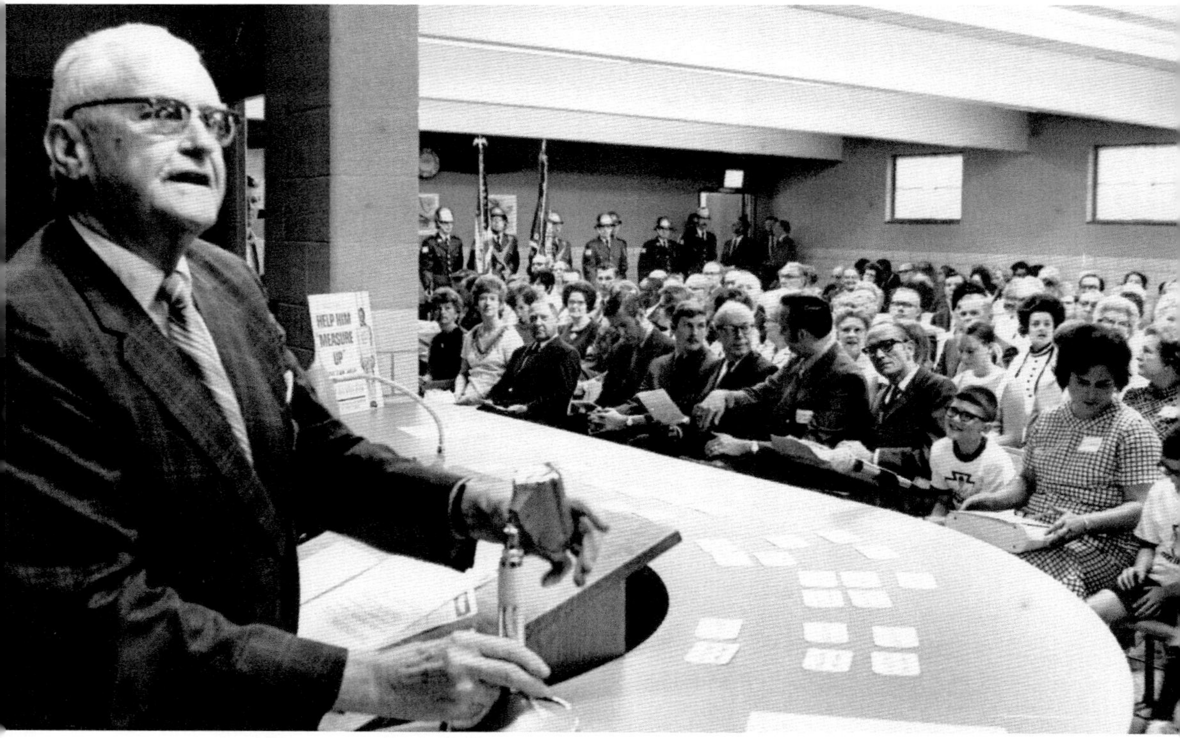
HELP HIM
'MEASURE
UP'

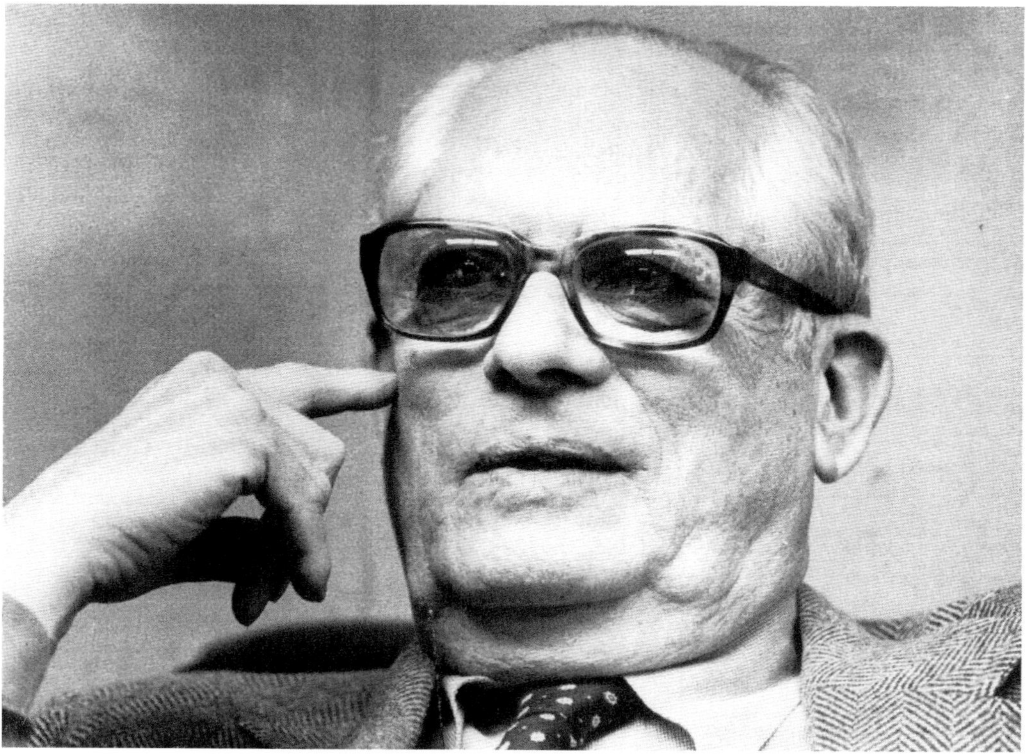

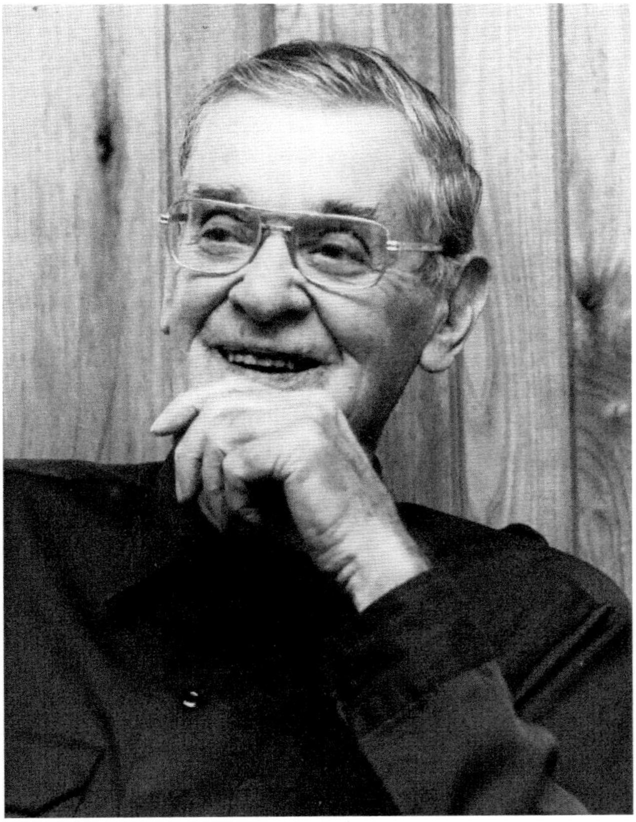

Wayne County political patriarch Milton J. Ferguson, who died in 1995 at age 92, was a skilled lawyer, a powerful politician, a knowledgeable historian, and, as his family and friends would gladly attest, a heck of a storyteller. Earning his law degree at West Virginia University in 1929, he served briefly in the legislature and began his career as a trial lawyer. After an unsuccessful bid for governor in 1956, he was appointed US attorney for the Southern District of West Virginia. At various times in his long career, he served as state tax commissioner, mayor of Wayne, and Wayne County prosecuting attorney. He served for 32 years on the Tri-State Airport Authority, which named its Milton J. Ferguson Field in his honor. (*H-D.*)

(OPPOSITE PAGE, TOP)
John W. Hereford (1897–1977) served as a circuit judge for Cabell County for nearly 28 years. Born on a farm in Mason County, West Virginia, he graduated from Louisa (Kentucky) High School before joining the Navy. After his discharge, he enrolled at West Virginia University, where he received his bachelor's degree in 1923 and his law degree in 1925. That same year, he came to Huntington, where he practiced law, serving as assistant prosecuting attorney and assistant US attorney. He became circuit judge in 1941 and served until 1968. Off the bench, he was founder and former president of the John W. Hereford Boys and Girls Club. He is shown here addressing a gathering at the club. (*H-D.*)

(OPPOSITE PAGE, BOTTOM)
Huntington's sweeping downtown urban renewal program of the 1960s had its foes and its fans. That made David W. Harris (1905–1994), director of the city's Urban Renewal Authority, either a villain or a visionary, depending on one's point of view. A Baltimore, Maryland, native, Harris came to Huntington in 1934 as the director of Depression-era federal relief and public works programs in 13 southern West Virginia counties. He worked in the defense industry during World War II and as a business consultant after the war. He became urban renewal director in 1961 and held the post for more than 20 years, retiring in 1983. Huntington's downtown riverfront park, an urban renewal project that is almost universally applauded, is named in his honor. (*H-D.*)

A leading figure in West Virginia politics for more than 50 years, Cecil Harland Underwood (1922–2008) had the distinction of having served as the state's youngest governor and its oldest. A native of Tyler County and a graduate of Salem College, he started out as a schoolteacher. Elected as a Republican member of the West Virginia House of Delegates in 1944, he became minority leader in 1949 and, at age 33, won election as governor in 1956. Barred from a second consecutive term by the state constitution (a prohibition later removed by state voters), Underwood in 1960 unsuccessfully ran for the US Senate, then accepted a position with Island Creek Coal Company in Huntington. He later worked for Monsanto Chemical and, from 1972 to 1975, served as president of Bethany College. He made two more unsuccessful bids for governor in 1964 and 1976 before winning the governor's race in 1996 and, at age 74, becoming the state's oldest governor. Losing a 2000 reelection bid, he returned to private life and community service. (*HQ.*)

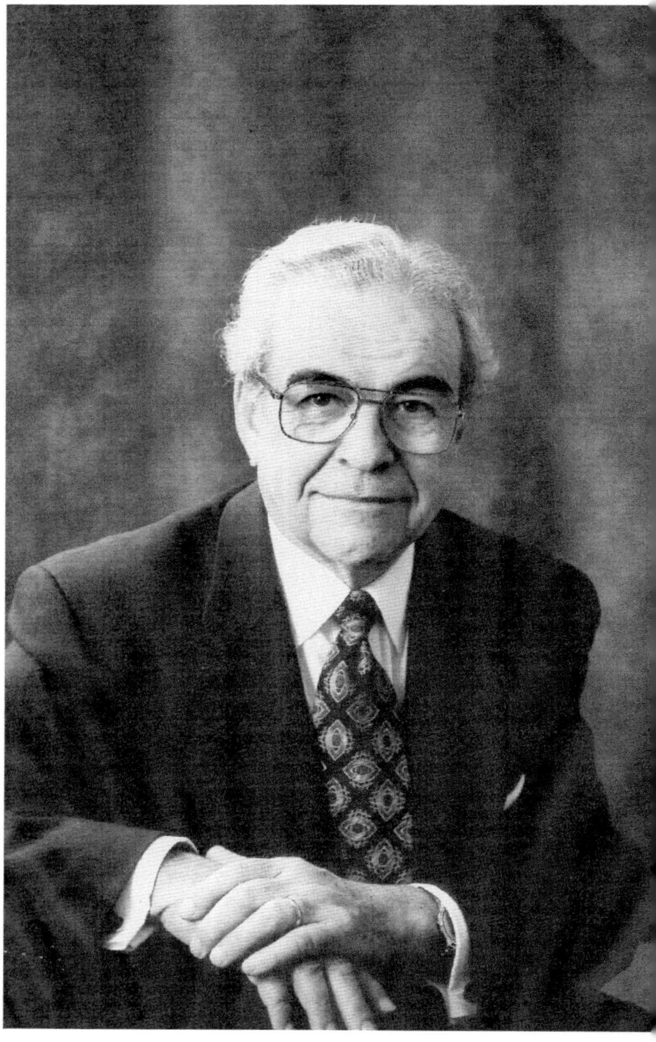

(OPPOSITE PAGE, BOTTOM)
David Ginsburg (1912–2010), valedictorian for the class of 1928 at Huntington High School, became a longtime Washington, DC, insider who led a presidential commission on the nation's race riots of the 1960s. Ginsburg was born in New York City. When the family's grocery on New York's East Side failed, the Ginsburgs started over in Huntington, where they had relatives. Ginsburg graduated from West Virginia University and then earned a law degree at Harvard. Over the years, he held various posts in the District of Columbia. During World War II, he helped draft laws on price controls and served as an adviser on reorganizing the German economy after the war. In 1967, after race riots engulfed a number of US cities, Pres. Lyndon Johnson appointed him director of the National Commission on Civil Disorders, known as the Kerner Commission after its chairman, Gov. Otto Kerner of Illinois. Ginsburg is shown on the left conferring with Johnson. (*H-D.*)

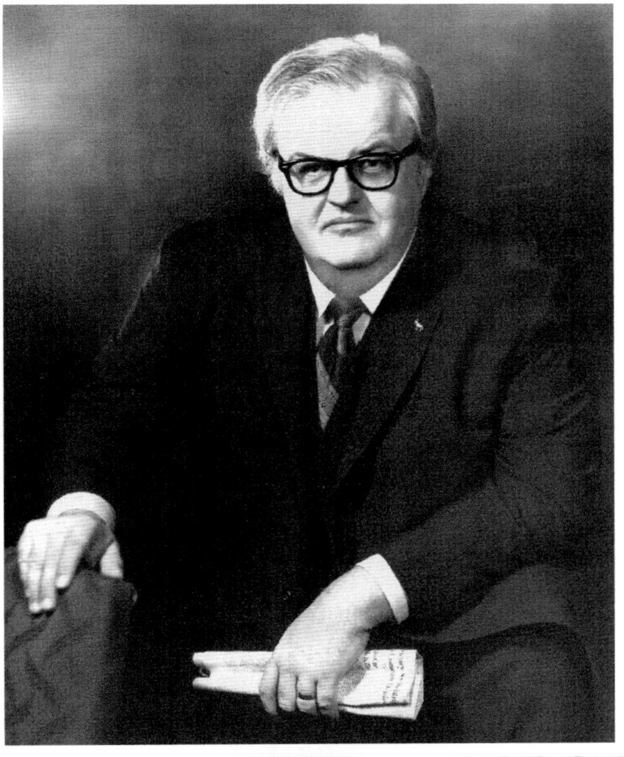

Huntington native Matthew Reese (1927–1998) was a pioneer in the field of political consulting. Reese graduated from Marshall College in 1950. He was heavily involved in John F. Kennedy's historic victory in West Virginia's 1960 presidential primary and the next year joined the Democratic National Committee as deputy chairman. In 1964, he directed get-out-the-vote efforts for Pres. Lyndon Johnson's successful campaign. In all, Reese worked on more than 450 political campaigns during his long career. He received a Distinguished Alumnus Award from Marshall in 1995 and was inducted into the Marshall Business Hall of Fame in 1997. (*H-D.*)

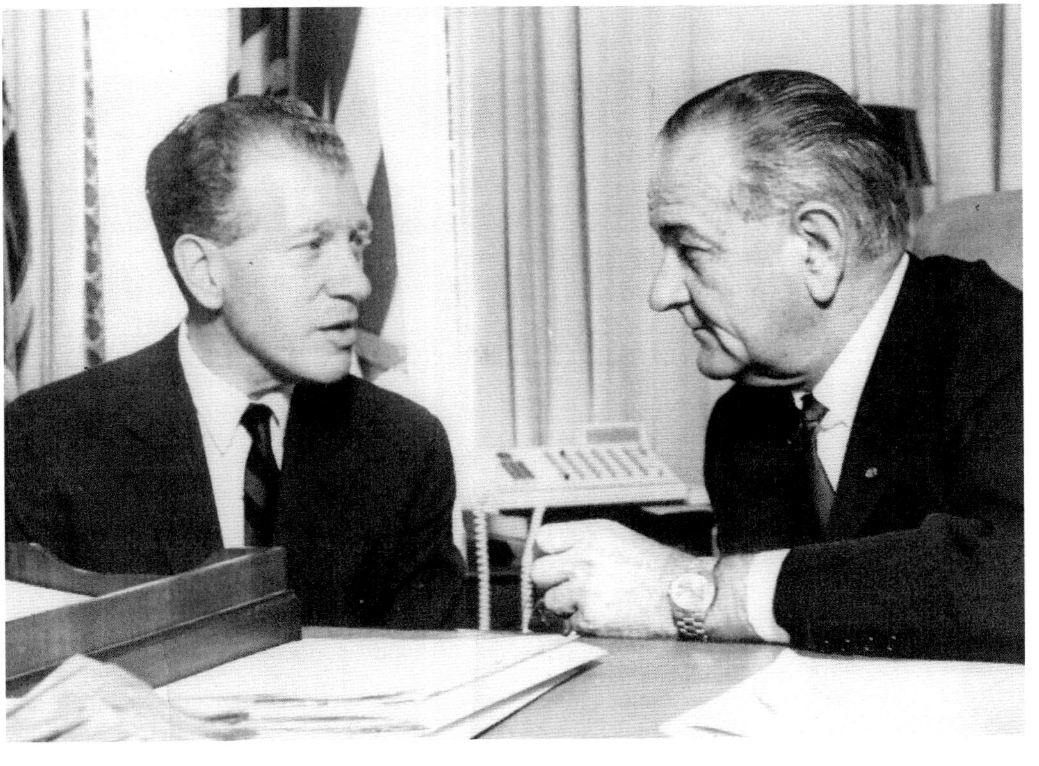

Nancy Cartmill, who served eight years as Barboursville mayor, has politics in her blood. When she was elected in 1993, she was not just the first woman to be mayor of the village just east of Huntington, she was also the first woman ever to seek the office. She has been a lobbyist in both Charleston and Washington, DC, for 25 years. Long active in state Republican politics, she now serves on the Cabell County Commission. She was the executive director of the West Virginia PTA for 20 years and is currently the executive director of the West Virginia Assisted Living Association. (*H-D.*)

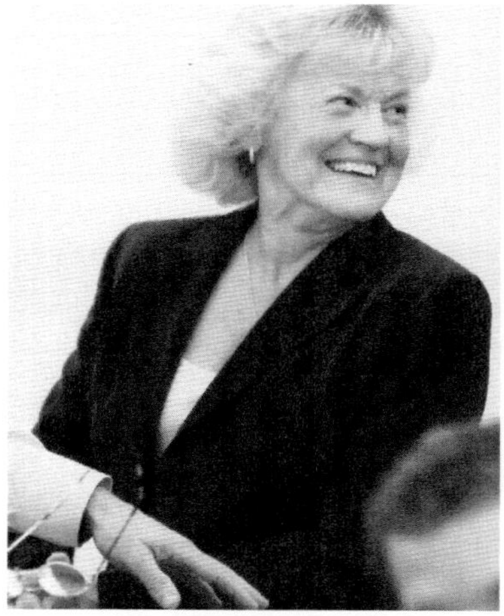

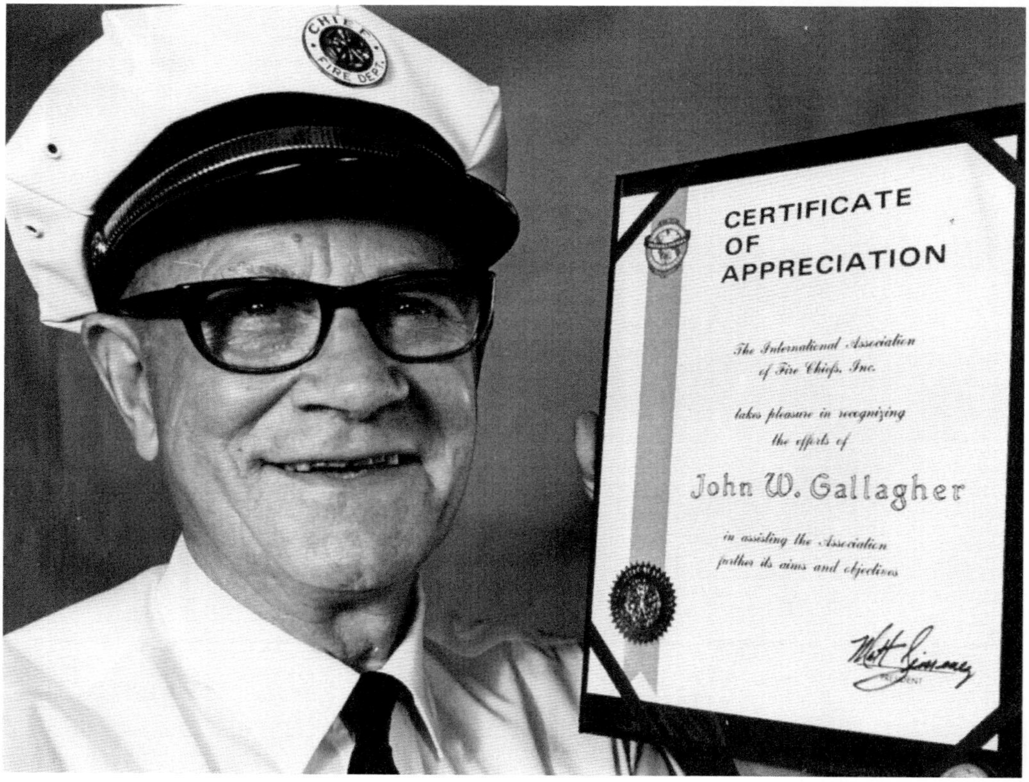

John Gallagher (1904–1974) joined the Huntington Fire Department in 1934 and rose through the ranks to become fire chief in 1954, a post he held until his retirement in 1969. Under his leadership, the city advanced from a Class 7 fire insurance rating to a Class 3, meaning cash savings for homeowners and other property owners. At his urging, the city constructed a new fire station at US Route 60 East and Washington Boulevard, the first new station built in the city since 1926. When the station opened in 1965, it was named in his honor. Gallagher is shown with a Certificate of Appreciation presented him by the International Association of Fire Chiefs in 1971. (*H-D.*)

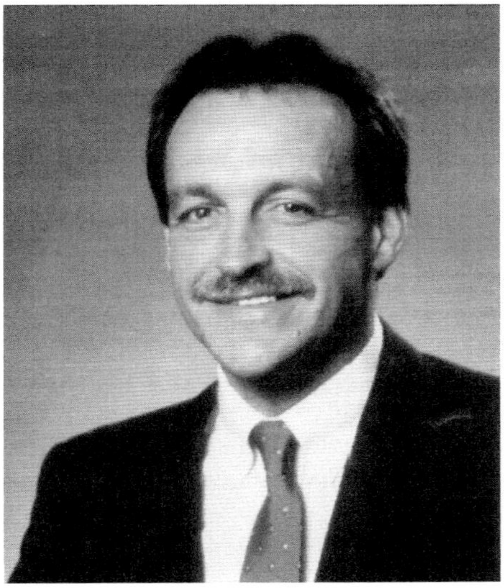

Judge Robert C. "Chuck" Chambers served 10 years as speaker of the West Virginia House of Delegates, from 1987 to 1996, the longest tenure in that office in state history. Nominated by Pres. Bill Clinton as a federal judge for the Southern District of West Virginia, Chambers was confirmed by the Senate and sworn in on October 17, 1997. Born in 1952 in Matewan, West Virginia, Judge Chambers received a bachelor's degree in political science from Marshall University in 1974 and a law degree from West Virginia University in 1978. He was first elected to the House in 1978 and reelected to eight successive two-year terms until he retired from the legislature in 1996. (Office of Reference and Information, West Virginia legislature.)

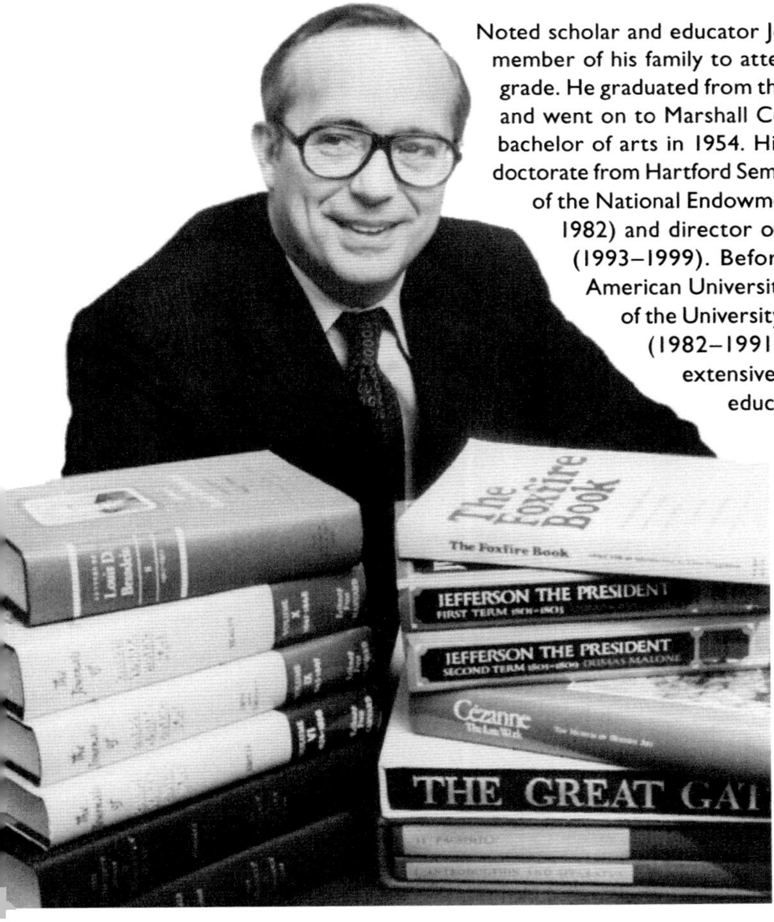

Noted scholar and educator Joseph D. Duffey was the first member of his family to attend school beyond the fourth grade. He graduated from the old Huntington High School and went on to Marshall College, where he received his bachelor of arts in 1954. His advanced degrees include a doctorate from Hartford Seminary. Dr. Duffey was chairman of the National Endowment for the Humanities (1977–1982) and director of the US Information Agency (1993–1999). Before that, he was president of American University (1991–1993) and chancellor of the University of Massachusetts at Amherst (1982–1991). Dr. Duffey has written extensively on issues relating to higher education and social and economic policy. He holds 14 honorary degrees. (*H-D.*)

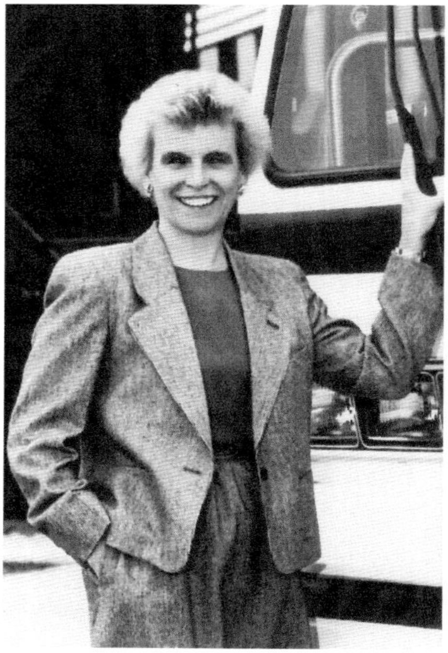

During her nearly 30 years at the helm of the Tri-State Transit Authority (TTA), Vickie Shaffer worked tirelessly to make sure the riding public was well served by the agency's buses. At her urging, TTA acquired and restored the city's blighted Greyhound bus terminal. And she spearheaded the successful effort to build Pullman Square, the entertainment/retail complex that is now a downtown jewel. She was attending Queens College in Charlotte, North Carolina, when she met her future husband, Edgar. She moved to Huntington to be with him and later finished her college work at Marshall, earning undergraduate and graduate degrees in political science and government relations. She retired as general manager at TTA in 2009. Upon her retirement, she was presented the Distinguished West Virginian Award. (*H-D.*)

New York native Ken Hechler graduated from Swarthmore College and later earned a doctorate degree at Columbia University. In World War II, he was a combat historian with the US Army in Europe. From 1949 to 1953, he served on Pres. Harry Truman's staff. In 1957, Hechler moved to Huntington to teach political science at Marshall College, and the following year he defeated Republican congressman Will E. Neal. He served 18 years in the US House of Representatives before running unsuccessfully for governor in 1976. Later attempts to regain his seat in Congress failed. In 1984, he was elected West Virginia's secretary of state and was reelected in 1988, 1992, and 1996. Hechler has written a number of books, including *The Bridge at Remagen*, which was made into a 1969 motion picture. (*H-D.*)

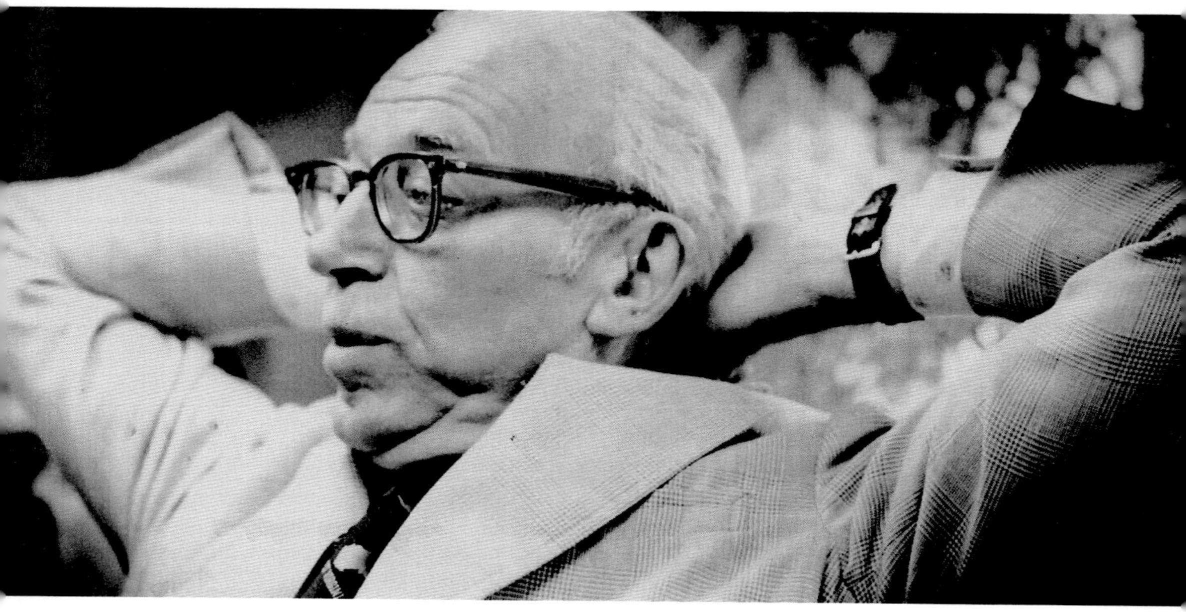

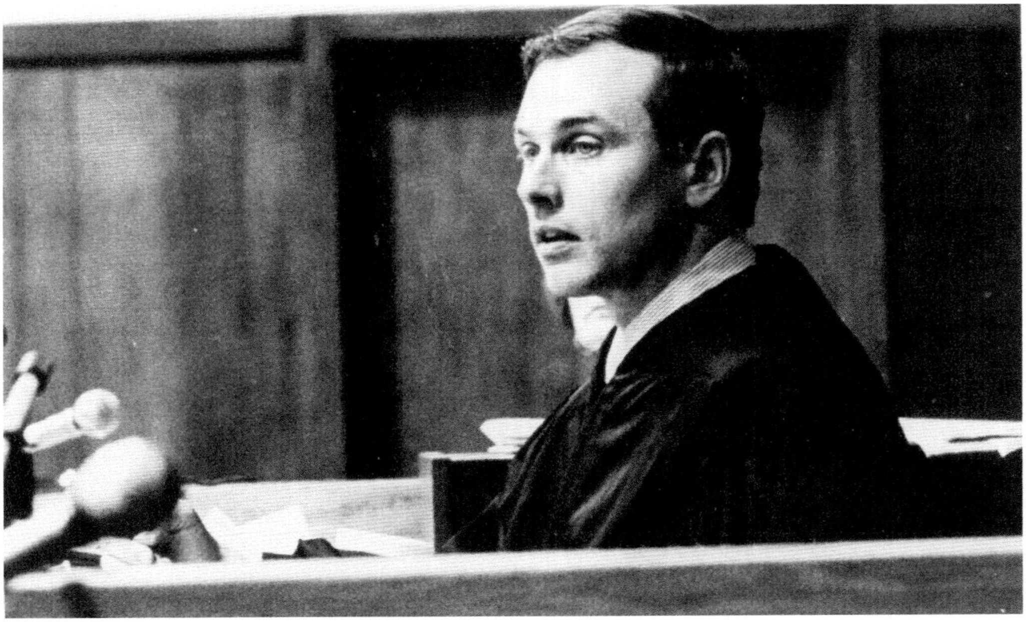

Dan O'Hanlon, who earned a bachelor's degree from Marquette University and a law degree from Arizona State University, came to Huntington in 1978 as coordinator of the Legal Assistant Program at what was then the Marshall Community College. He liked what he found and put down roots. In 1984, he won election as a Cabell County Circuit Court judge, a post he held for the next 25 years, with the voters regularly returning him to office. Along the way, he became one of the most popular public figures in the community. Retiring from the bench in 2010, he accepted a job coordinating technology for the West Virginia Higher Education Policy Commission. (*H-D.*)

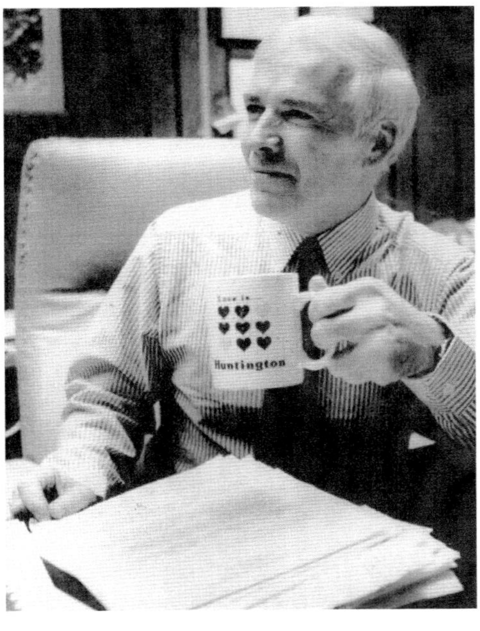

Robert "Bobby" R. Nelson has long been a key player in Huntington-area politics. He was an administrative assistant to Ken Hechler when Hechler served in the US House of Representatives. He represented Cabell County in the West Virginia House of Delegates from 1965 to 1970 and then moved to the state senate, where he served from 1971 to 1985. After that, he became Huntington's first elected mayor in 30 years when voters junked the city's council-manager form of government and approved a new charter placing a politically elected mayor in charge at city hall. Nelson was mayor from 1986 to 1993. Today, he hosts a call-in talk show on WRVC Radio. (*H-D.*)

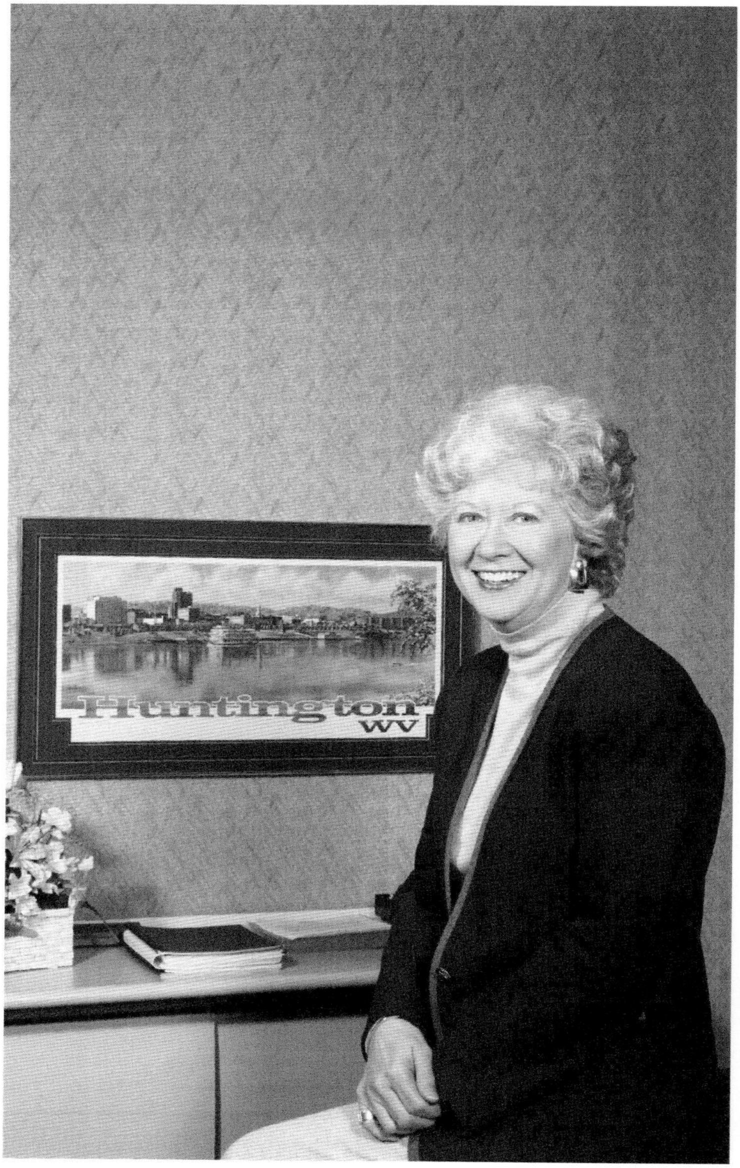

Born in London, England, Jean Dean came to Huntington to live in 1956. Thirteen years later, she became a naturalized American citizen (while still maintaining her British accent). Over the years, she steadily climbed the ladder at Huntington City Hall. She started as the executive secretary to the city manager before becoming assistant city manager and after that acting city manager. When the city switched from council-manager government to a strong mayor charter, she became the no. 2 person in Mayor Bobby Nelson's administration. Then, she and Nelson had a highly publicized falling out, prompting her to exit his administration and, two weeks later, announce her candidacy for mayor. She went on to win that election and was elected to a second term as well. After leaving city hall, she became the host of a popular call-in show on radio station WRVC. (*HQ.*)

Business and Civic Leaders

The businessmen who were attracted to Collis P. Huntington's new town in its earliest years laid down a solid foundation for the city's growth, but it was up to those who came after them to successfully build on that foundation. Fortunately for Huntington, there proved to be no shortage of individuals equal to that task. They built a busy downtown with handsome structures of steel and glass and wide streets and avenues. They opened banks, factories, wholesale firms, and retail stores designed to serve not just the people of Huntington but also shoppers from a wide region. And the dollars generated by those businesses were put back to work in the community to build homes, schools, churches, hospitals, an expansive park system, and other amenities. It is thanks to the efforts of business leaders such as J.L. Caldwell, Walter Lewis Sr., Herman P. Dean, Max Jones, Leonard Samworth, Raymond Salvati, David L. Francis, Andrew J. Houvouras, and many, many others that Huntington developed a well-deserved reputation as a vibrant, progressive city. Today's business leaders—Marshall Reynolds, Art Weisberg, Bob Shell, and others— continue to work on the community's behalf.

James Lewis Caldwell (1846–1923) was one of the first to see the possibilities of the rich coalfields of southern West Virginia and built the Guyandotte Valley Railway to tap that natural wealth. He was born in Elizabeth, Wirt County, fought in the Union Army, and traveled the state selling insurance after the war. When Collis P. Huntington founded his new town, Caldwell moved to Huntington and quickly took advantage of the opportunities it presented, investing in a number of business ventures, including the city's first streetcar line. In 1884, he and his partners organized the First National Bank of Huntington with Caldwell as president, a post he held until his death nearly 40 years later. In 1914, the bank constructed a 12-story building at Fourth Avenue and Tenth Street that is still a downtown landmark. (MU.)

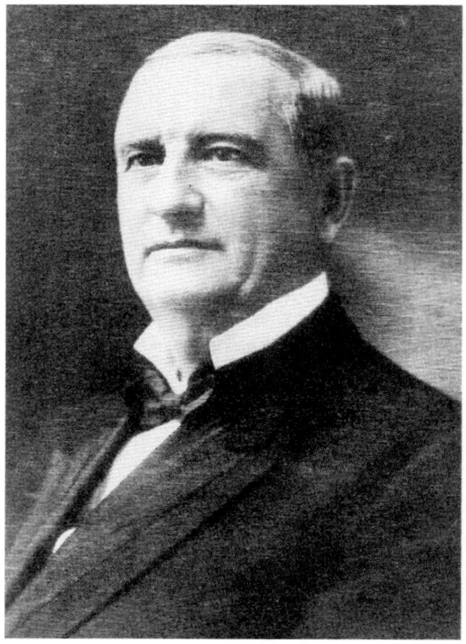

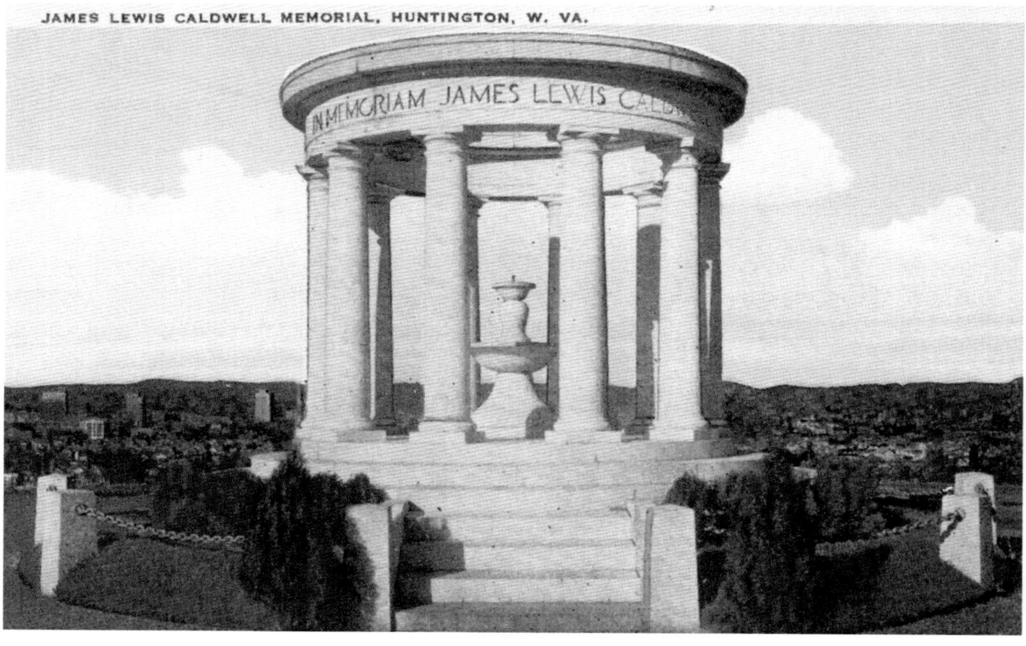

In 1926, the Huntington Board of Park Commissioners granted the family of J.L. Caldwell permission to erect in Ritter Park a marble fountain honoring the late business leader. The fountain, said to have cost $20,000, was located on the hill known as Gobbler's Knob. Over time, its isolated location made the memorial a tempting target for vandals. In 1939, one of Caldwell's daughters, Ida Caldwell McFaddin of Beaumont, Texas, said that on a visit home she was "shocked and hurt" to see the monument's sad state. She asked that it be repaired or torn down. The park board ignored her request, apparently hoping she would abandon her pursuit; instead, she continued to pepper the board with angry complaints. Finally, in 1945, the board ordered the memorial dismantled. (Author's.)

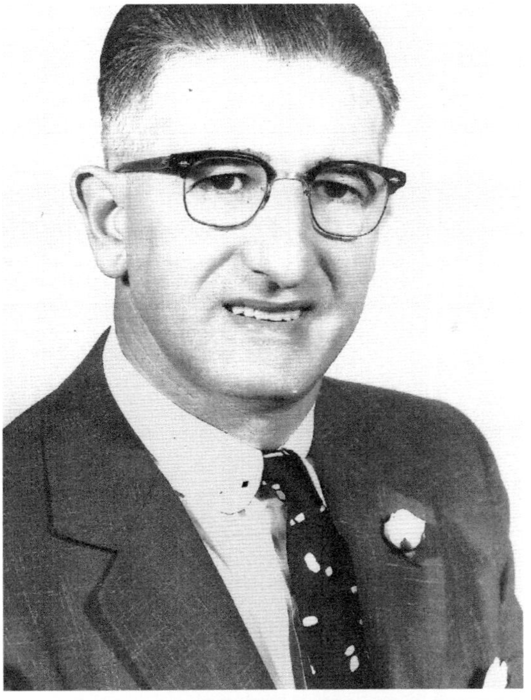

Michael Raymond Prestera was one of the victims aboard the chartered jetliner that crashed at Tri-State Airport on November 14, 1970, killing all 75 Marshall football players, coaches, and fans aboard. Born in 1909, he was a successful businessman (the president of Whitten Transfer Company and the Prestera Trucking Company), served as chairman of the KYOVA Interstate Planning Commission, and was the founding president of the Southwestern Mental Health Center. In 1981, it was renamed the Prestera Center for Mental Health Services to honor his dedication. (*H-D.*)

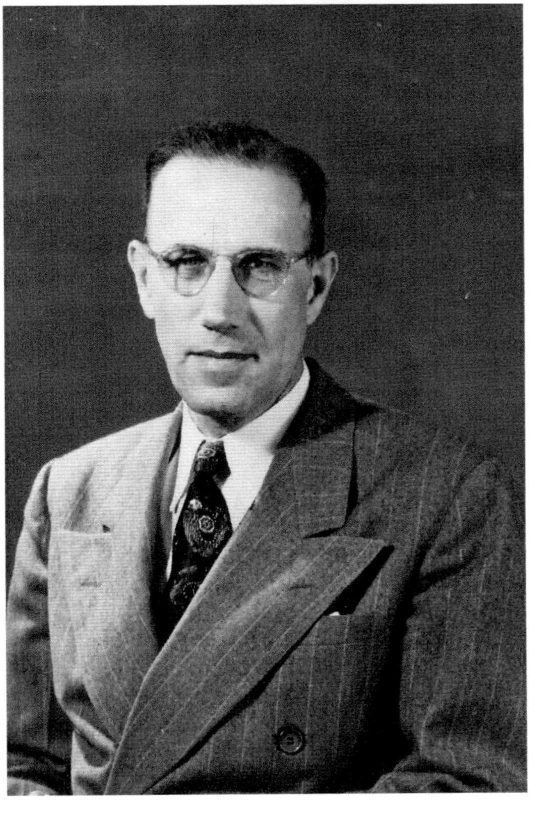

Huntington businessman D. Sterling Diddle (1896–1980) was chairman of the board and founder of both the Guaranty National Bank of Huntington and Huntington Steel and Supply Company. He and his father, James A. Diddle, founded Huntington Boiler and Supply in 1904. The name was later changed to Huntington Steel and Supply. He founded the Guaranty Bank and Trust Co. in 1939. The bank became the Guaranty National Bank in 1954. He served as president of the Huntington Chamber of Commerce, was a 50-year Shriner and Mason, and a 50-year member of Huntington Lodge No. 313, BPO Elks, and the United Commercial Travelers. This photograph is undated but appears to have been taken in the 1940s. (*H-D.*)

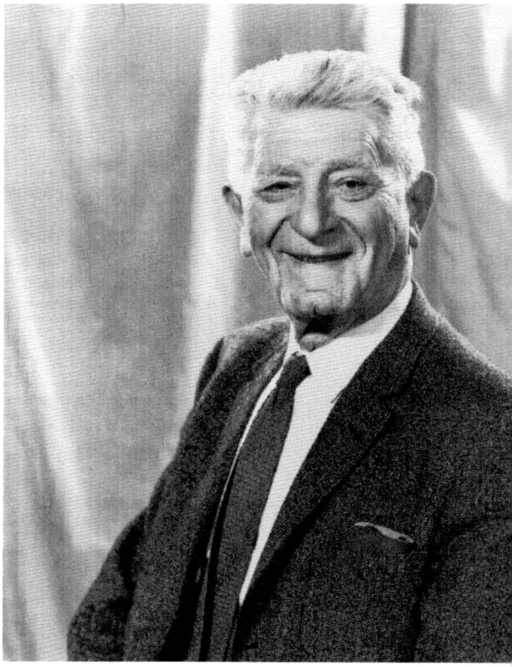

Walter Lewis Sr. (1885–1970) was born in Lithuania, came to the United States as a child, and lived for several years in Texas before moving to Huntington in 1908. Upon his arrival, he established a furniture store that grew into a chain of stores in West Virginia, Ohio, and Kentucky. He was also active as a real estate developer. The former Lewis Arcade and the Belford Village condominiums were just two of his many real estate projects. Long active in civic and philanthropic affairs, he was one of the founders of Ohev Sholom Temple. He spent much of his time on his Mason County farm, where he was one of the early breeders of pure Hereford cattle. (*H-D.*)

In 1955, Walter Lewis Sr. constructed the City Parking Port in the heart of downtown Huntington at Fourth Avenue and Tenth Street, providing nearly 500 badly needed parking spaces for downtown shoppers and workers. When it opened, the garage housed an S.S. Kresge store on the first floor. When the five-and-dime store closed, it was briefly replaced by a furniture store. In recent years, the space has been occupied by a series of restaurants. (Author's.)

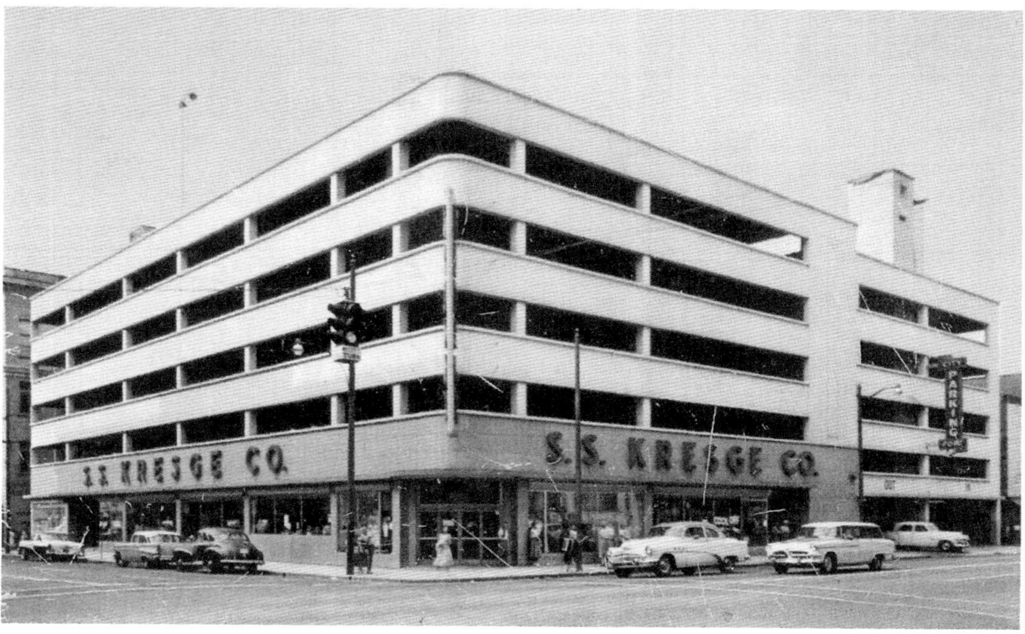

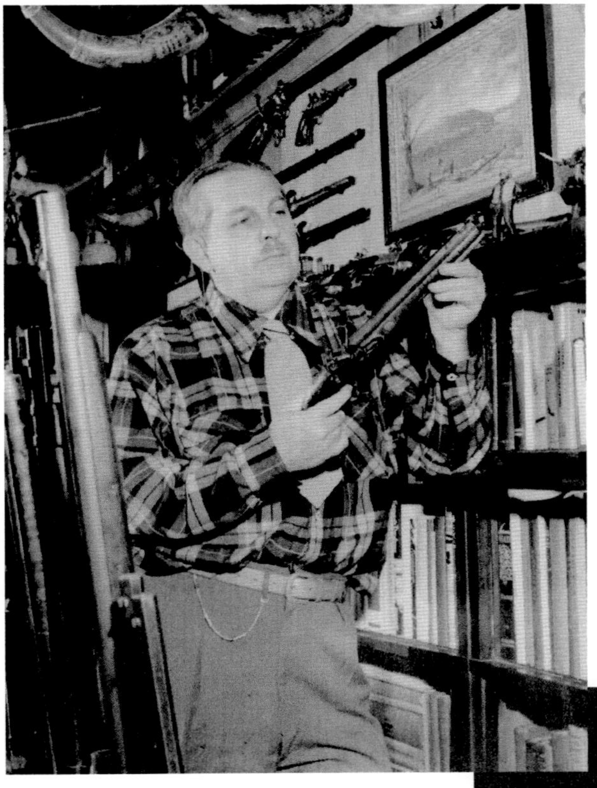

Herman P. Dean (1897–1978) packed several lifetimes of experiences into his busy eight decades. A businessman, he owned Huntington's former Standard Printing & Publishing Co. A newspaperman, he published the weekly *Wayne County News*. A church and civic leader, he taught Sunday school at Huntington's Central Christian Church for 30 years and aided a long list of charitable endeavors. A world traveler, he visited not just familiar tourist spots but such remote regions as the Canadian Yukon, where he even lived with Eskimos for two years. He loved hunting, fishing, and collecting antique guns. He spent a lifetime amassing his collection of firearms and then presented it to the Huntington Museum of Art for future generations to admire and enjoy. (Huntington Museum of Art.)

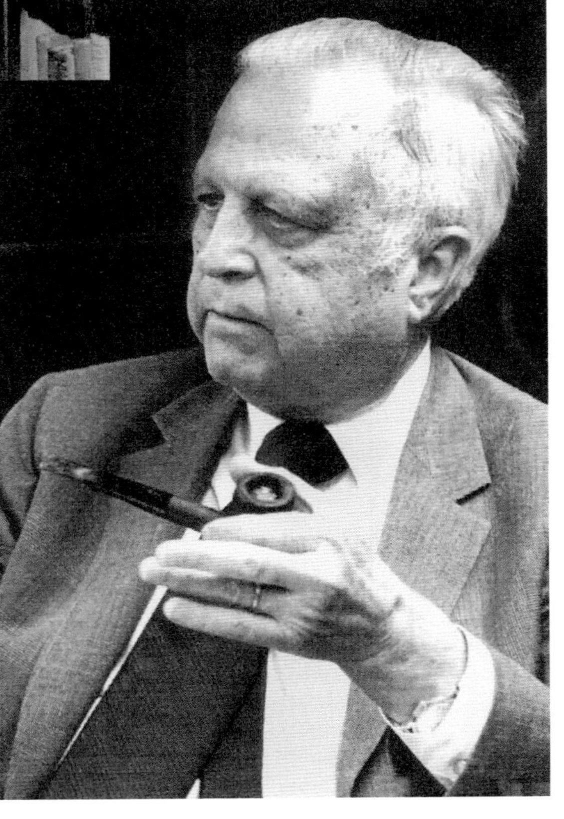

Max Jones, who died in 1980 at age 78, was manager of the old Huntington Water Company, which is now part of West Virginia American Water, and was one of the city's best-known business and civic leaders. As chairman of the Cabell County Recreation Board, he played a major role in construction of Veterans Memorial Field House. And as chairman of the Cabell County Hospital Board, he was a key figure in the creation of Cabell Huntington Hospital and helped foster its growth in its earliest years. (*H-D.*)

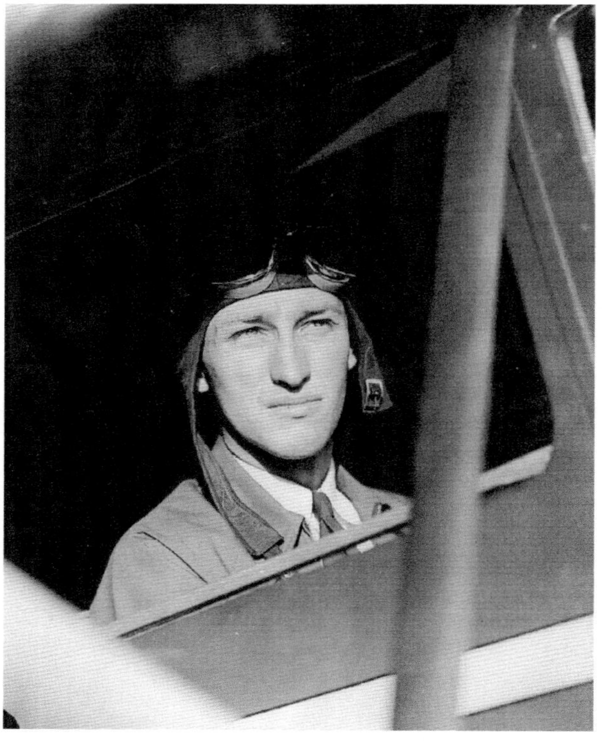

The son of Howard G. Mays Sr., the manager-operator of the Chesapeake, Ohio, Airport, Capt. Howard G. Mays Jr. followed in his father's footsteps. The younger Mays learned to fly at age 14, flew for the Air Transport Command in World War II, and joined United Airlines after the war, where he rose to become vice president of flight operations. He and wife, Fran, met at Huntington High School in the 1930s. His career took flight, and eventually, after living in Chicago, Denver, New York, Miami, and Washington, DC, they returned home to Huntington, where he shared his experience and knowledge of aircraft and airports as a member of the Tri-State Airport Authority. Mays died in 2011 at age 93. (*H-D.*)

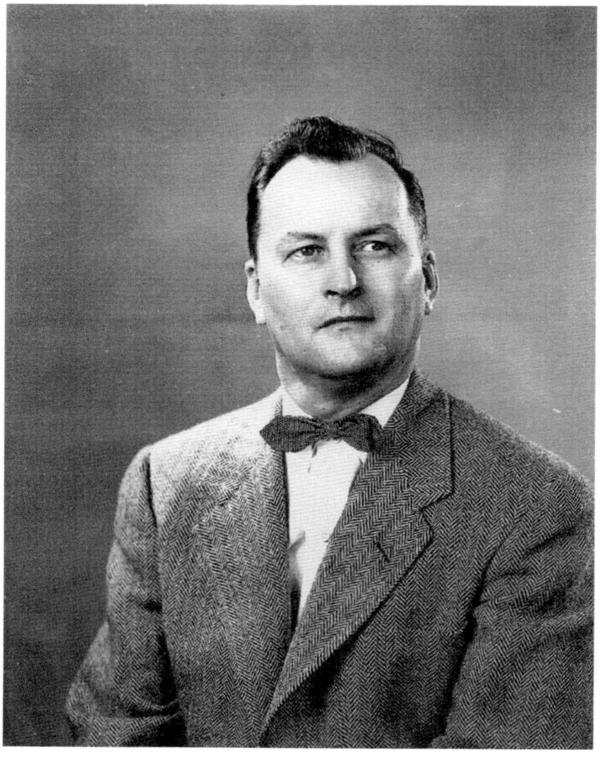

In the late 1930s, Fred W. Samworth, president of the company that operated the city's streetcars, decided it was time to replace them with buses. So the old Ohio Valley Electric Railway Company vanished into history, replaced by the Ohio Valley Bus Company. On November 7, 1937, Huntington became the first city in West Virginia to be served entirely by buses. When Fred Samworth died in 1939, his son Leonard Samworth (1913–1990) became the company's treasurer. Five years later, he took over as its president and, for the next three decades, would be "Mr. Bus" in Huntington. (*H-D.*)

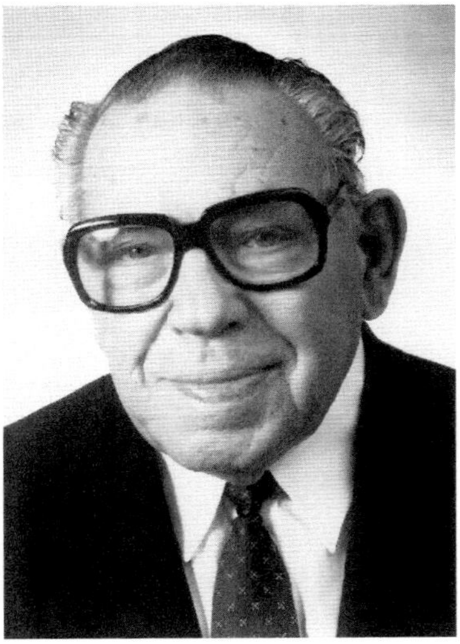

A star football player at Ohio State University in the late 1930s, Alex Schoenbaum (1915–1996) also became a star in the world of business as the founder of the Shoney's restaurant chain. He was born in Richmond, Virginia, but moved with his family to Huntington when he was 10. His father owned Arcade Recreation, a bowling alley and poolroom in downtown Huntington, and young Alex worked there as a pin boy. After college, he moved to Charleston to manage the family's bowling business there. It was in Charleston, in 1947, that he opened his first restaurant. The rest, as they say, was history. At its peak, the Shoney's chain had 1,800 restaurants in 36 states. He retired in 1985 and spent much of his time during his final years distributing millions of dollars in charitable donations. (*H-D.*)

Harold Frankel (1916–2002) is remembered for his accomplishments in both business and politics. In business, he took over his father's clothing store, branched out into the appliance business, established a highly successful Holiday Inn on US 60 East, and then invested everything he had—and everything he could borrow—in construction of a new downtown hotel, the first built in the city in decades. In politics, Frankel was a member of Huntington City Council for 16 years, served four one-year terms as mayor under the city's former council-manager form of government, and was Cabell County sheriff for four years. He is pictured with his wife, Dodi, his partner not only in marriage but also in everything he did. (*H-D.*)

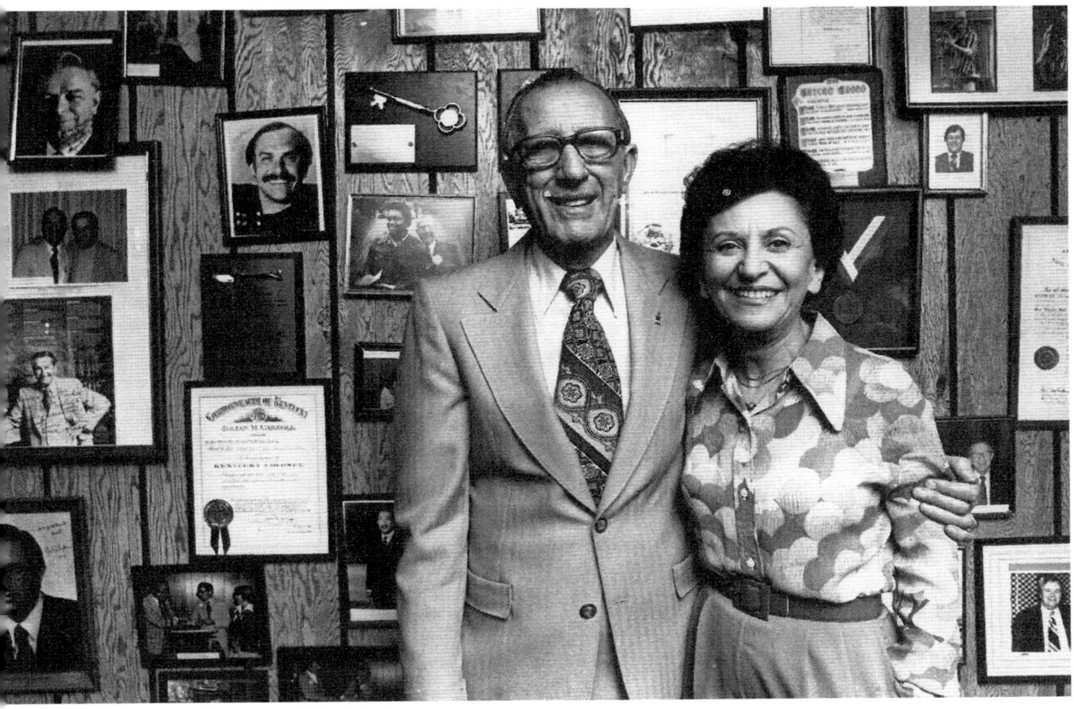

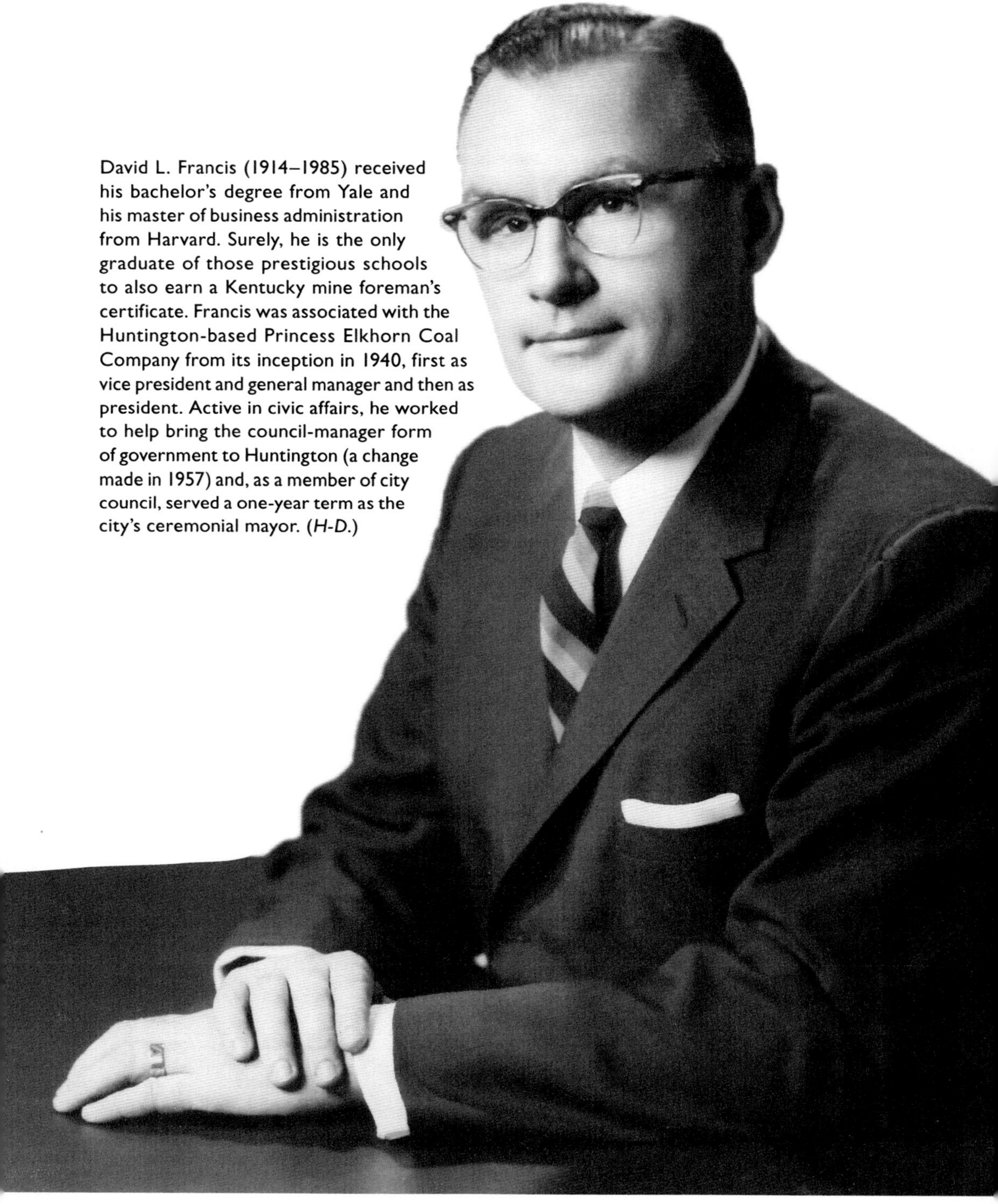

David L. Francis (1914–1985) received his bachelor's degree from Yale and his master of business administration from Harvard. Surely, he is the only graduate of those prestigious schools to also earn a Kentucky mine foreman's certificate. Francis was associated with the Huntington-based Princess Elkhorn Coal Company from its inception in 1940, first as vice president and general manager and then as president. Active in civic affairs, he worked to help bring the council-manager form of government to Huntington (a change made in 1957) and, as a member of city council, served a one-year term as the city's ceremonial mayor. (*H-D.*)

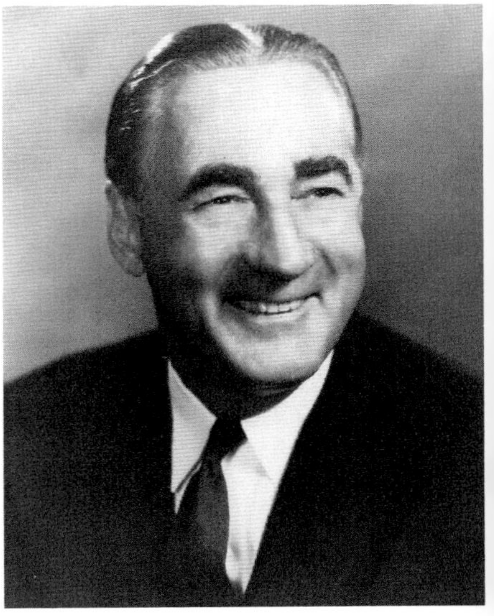

Raymond Salvati (1899–1982), who headed Island Creek Coal Company when it was headquartered in Huntington in the 1950s and 1960s, was born in Monongah, West Virginia. He began his career with Island Creek after graduating from West Virginia University in 1922. He worked his way up through the ranks until becoming the company's president and CEO in 1949. He retired in 1964. In 1948, he was honored with the Horatio Alger Award, given to honor individuals who have risen from humble beginnings to achieve success and shared that success with others through their philanthropic efforts. (*H-D.*)

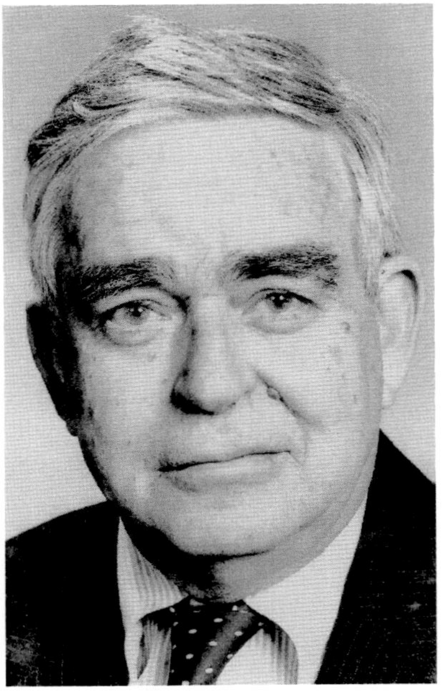

Long active in local and state politics, Robert K. Emerson, who died in 1991 at age 69, served on John F. Kennedy's campaign staff during West Virginia's historic 1960 presidential primary. A native of San Francisco, he grew up in Illinois and served in the Navy in the South Pacific during World War II. He graduated from the University of Virginia Law School in 1949 and became a partner in the Huntington law firm now known as Campbell Woods, PLLC. Active in civic affairs, he served on the boards of United Way, the Boy Scouts, and the Huntington Museum of Art, where his wife, Roberta, was director. (*H-D.*)

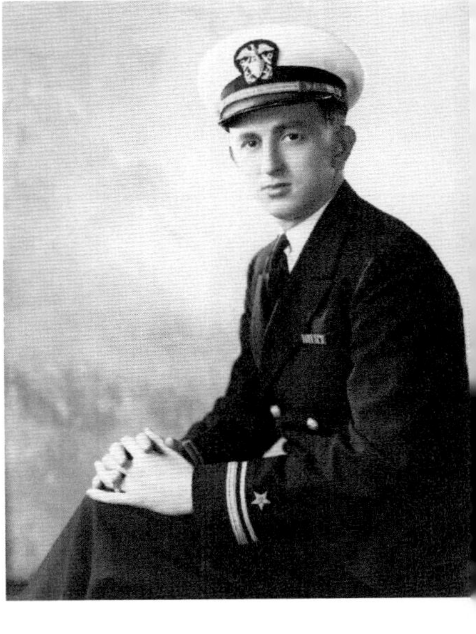

This photograph of a young Andrew John Houvouras (1919–2003) wearing his Navy uniform is a favorite of his son Jack. A proud veteran of World War II, Houvouras earned a commendation for shooting down a Japanese kamikaze during the Okinawa invasion. After the war, he helped form several local companies, including Huntington Plating, Sterling Supply, C.I. Thornburg, and Steel of West Virginia. A Democrat, he was deeply involved in John F. Kennedy's landmark win in West Virginia's 1960 presidential primary. He was named to the Huntington Wall of Fame in 1997. (*HQ.*)

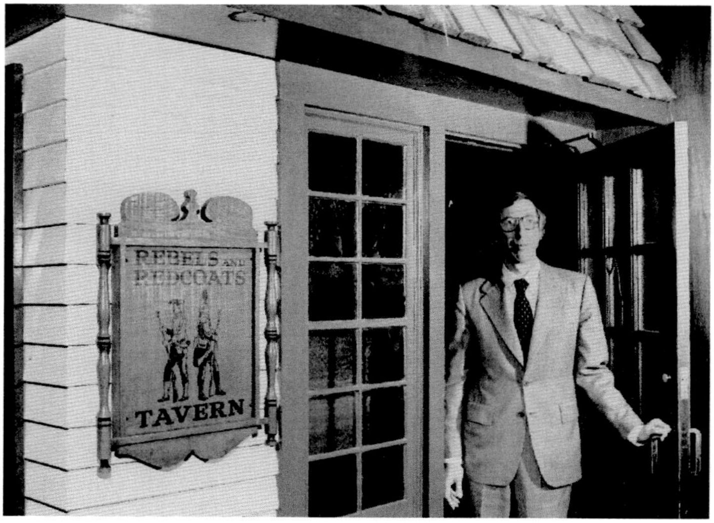

"You're kidding me, right? You're telling me one of the best restaurants in town is in a bowling alley?" Over the years, people in Huntington took great delight in introducing disbelieving out-of-town visitors to Rebels & Redcoats Tavern. Restaurant owner Lloyd Frankel took equal delight in welcoming them to his nationally acclaimed restaurant housed under the same roof as Colonial Lanes. For 20 years, until his death in 1986, Frankel personally presided over the restaurant, which offered a gourmet menu and wine list in a Williamsburg-style setting. (*H-D.*)

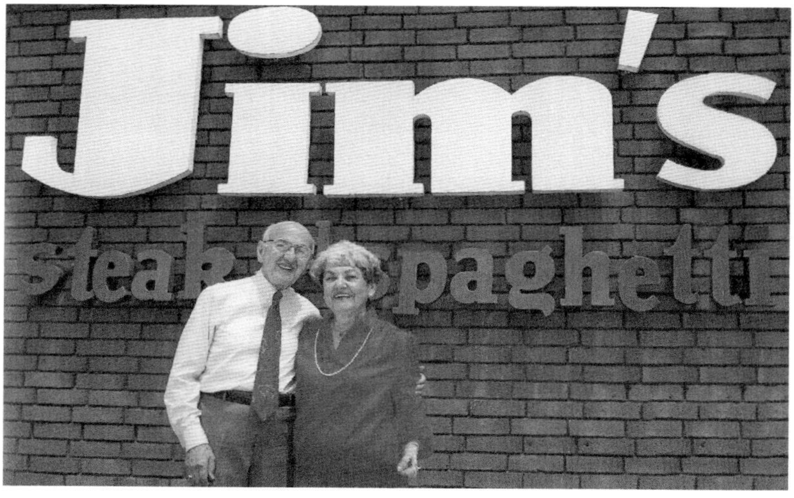

In 1938, James A. "Jim" Tweel (1915–2005) purchased the Kennedy Dairy Store on the 900 block of Huntington's Fifth Avenue. There, he and his wife, Sally, sold cheeseburgers, ice cream cones, and milk shakes. Business steadily grew, and over the years the restaurant expanded in size, added items to its menu, and went through a couple of name changes. Today, Jim's Steak and Spaghetti House is a Huntington institution, a lunchtime and dinnertime favorite for generations of local residents. Framed photographs of celebrities who have dined at Jim's line the walls. Jim's daughter Jimmie Tweel Carder now manages the restaurant. (Bulldog Creative Services.)

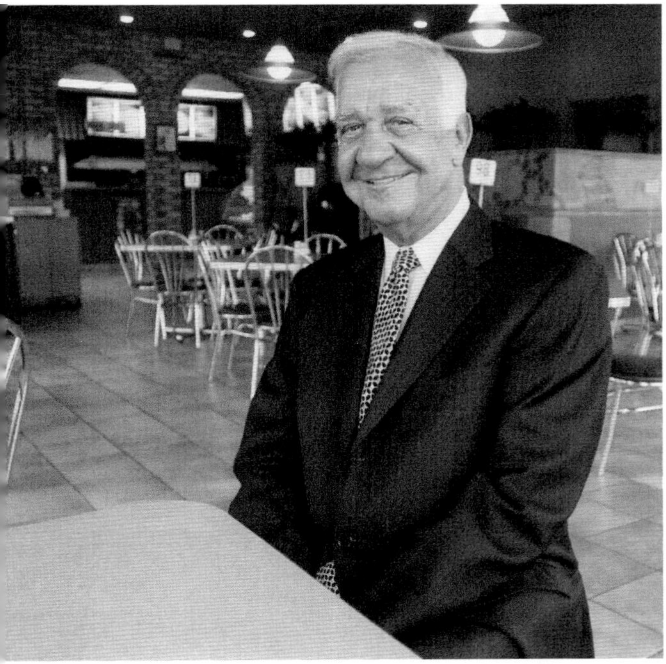

Fifty-plus years ago, Huntington's Kenny Grant had a dream: he wanted to open a pizza shop. When he shared his dream with his wife, Vivian, she laughed. "You can't even fry an egg," she said. Nevertheless, Grant learned to make a tasty pizza and, in 1961, opened Gino's, the shop he had long dreamed of. Next, he opened another shop and then another in a process repeated over and over. Today, Grant is the region's uncrowned king of pizza, presiding over a mini-empire of 70 Gino's locations. Retirement? That does not seem in the cards for Grant. In 2004, he told an interviewer that he intended to keep working until he turned 100—and then would slow down. (*H-D.*)

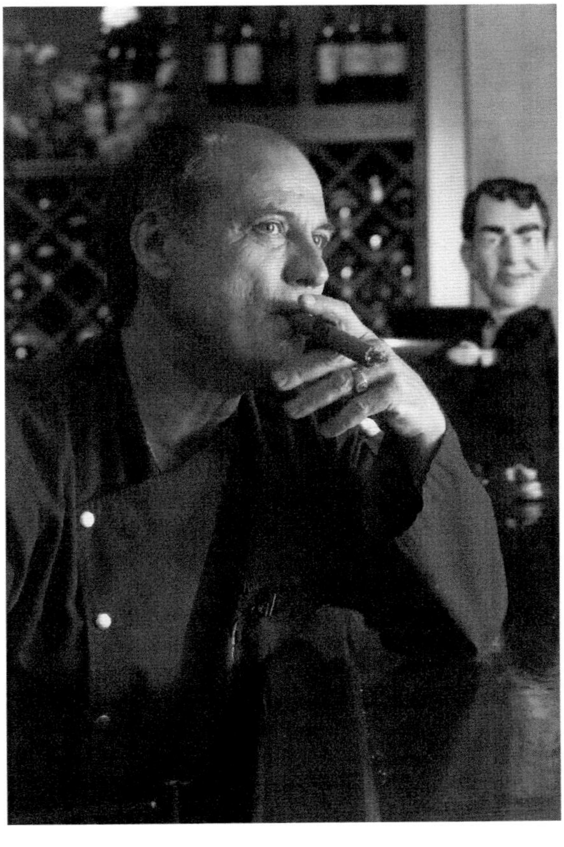

Early on, it appeared that Clarksburg, West Virginia, native Rocco Muriale's career might be in music. He majored in music at Fairmont State University and played in the US Army Band. But as a teenager, he worked at Minard's, a popular Clarksburg restaurant, and that planted the seed of a dream for him. In 1977, he came to Huntington and opened Rocco's, a small Italian restaurant on Main Street in Ceredo. Since then, Rocco's has grown significantly, both in size and reputation. Today, it is one of the region's most popular restaurants. In 2005, he began selling a selection of Italian specialty food items in the region's supermarkets. (*HQ.*)

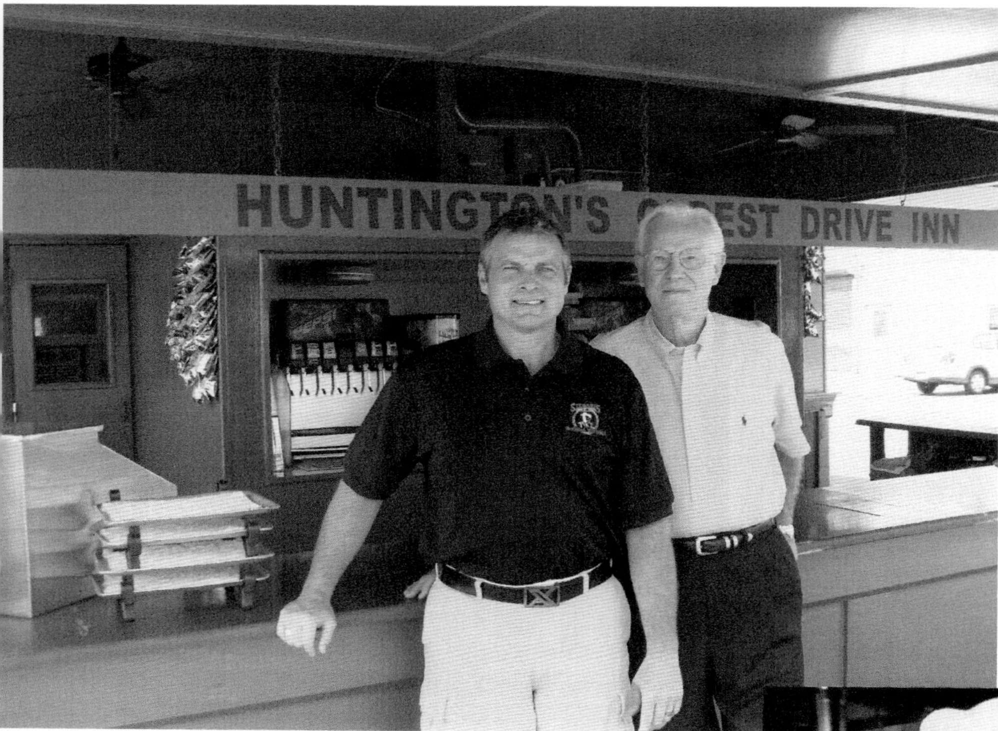

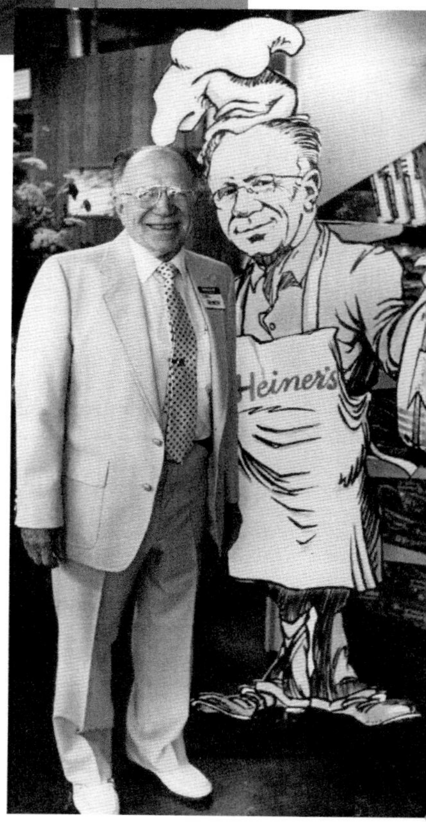

Established by John Lewis Mandt and his wife, Gertrude, in 1932, Stewart's is Huntington's oldest drive-in restaurant and one of its oldest restaurants of any type. Today, Stewart's is known for its distinctive hotdogs and its work in the community, including helping organize the annual West Virginia Hotdog Festival, and is still family owned. John Mandt Sr. (at right) is the grandson of the restaurant's founders and is its CEO. With him is his son John Mandt Jr., the restaurant's president. (*H-D.*)

Earl Heiner Sr. (1905–1990), shown here playfully posing with a life-sized cartoon likeness of himself, took over the bread business his father, Charles, began in 1905. At first, the elder Heiner went from door to door selling bread from a basket he carried on his arm. Later, a horse-drawn delivery wagon was put in service. Today, that tiny bakery has evolved into a big business with a sprawling block-long plant, more than 400 employees, and dozens of trucks that deliver bakery products in four states. (*H-D.*)

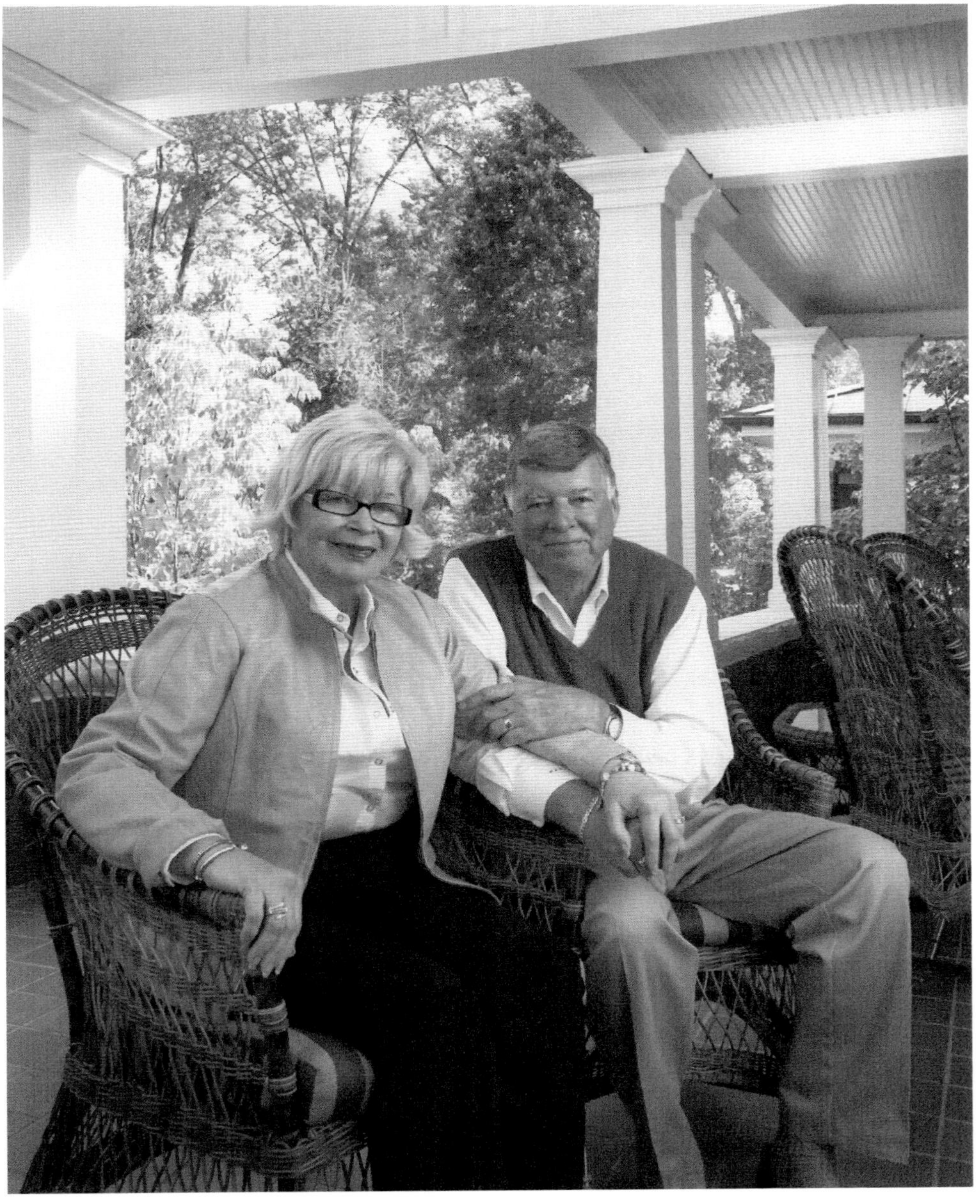

Originally from Elkview, West Virginia, Verna Gibson graduated from Point Pleasant High School and then came to Huntington to attend Marshall College, where she met her husband, Jim, and earned an associate's degree in 1962. She started her retail career selling dresses at a downtown Huntington shop. Jim's career took him to Columbus, Ohio. There, in 1971, Verna landed a job as an assistant buyer with a new women's clothing store, The Limited, under the leadership of Leslie Wexner. The Limited grew to be a nationwide chain, and Verna steadily rose in its ranks. By 1985, she was its CEO, the nation's first female CEO of a Fortune 500 company. When she retired in 1991, the Gibsons bought a home in Huntington, where they have been generous supporters of Marshall and leaders in the effort to revitalize the community. (*HQ*.)

Charles R. "Charlie" Neighborgall III is the chairman of Neighborgall Construction Company of Huntington. He is a graduate of Christchurch School in Christchurch, Virginia, and a 1967 cum laude graduate of Marshall University. He started working with Neighborgall Construction, the family business, when he was only 14, carrying water to the workmen. He gradually moved up the ladder, taking charge of the company in 1983. He is a member of the Marshall Business Hall of Fame. (MU.)

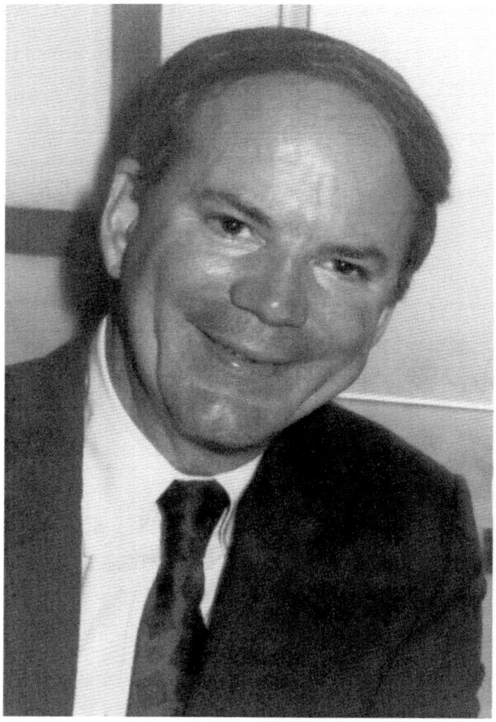

Phillip E. Cline made his mark early at Marshall University, where he was elected student body president. He has gone on to make his mark in the business world as well as vice president of J.H. Fletcher and Company and then as president and CEO of Broughton Foods Company, along with numerous other business ventures. Significantly, he has shown a deep-seated willingness to share the fruits of that success with others. Huntington's Phil Cline Family YMCA, a new $1.3-million facility dedicated in 2010, is but one example of his remarkable generosity. Long affiliated with Alderson-Broadus College at Philippi, Cline served as its acting president in 2010–2011 while a search was underway for a new president. Shortly thereafter, he purchased the former Broadus Hospital building and presented it to the school. (*H-D.*)

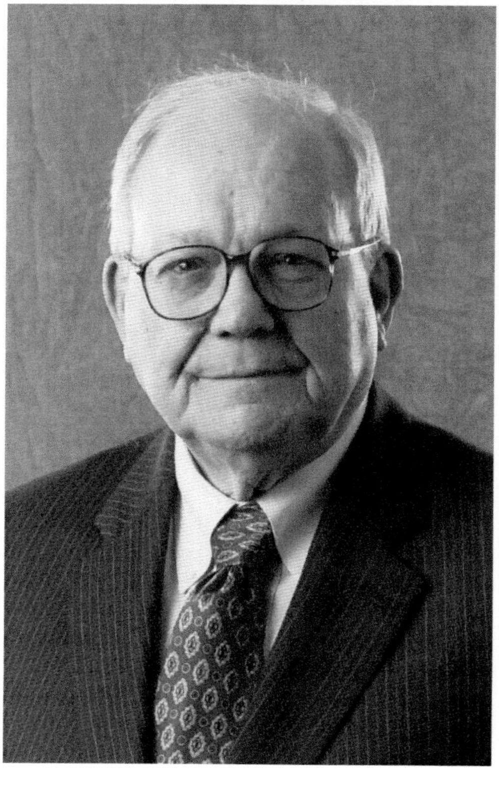

Architect E. Keith Dean (1926–2011) and his brother Brooks carried on the business that had been founded by their father, Levi Dean, one of the city's early architects. A few of the many buildings he designed were the Memorial Student Center, Smith Hall, Corbly Hall, Harris Hall, and the Campus Christian Center on the Marshall University campus; the Cabell County Public Library; Huntington Federal Bank; and several buildings for the Prestera Center. A 1944 graduate of Huntington East High School, Dean enlisted in the Navy just 30 days after getting his diploma and was assigned to a destroyer, the USS *Register.* He is shown here in a 2008 newspaper interview in which he recounted his wartime experiences. He was the husband of former mayor Jean Dean. (*H-D.*)

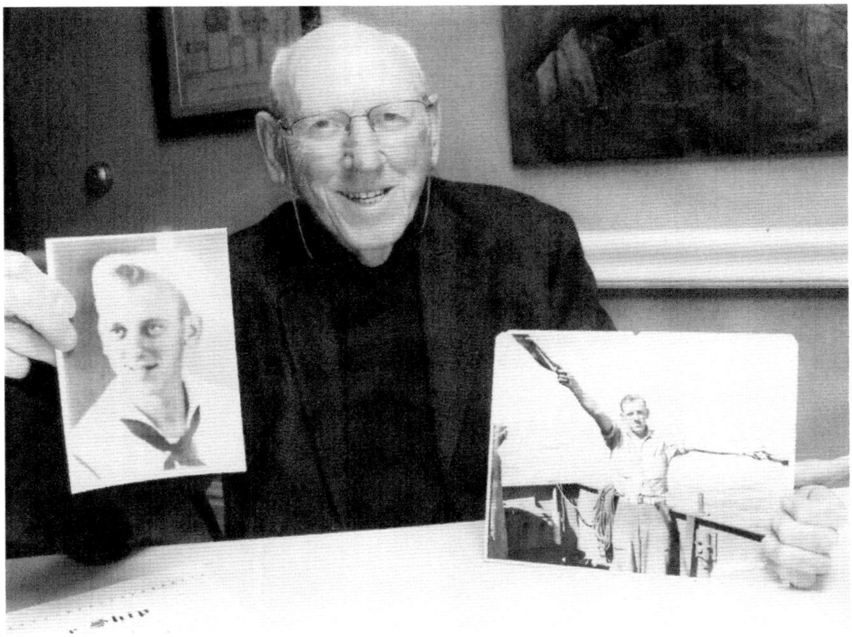

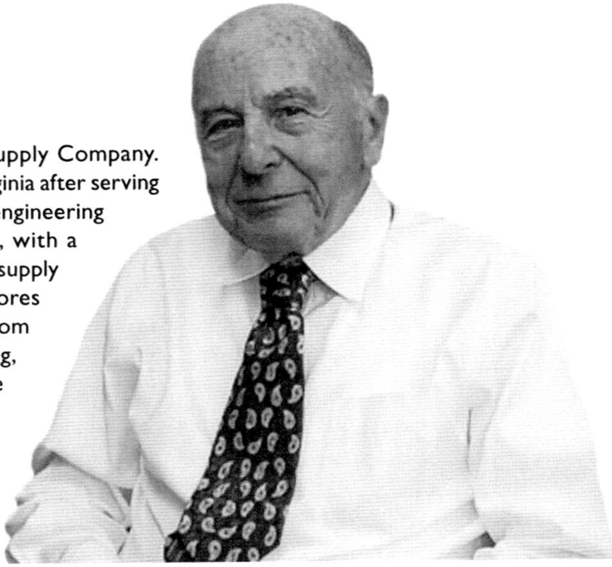

Art Weisberg is the founder of State Electric Supply Company. Brooklyn-born Weisberg made his way to West Virginia after serving in World War II and earning a degree in electrical engineering from the City University of New York. In 1952, with a bankroll of $2,500, he started a one-man electrical supply business, calling on small grocery and hardware stores and selling lightbulbs, extension cords, and fuses from the back of his truck. From that humble beginning, Huntington-based State Electric has evolved into one of the nation's biggest and best-known electrical distributors, with more than 50 locations in a half-dozen states. Noted for their charitable giving, he and his wife, Joan, have donated millions of dollars to Marshall University and other recipients. (State Electric Supply Company.)

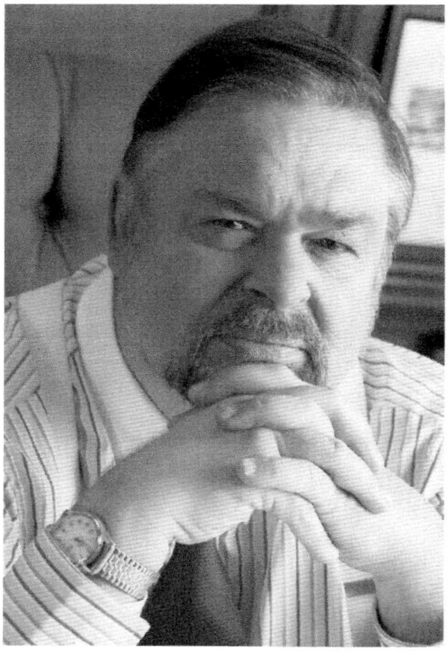

Huntington's Bob Shell presides over business interests that stretch from Logan, West Virginia, to Tianjin, China. Raised in Logan, he says he enrolled at Marshall University with a dream of becoming an astronomer but could not do the math; instead, he left Marshall and followed in his father's footsteps in the mining equipment business. Ironically, he has clearly had no trouble dealing with the math in multimillion-dollar business deals. Today, his company, Guyan International, Inc., is a leading manufacturer of high-pressure pumps used in mining, construction, drilling, timbering, and other industries. Guyan has manufacturing sites in the United States and China, with distribution in the United States, China, Europe, and Africa (*HQ*.)

When Gilbert, West Virginia, native Huey Perry was hired as director of the Mingo County Economic Opportunity Commission, he soon butted heads with local politicos who saw the antipoverty organization as a threat to their power. Perry's book about that clash, *They'll Cut Off Your Project*, caused quite a stir. His next book also raised eyebrows when he teamed with stripper Blaze Starr to write her life's story, *Blaze*. The book later became a movie with Paul Newman as Louisiana governor Earl Long, who carried on an affair with Starr. When Perry moved to Huntington, he bought the tallest building in town, the 15-story West Virginia Building, and opened Permons, a plush restaurant, on the top floor. The restaurant proved short-lived, and Perry later sold the building. (*H-D*.)

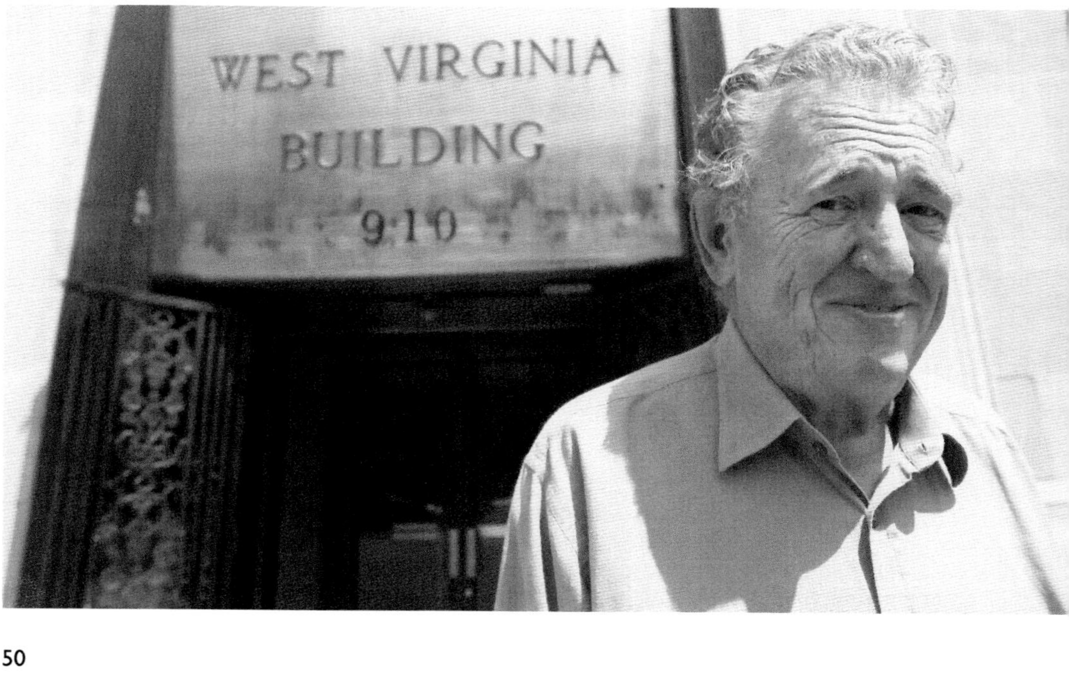

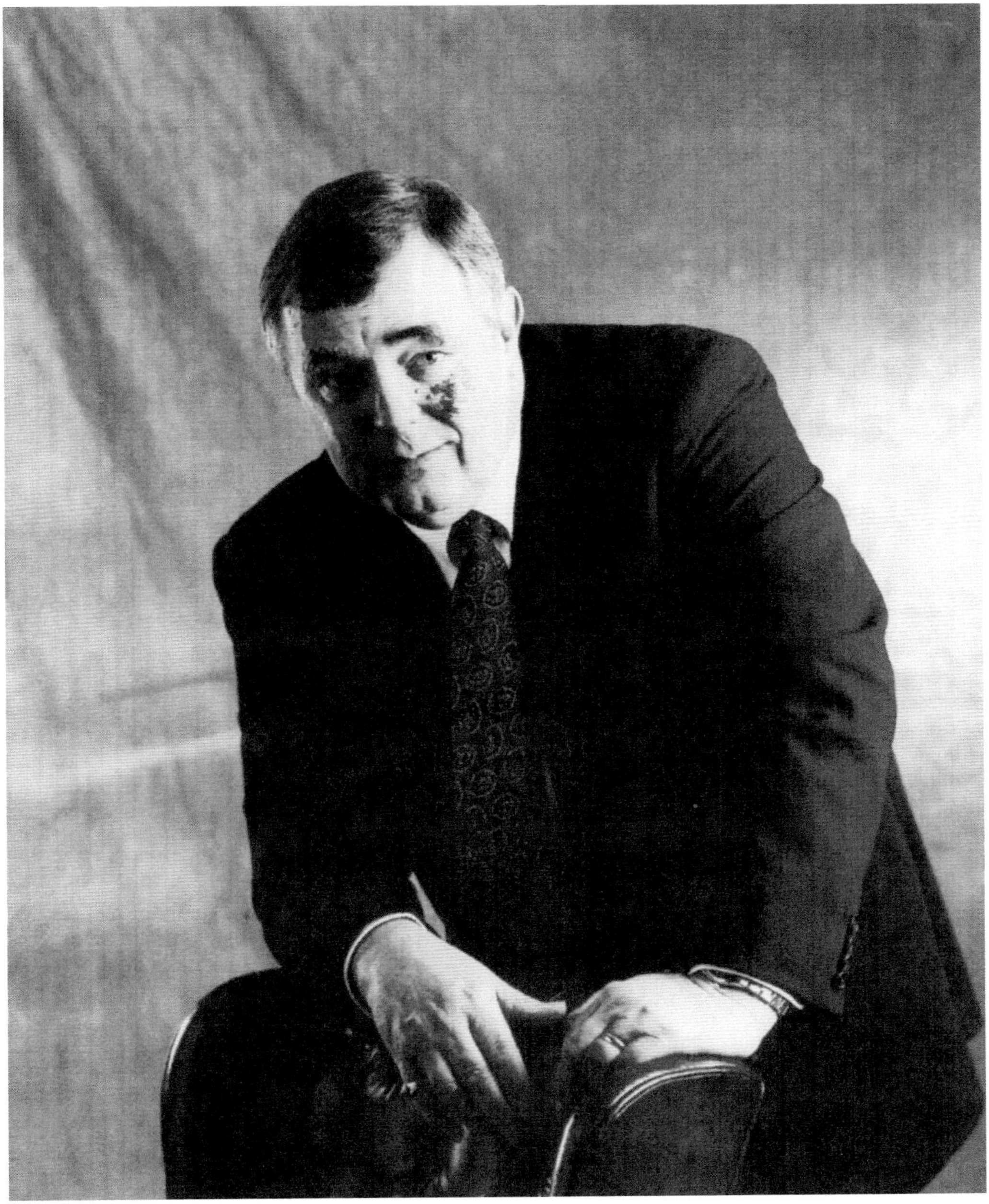

When the First Huntington National Bank denied a young West Huntington businessman a modest $2,500 loan for his business, he stormed out of the bank, vowing, "I'll own this damn bank one day." Fifteen years later, Marshall Reynolds made good on that pledge. Reynolds is one of West Virginia's best-known and most successful entrepreneurs. Starting with Chapman Printing, where he once worked as a delivery boy, he has assembled a network of printing properties, banks, manufacturing companies, real estate holdings, a hotel (downtown Huntington's Pullman Plaza), and other ventures. In 2007, he realized a longtime dream when he purchased Huntington's *Herald-Dispatch* newspaper. (*HQ*.)

Now retired, A. Michael Perry was a key leader in the West Virginia business community throughout his long career. As chairman and CEO, he helped guide Key Centurion Bancshares, the state's first billion-dollar banking organization, through its growth to become Banc One (now a unit of J.P. Morgan Chase). Active in a long list of organizations, he served as chairman of both the West Virginia Bankers Association and the West Virginia Chamber of Commerce. On weekends, he happily shed his suit and tie, donned work clothes, and prowled antique stores and estate sales looking for vintage items to add to his growing collection. (*H-D.*)

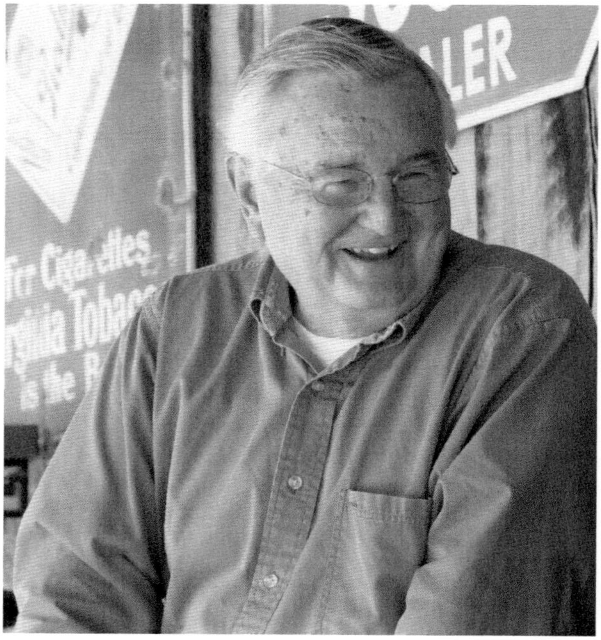

As Mike Perry and his wife, Henriella, added antiques to their collection, they quickly ran out of room in their Wayne County home. Then, they filled their barn. Eventually, they started buying log buildings, disassembling them, and moving them to their 500-acre farm. Today, Heritage Farm Museum is a major tourist attraction that features 16 exhibit-filled buildings, including this historical church. Each year, the farm attracts thousands of visitors who get a glimpse of what daily life was like in pioneer days. (*H-D.*)

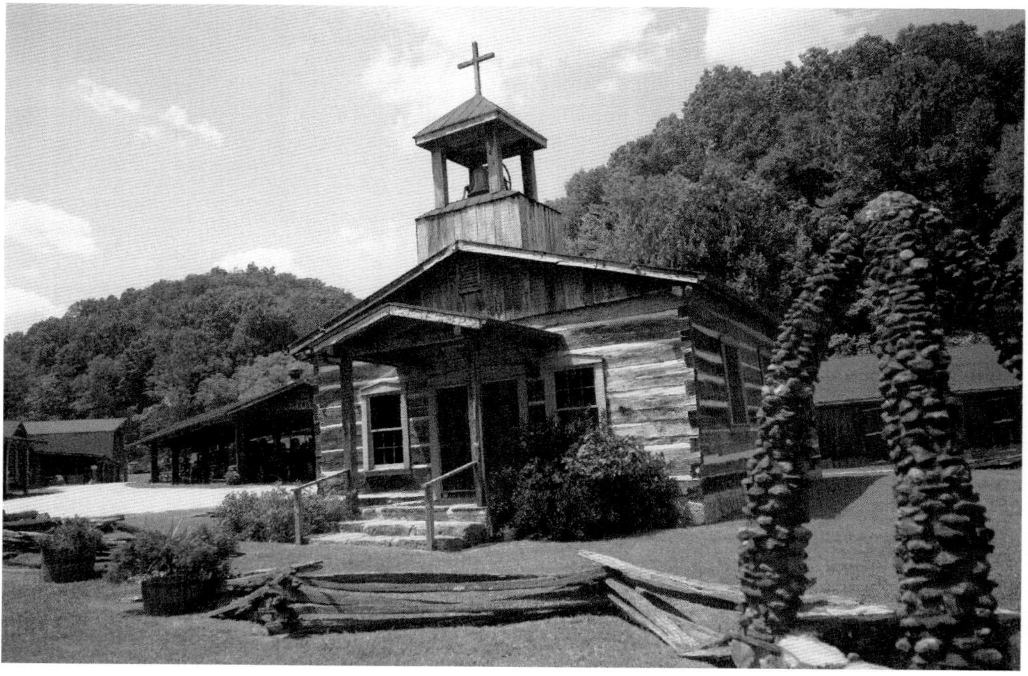

Familiar Names, Familiar Faces

"Did you read what Ernie said in his column?" For decades, the question was a familiar one that could be heard around countless kitchen tables and coffee-shop counters as people talked about Huntington sportswriter Ernie Salvatore's latest newspaper essay. Some people loved what he wrote, and some people hated it, but nearly everybody read it. If one was a dyed-in-the-wool Marshall University sports fan, Ernie Salvatore's columns were required reading. Over the years, his was just one of many bylines familiar to readers of Huntington's newspapers. Catherine Bliss Enslow chronicled the latest doings of the city's social set, Jack Hardin served up the latest bulletins from the police beat, and Bill Belanger provided doses of art and culture to the mix. In 1949, when WSAZ signed on as West Virginia's first television station, the station's familiar faces were added to the mix. Veteran news anchor Bos Johnson, sportscaster Jim Thacker, farm director William D. Click, and others became video visitors to thousands of Huntington-area homes. And the fun-filled antics of WSAZ's "Mr. Cartoon" should not be forgotten.

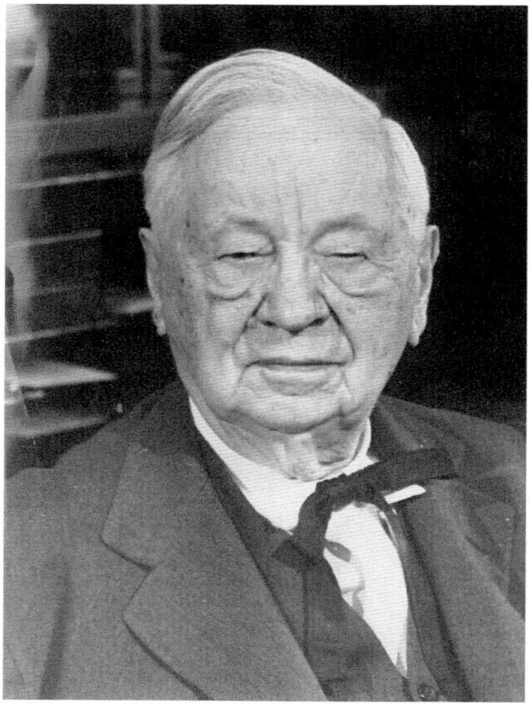

Pennsylvania-born Joseph Harvey Long (1863–1958) moved to Wheeling in 1881 to become a printer at a newspaper there. Moving to Huntington in 1893, he purchased the *Herald*. Two years later, he sold it and acquired the *Advertiser*, a small daily that became the first building block in what would become a local media empire. For a number of years, Long's afternoon *Advertiser* slugged it out with the morning *Herald-Dispatch*, owned by Dave Gideon. In 1924, Colonel Long (the title was strictly honorary) bought a corner lot at Fifth Avenue and Tenth Street and erected a new building for his paper. Not be outdone, the *Herald-Dispatch* built a new home just a few doors down. Shortly thereafter, the two newspapers declared a truce and merged as the Huntington Publishing Company, with Long as chairman and Gideon as president. The mechanical and business operations were combined, while the two news staffs operated independently. (*H-D.*)

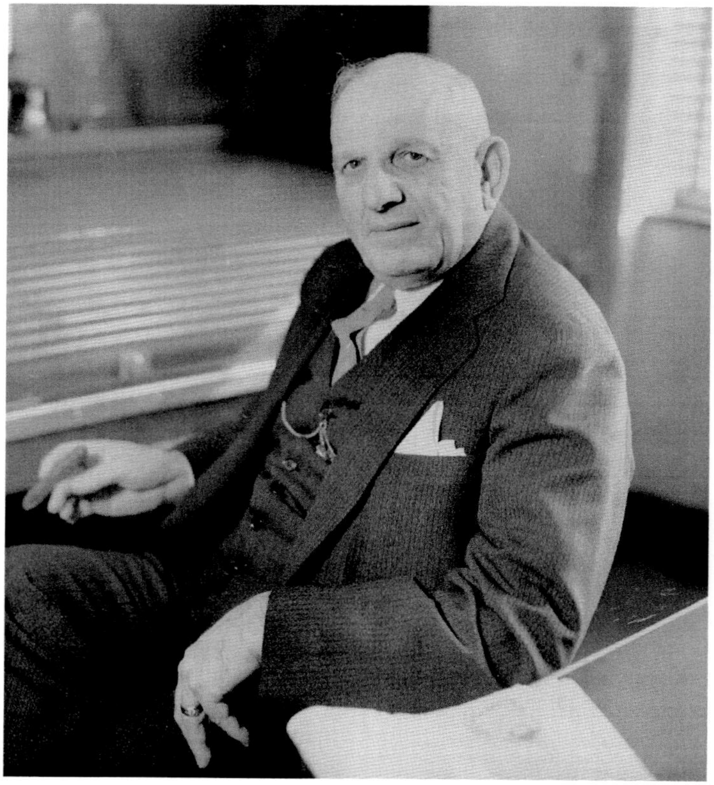

Dave Gideon (1873–1950) would, like his father Sam, play an outsized role in the city's affairs. Born upstairs over the family clothing store, Dave became a clerk in the store and later his father's partner. In 1913, he bought a part-interest in the *Herald-Dispatch* and, in 1920, was named the newspaper's publisher. Later, the *Herald-Dispatch* and the *Advertiser* merged to form the Huntington Publishing Company, and he became president of the merged company. Active in Republican politics for many years, Dave Gideon served as a respected informal adviser to many political figures on the local, state, and national levels. (*H-D.*)

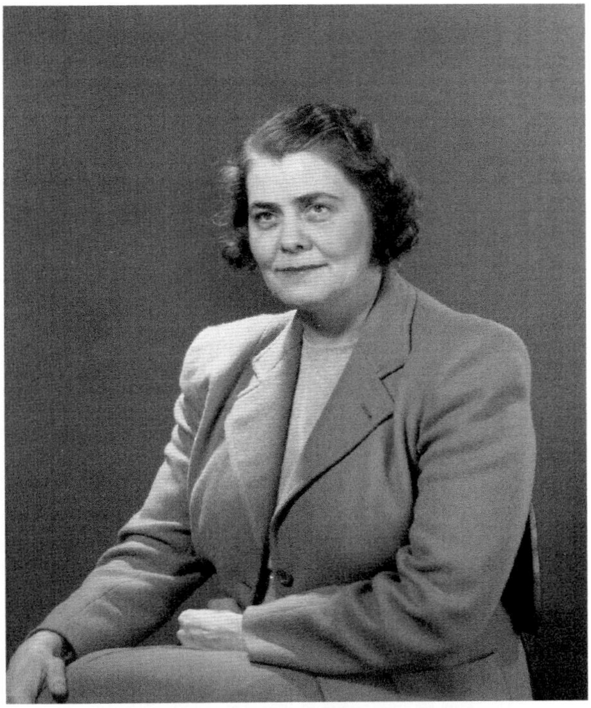

Back in the day, when newspapers had "society pages," Catherine Bliss Enslow (1899–1973) was the woman one needed to see to have news of one's social event published. Born into a locally prominent family, she went to work as a reporter at the *Advertiser* shortly after her graduation from Huntington High School in 1917. She briefly left her newspaper career but rejoined the *Advertiser* in the 1930s as its society editor. Despite her official retirement in 1966, she continued to write her popular name-filled columns until shortly before her death. (*H-D.*)

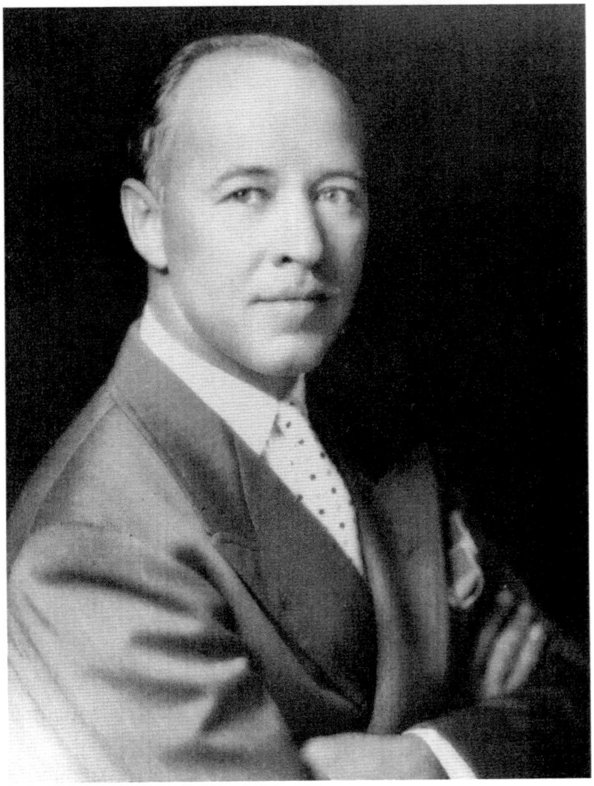

Illinois farm boy H.R. "Punk" Pinckard (1897–1972) began his newspaper career in 1919 at the former *Morning Press* in Danville, Illinois, while a student at the University of Illinois. He came to Huntington in 1922 to join the staff of the *Advertiser*. He would be a fixture at Huntington's newspapers for the next 49 years, holding down nearly every job in the newsroom: reporter, city editor, telegraph editor, Sunday editor, and editorial-page editor. He wrote a Sunday personal column from 1939 until shortly before his death. Active in civic affairs, in 1944 he was the founder and first president of the Friends of the Cabell County Public Library. (*H-D.*)

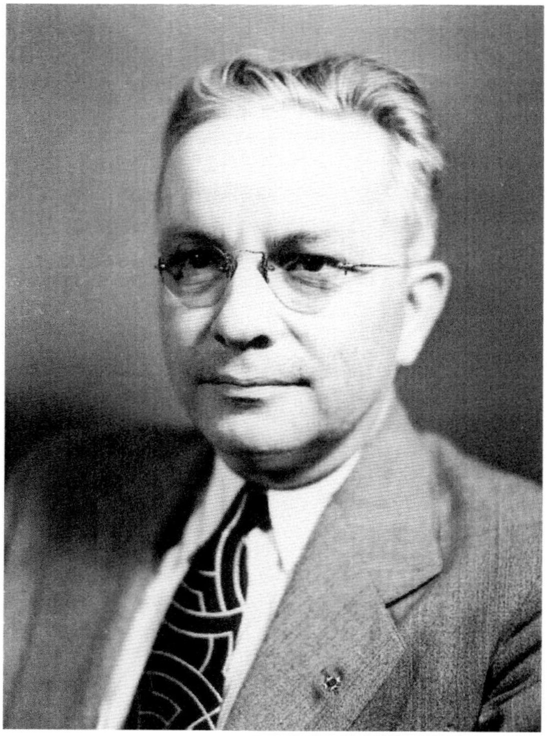

The face of the artist may not be familiar, but many longtime Huntington newspaper readers will recognize his cartoon creation pictured on this page. The cartoons of Irvin Dugan (1892–1982) enlivened the pages of Huntington's papers for 30 years, from the late 1920s through the 1950s. Born in Guyandotte, Dugan studied at the Chicago Academy of Fine Arts and the New School of Design in Boston. During World War I, he worked as a draftsman for the Navy. After the war, he returned to Huntington to work for an engraving firm and, in 1927, joined the Huntington Publishing Company as staff artist. After his retirement in 1957, he moved to Phoenix, where he died at age 90. (*H-D.*)

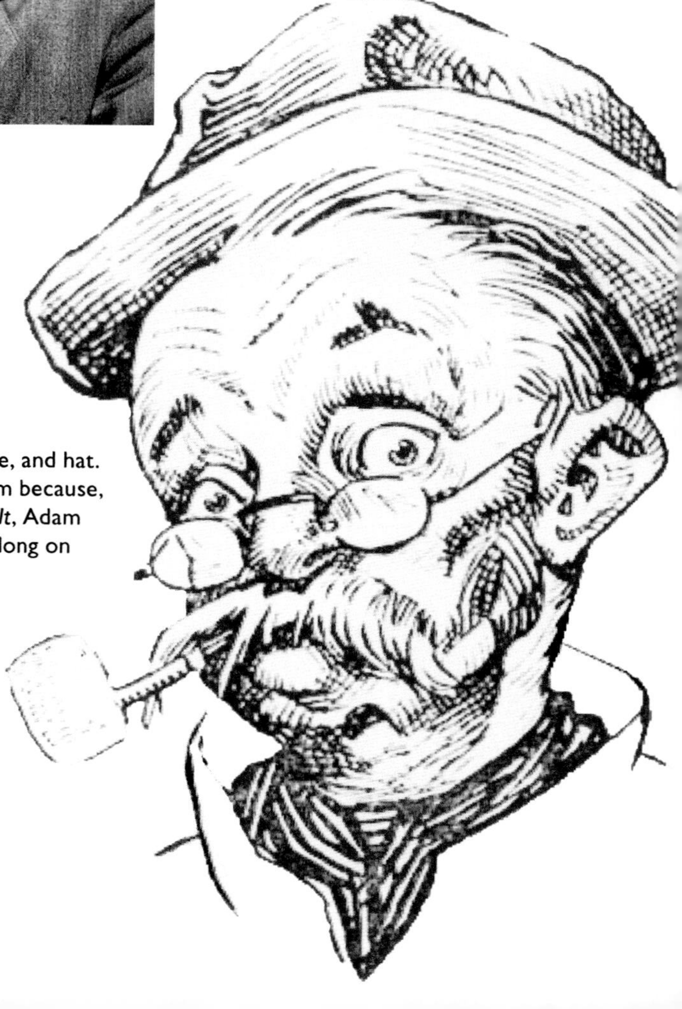

Virtually all of Dugan's editorial-page cartoons featured his alter ego, Adam Goodfellow, easily recognizable by his flowing mustache, glasses, corncob pipe, and hat. Dugan said he named his creation Adam because, like Adam in Shakespeare's *As You Like It*, Adam Goodfellow was "short of stature and long on wisdom." (*H-D.*)

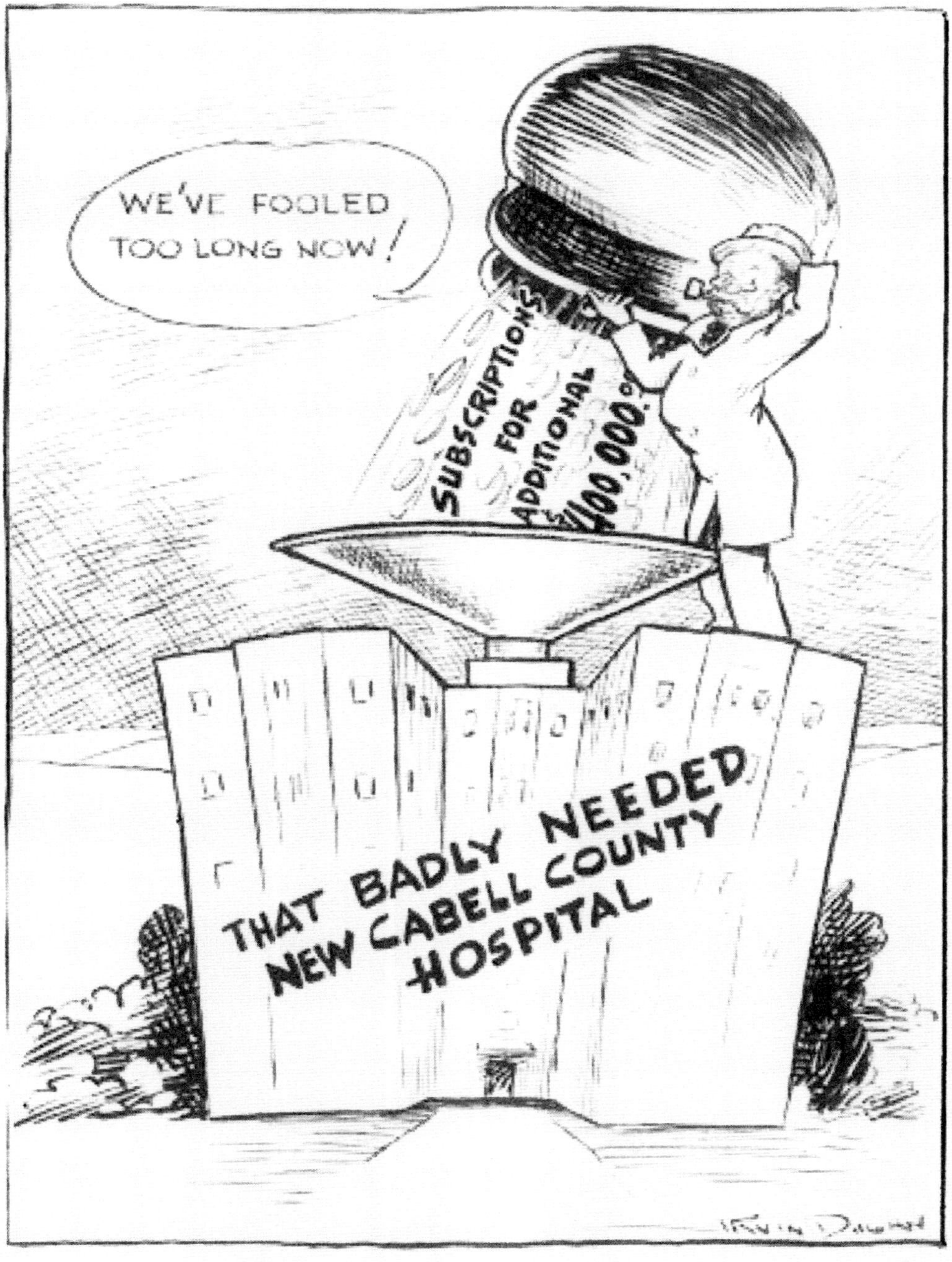

Dugan's cartoons championed construction of a number of important projects, including the city's flood wall, Tri-State Airport, and, as seen in this cartoon, Cabell Huntington Hospital. He frequently cartooned about his own pet project, an underpass at the railroad tracks at Twenty-third Street, but it was never built. (*H-D.*)

In his half century of reporting for Huntington's newspapers—first for the *Advertiser* and later for the *Herald-Dispatch*—Hardin (1926–2011) wrote untold thousands of news stories of all kinds, but what he truly excelled at were stories from the police beat. He demonstrated that early when, in 1955, he won the Pall Mall Big Story Award for convincing an escaped murderer into surrendering. Knowing every local police officer and firefighter by their first name gave him unprecedented access to news events—his loyal readers were the beneficiaries. (*H-D.*)

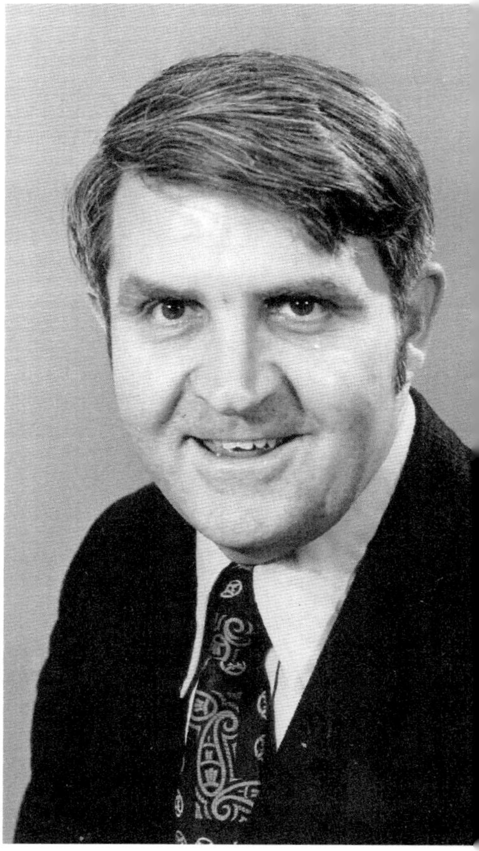

Ernie Salvatore was a Connecticut Yankee who came to Huntington, fell in love with the place, and never left. Salvatore, who died in 2009 at age 87, was a sportswriter, columnist, and editor at Huntington's newspapers—first the *Advertiser* and then the *Herald-Dispatch* after the two papers consolidated—for nearly 60 years. He once estimated he had written 7,000 columns and that likely was shy of the real total. Salvatore came to Huntington to enroll in Marshall College in the 1940s and stuck around to marry newspaperwoman Joanne Pinckard. He won his first statewide journalism award in 1952 and kept right on winning them, year after year. In 2008, the press box at Marshall's Joan C. Edwards Stadium was named in his honor. (*H-D.*)

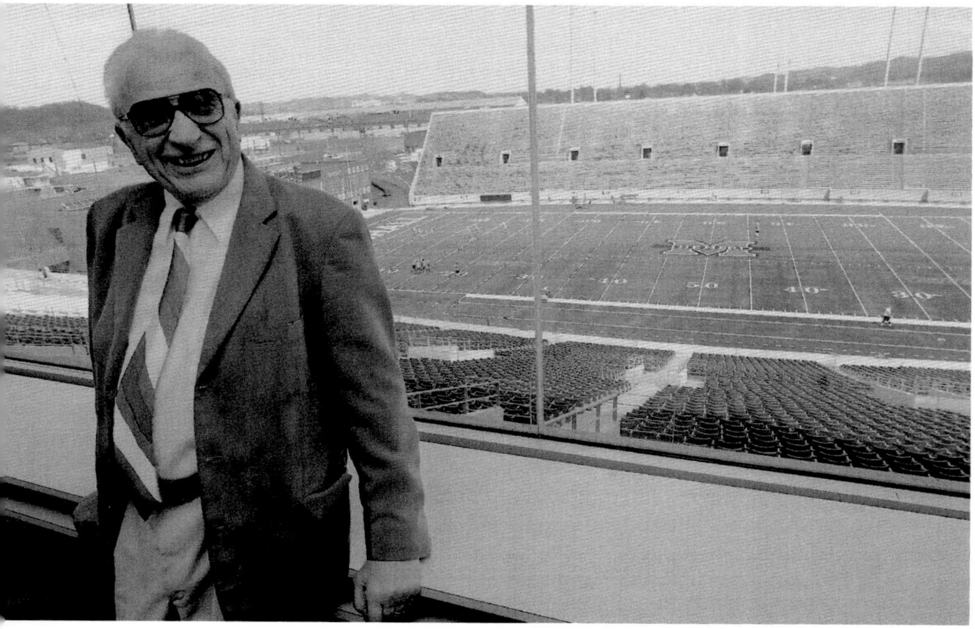

Estelle Belanger (1914–2000), better known as "Bill" to her friends and readers alike, frequently noted that she had gone into newspaper work at a time when "women were supposed to know their place." But as a reporter and editor for Huntington's newspapers for more than 50 years, she refused to be relegated to typical female assignments. She proved she could do just about any newspaper job, whether it was editing copy under deadline pressure or writing a first-person account of what it was like to climb into a jet fighter and fly with the Navy's Blue Angels, which she did in 1963. First hired as the assistant Sunday editor in 1942, she held a series of posts over the years. She retired as the fine-arts editor for the *Herald-Dispatch* in 1977 but continued to write columns and features until shortly before her death. (*H-D.*)

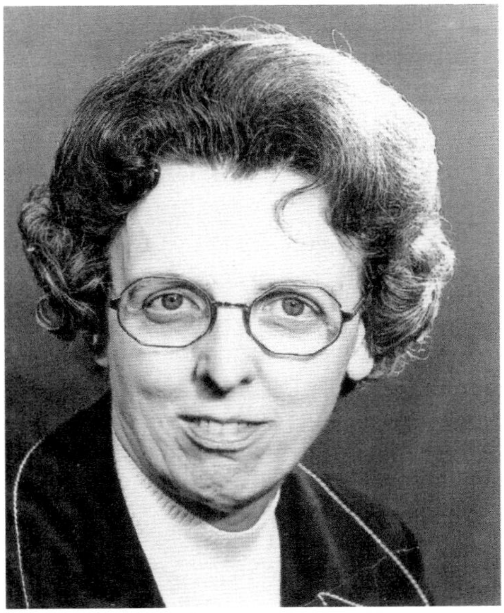

Don Hatfield started out in journalism in the 1950s working as a part-time sports assistant for the *Advertiser*, being paid a few dollars out of petty cash. He steadily rose through the ranks to eventually become executive editor, president, and publisher of the *Herald-Dispatch*. He followed that by becoming vice president of Gannett West in Arizona in charge of newspapers in El Paso, Sante Fe, Tucson, and a *USA Today* printing site in Chandler, Arizona. When he retired from 47 years of "newspapering," he and his wife, Sandy, moved from Tucson back to Huntington. (*H-D.*)

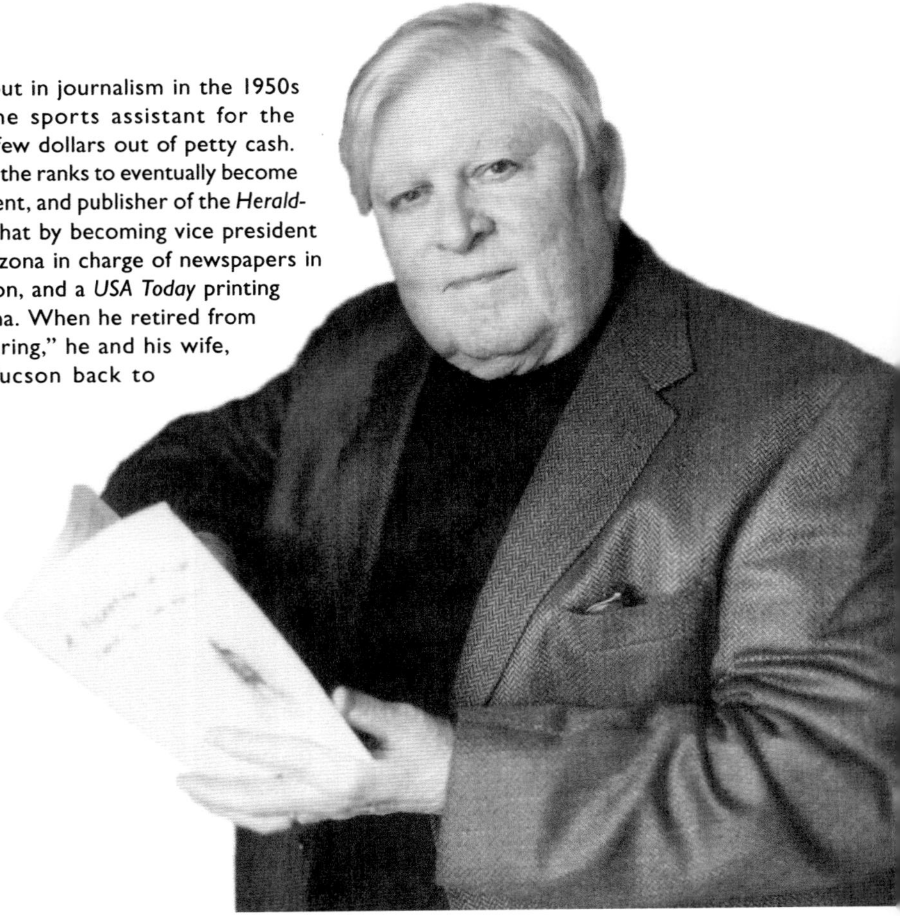

In 1949, the Huntington Publishing Company started one of the nation's first television stations, WSAZ. In those early days of television, the networks provided no daytime programming, and stations filled the void by airing locally produced programs such as WSAZ's *Coffee Time*, a live variety show. On-air personalities appearing on the show included, among others, D.J. Schroeder, Sue Chambers, Jule Huffman, Dean Sturm, and musical director Brownie Benson (seated at the piano). Fritz Leichner was the show's director. Most of them would be with the station for years. (WSAZ.)

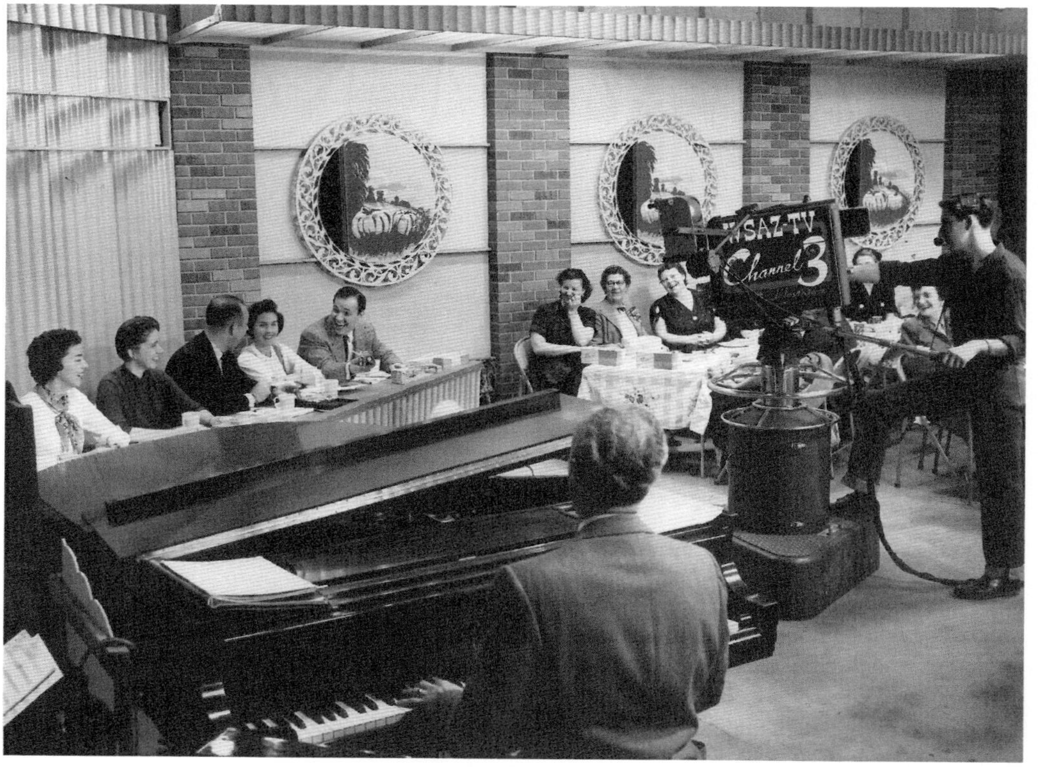

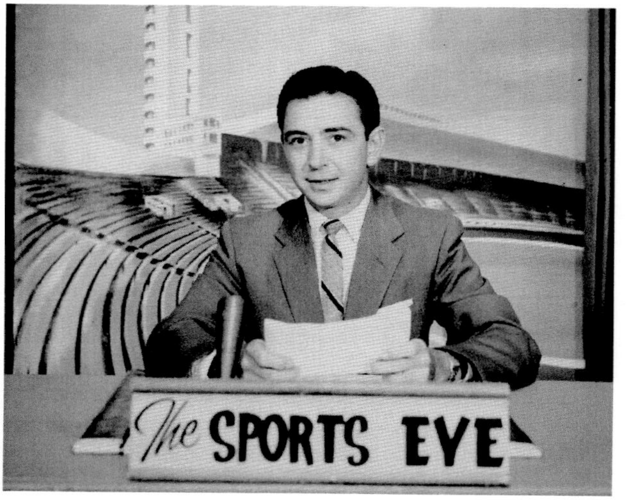

Jim Thacker joined WSAZ as sports director in the mid-1950s and was named Outstanding Sportscaster in the nation in 1962. He moved on to North Carolina, where he was sports director at WBTV in Charlotte and did frequent network sports assignments. He retired in 1981 and died in 1992. (WSAZ.)

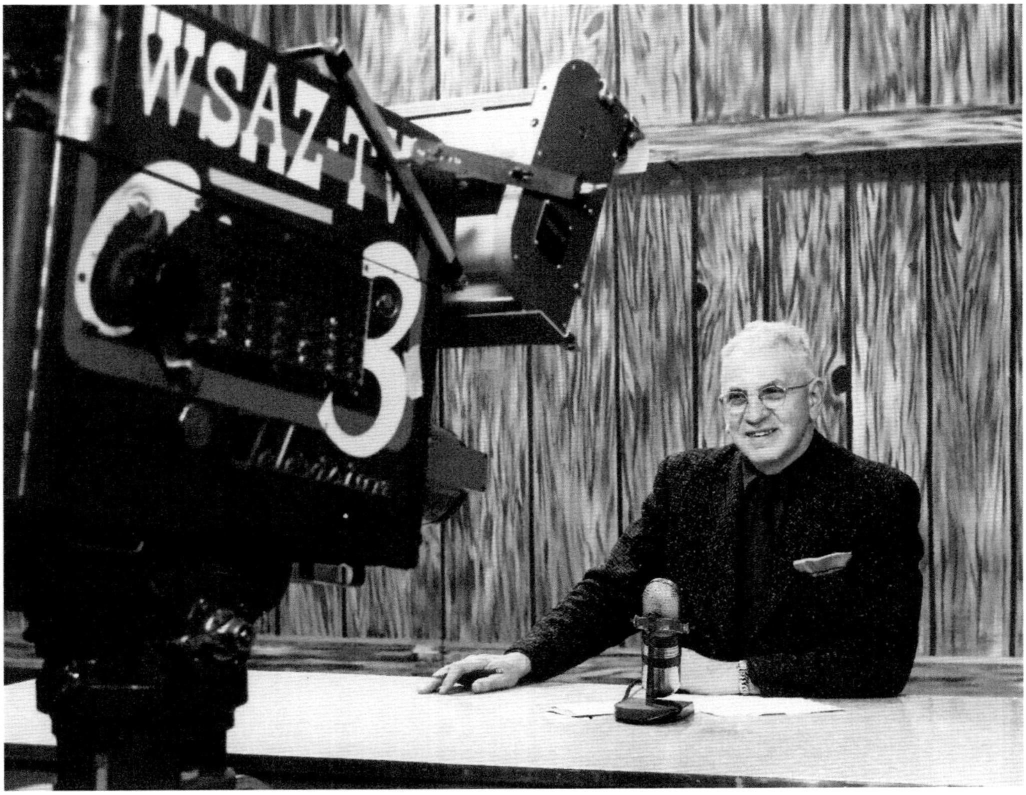

The *Herald-Dispatch* farm-and-garden column written by William David Click (1889–1960), better known as "Farmer Bill," was one of the newspaper's most popular features, and his regular broadcasts on WSAZ radio and television were equally popular. Born in Jackson County, Kentucky, the youngest of 12 children, he graduated from Berea College. In 1914, he came to West Virginia as an agricultural extension agent in Nicholas County. He moved to Lincoln County in 1919, to Wayne County in 1921, and Cabell County in 1930. He retired from the Extension Service in 1952 and then devoted all his time to his newspaper column and broadcast activities. (*H-D.*)

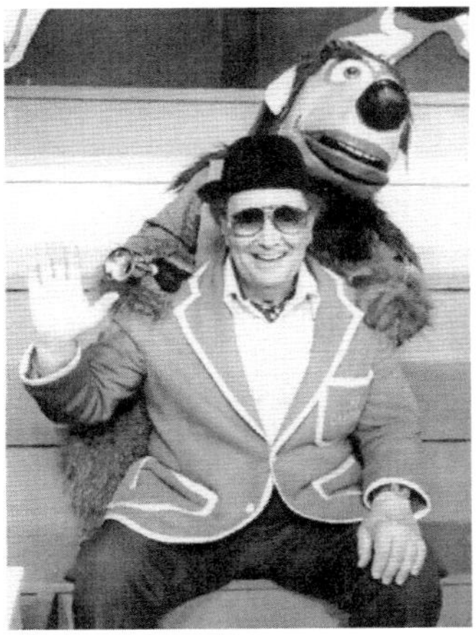

In his 40-plus years at WSAZ, Jule Huffman played many roles. In the station's early days, he was a singer and announcer. He was also the station's morning weatherman for years, but most longtime viewers remember him as (pictured here) Mr. Cartoon, the jovial host of WSAZ's afternoon cartoon show. Huffman began playing Mr. Cartoon in 1969 and continued until his retirement in 1995. (WSAZ.)

A Marshall College graduate and former reporter with the *Herald-Dispatch*, Marvin L. Stone (1924–2000) maintained close ties with the school and the community throughout his distinguished career. A Vermont native, he came to Huntington in 1941 to enroll at Marshall and talked his way into a reporting job at the newspaper. He spent two years at Marshall before leaving to join the Navy. Returning to Marshall and his reporting job, he graduated in 1948 and left Huntington to enter graduate school at Columbia University in New York. Graduating from Columbia in 1949, he worked as a European correspondent for the old International News Service and, in 1960, joined *US News & World Report*, where he rose to become the magazine's chief editor from 1976 to 1985. He followed that with four years as deputy director of the US Information Agency. (*H-D.*)

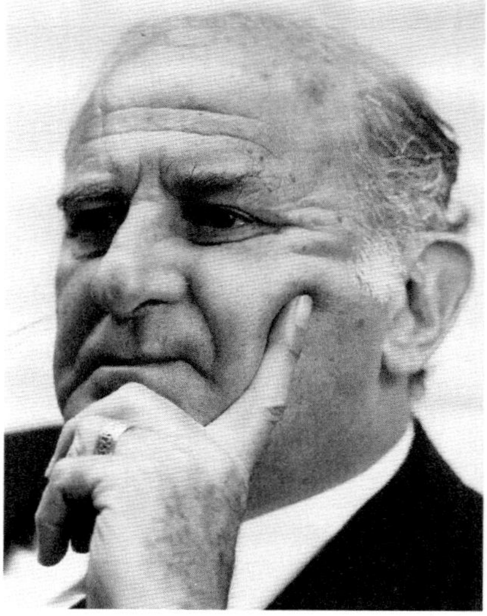

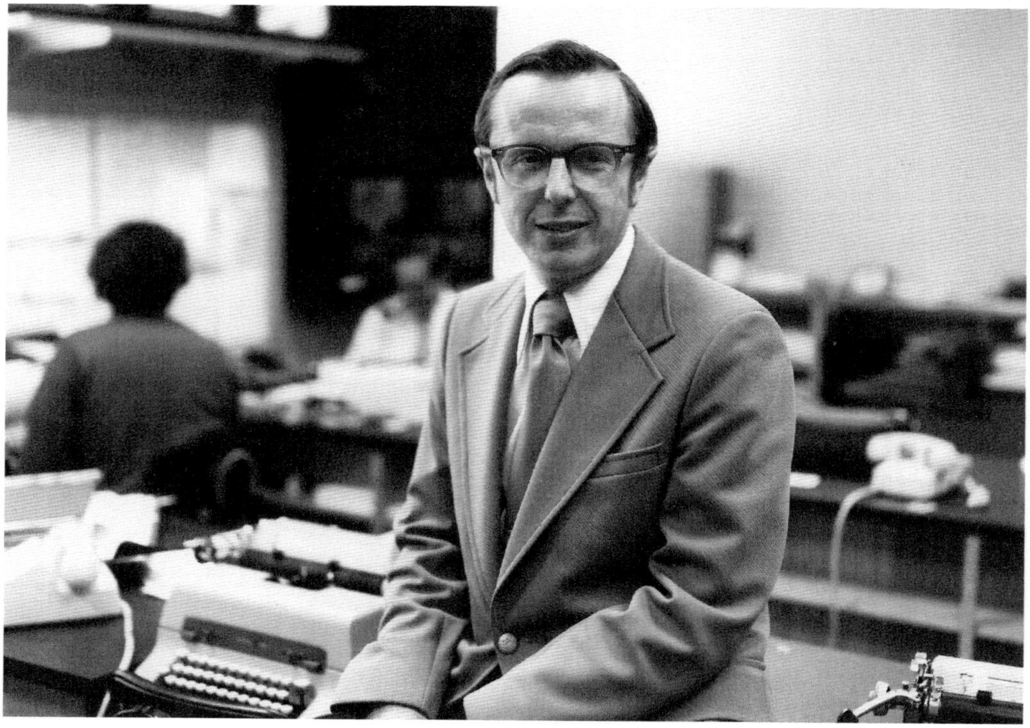

In the 1960s and 1970s, Bos Johnson was a daily video visitor in tens of thousands of Huntington-area homes as the news director for WSAZ-TV. During those years, he was a mentor to dozens of young journalists who went onto network news slots or jobs at stations in major metropolitan areas. Widely respected in the broadcast industry, he served as president of the Radio-Television News Directors Association (RTNDA) and, in that role, arranged and presided over Pres. Richard Nixon's last televised news conference in 1974. Two years later, he left WSAZ to join the journalism faculty at Marshall University. (*H-D.*)

School Days

Favorite teachers are also memorable, and no book this size could begin to hold all of Huntington's instructors. Instead, what is presented here are the names and faces of some who played important roles in administering Huntington's schools, either from the principal's office or the superintendent's chair at the school board's central office. Two names stand out: John Hunt Oley and Cater G. Woodson. Oley was a former Union general in the Civil War who had been stationed in West Virginia, liked what he saw, and stayed on after the war. Collis P. Huntington hired him as a sales agent for his Central Land Company. When the city conducted its first municipal election, Oley was elected town recorder and treasurer, which put him in charge of the city's schools, a task he took seriously. He urged construction of the city's first school building, and when he died as it neared completion, the school was named for him. Carter G. Woodson attended the city's all-black Douglass High School and later returned to the city as its principal. Today, he is widely credited with originating Black History Month.

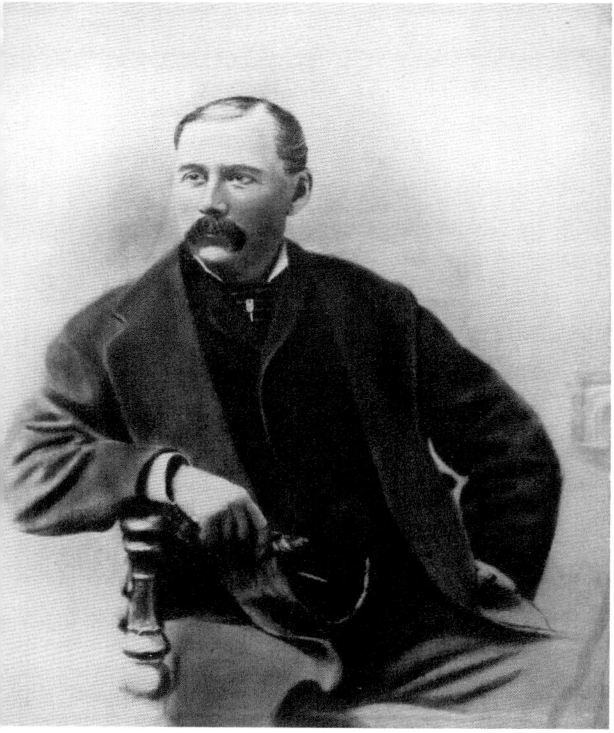

Gen. John Hunt Oley (1830–1888) was elected recorder and treasurer in the new city of Huntington's first election. As recorder, he was in charge of the city's schools. A native of Utica, New York, Oley served in the 7th Regiment of the New York National Guard and was posted to what would become the new state of West Virginia. He served gallantly and was promoted to brevet general. After the war, he stayed on in Charleston. In 1871, he moved to the fledgling community of Huntington, where Collis P. Huntington employed him as an agent for his Central Land Company. (*H-D.*)

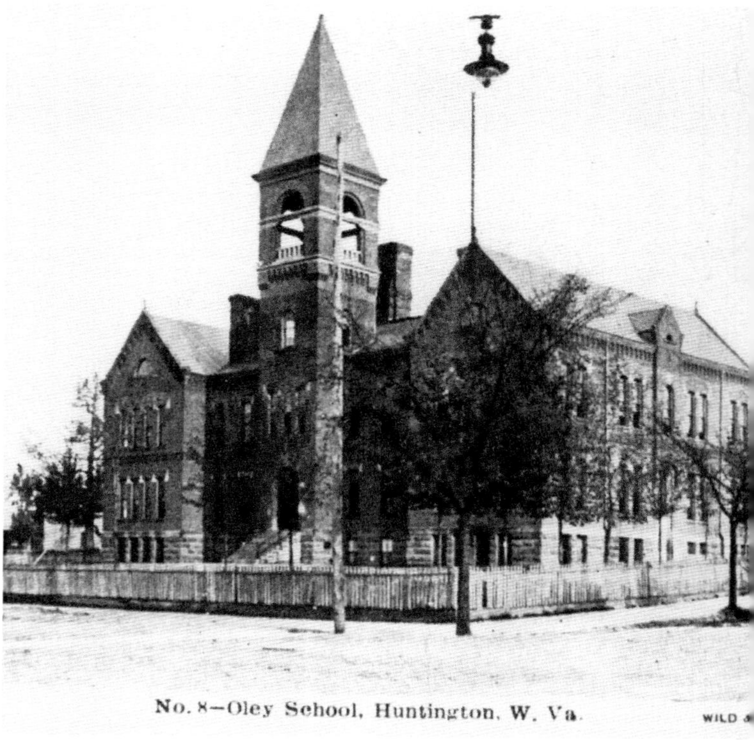

Huntington's schools originally met in makeshift quarters. Finally, a decision was made to construct a handsome new school building. When General Oley died as the school was nearing completion, it was decided it should be named in his honor. This photograph shows the school as it appeared in the 1890s. Originally, the school housed all 12 grades. With the construction of Huntington High School in 1916, Oley lost its older students, and its name was changed to Central School. In the early 1930s, the name was changed back to Oley. The building was demolished a number of years ago. (*H-D.*)

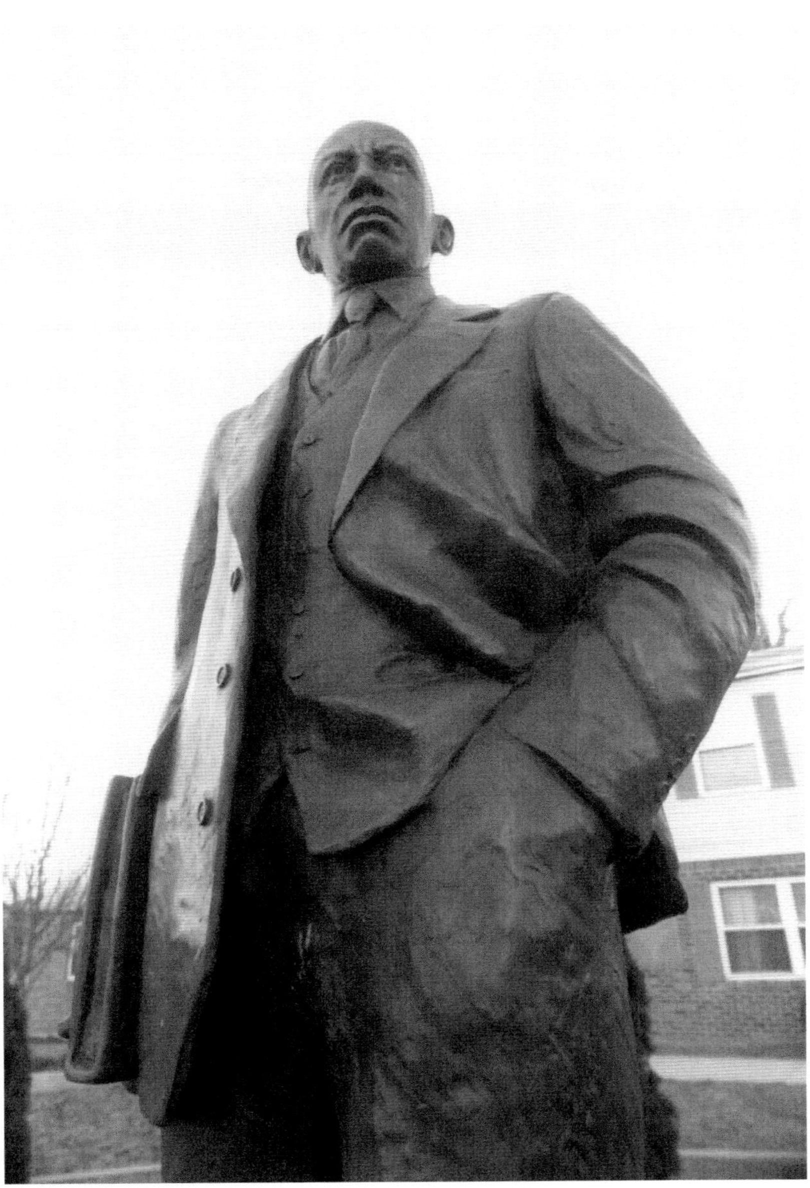

Carter Godwin Woodson (1875–1950), acknowledged as the "father of Black History Month," was born in Virginia to parents who were former slaves. The family moved to Huntington in 1893 after Carter and his brother Robert had migrated to West Virginia to work in the coal mines. Woodson attended Douglass High School in Huntington, graduating in 1896. He studied at Berea College in Kentucky and returned to Huntington as principal of Douglass in 1900. In 1903, he taught in the Philippines; during 1906–1907, he traveled around the world, studied at the Sorbonne, and returned to continue his education at the University of Chicago and at Harvard, receiving a doctorate from Harvard in 1912. As an author, publisher, and educator, he spent the rest of his influential life promoting the systematic collection and dissemination of black historical information. In 1995, the Carter G. Woodson Memorial Foundation erected this statue of him on Hal Greer Boulevard in Huntington. (*H-D.*)

A native of Mannington, West Virginia, Roy Straight (1911–1986) was a teacher and administrator at a number of Huntington schools and the assistant football coach at Marshall College from 1937 to 1949. Straight began his teaching career in Harrison County in 1935 before coaching at Marshall. After a one-year coaching stint at the University of North Carolina, he returned to Huntington to teach at Huntington East High School. From 1951 to 1953, he taught at Enslow Junior High and returned the following school year to Huntington East. A year later, he became principal at West Junior High School and served there until he was named principal at Huntington High in 1967. (*H-D.*)

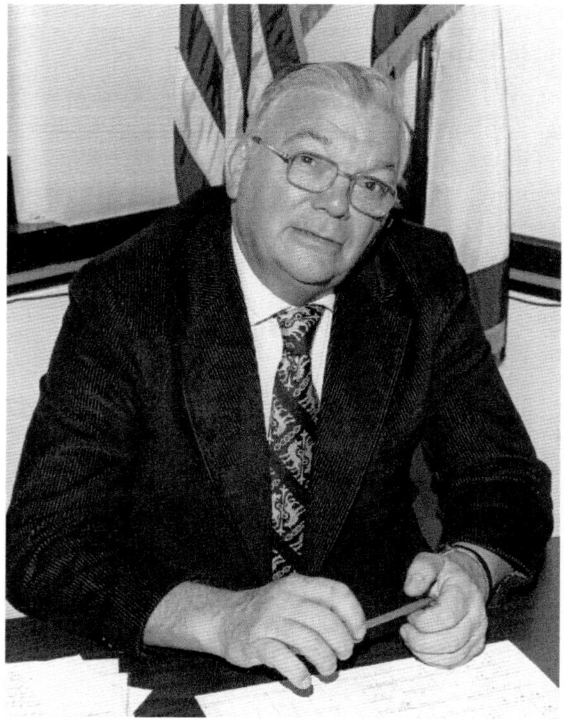

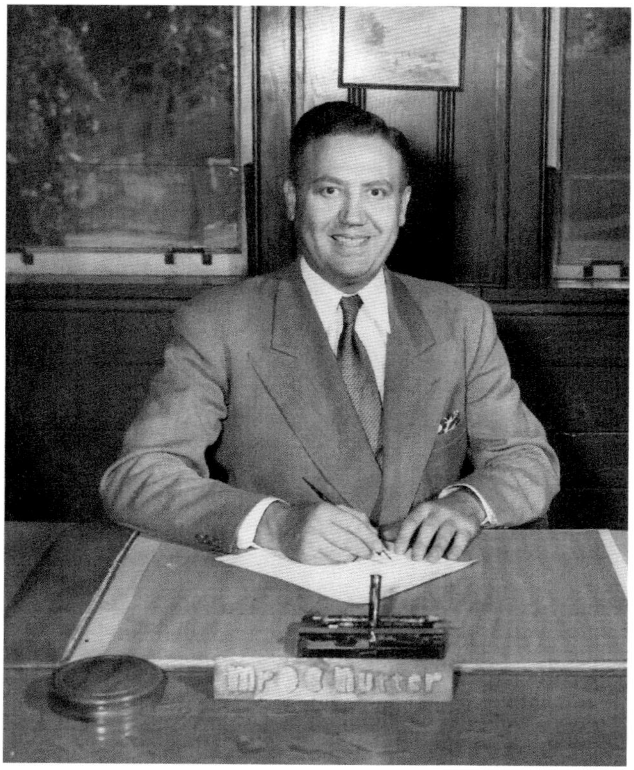

Greenbrier County native Olin C. Nutter (1903–1987) was Cabell County superintendent of schools for 32 years, a tenure unmatched in the county's history. A graduate of Morris Harvey (now the University of Charleston) and the University of Cincinnati, Nutter came to the county in 1922 to be superintendent of schools in Milton's Grant District. That was before West Virginia went to its current system of county-wide school systems. He was named assistant county superintendent in 1933 and superintendent in 1938. This undated photograph shows him early in his tenure. Often the center of controversy, the retiring Nutter said at his final school board meeting in 1970 that Huntington had hundreds of doctors, lawyers, and ministers "but only one school superintendent, and he can get more hell than any of them." (*H-D.*)

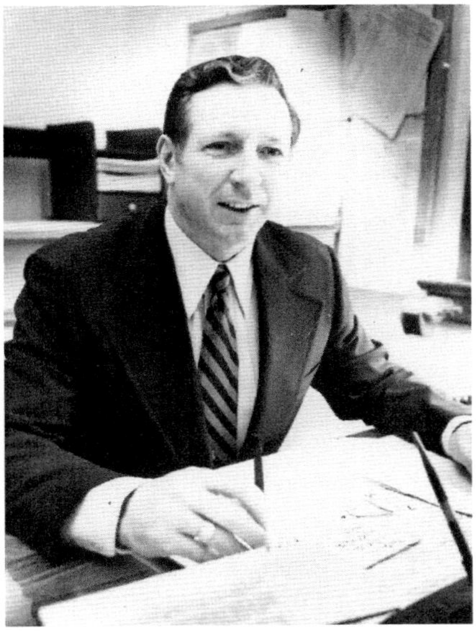

A graduate of Marshall University and a veteran of the US Marine Corps, Joe Avis was a teacher and principal in Cabell County's schools for nearly 30 years before he retired in 1979. He began his teaching career at Milton High School in 1950 and served as band director at Milton and Barboursville High School for 16 years before becoming a principal. He held that post at the former Ona and West Junior Highs before becoming principal at Huntington East in 1973. When he retired, he moved to Florida, where he died in 1991. (*H-D.*)

In 1977, Joseph A. Slash (1919–1986) made history when he took the oath of office as Cabell County superintendent of schools—becoming the first black school superintendent in West Virginia. Slash graduated from Douglass High School, the county's all-black high school in 1937, and continued his education at Bluefield State Teachers College, the University of Pittsburgh, Case Western Reserve University, Ohio University, and Marshall University. In 1956, he returned to Douglass High as principal shortly before it was closed due to school desegregation. Slash died when he suffered a heart attack during a Marshall University football game at old Fairfield Stadium. (*H-D.*)

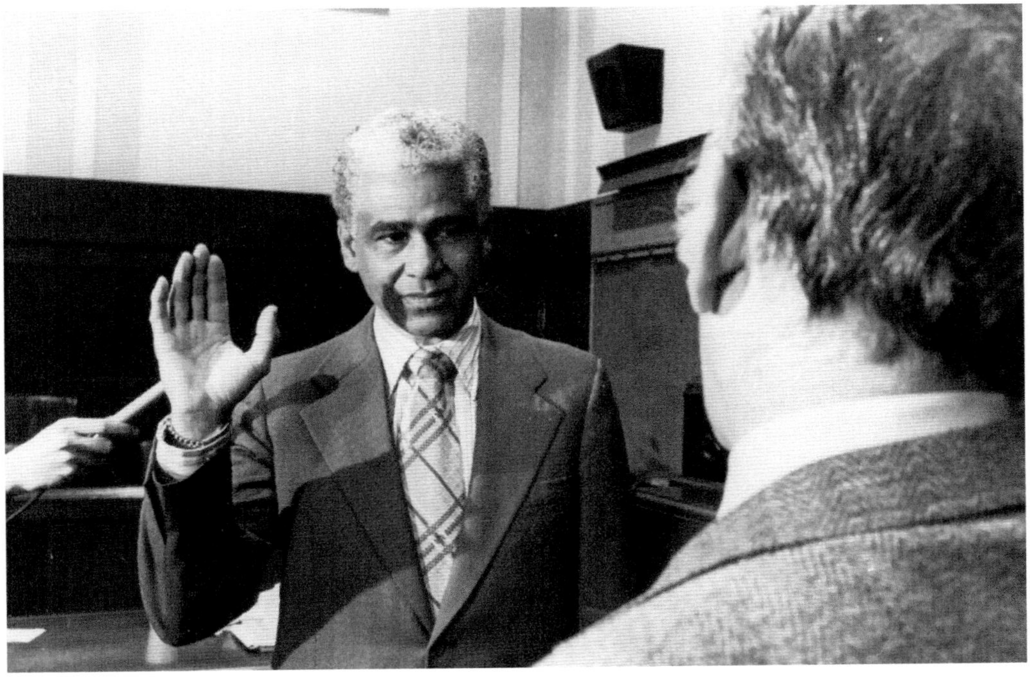

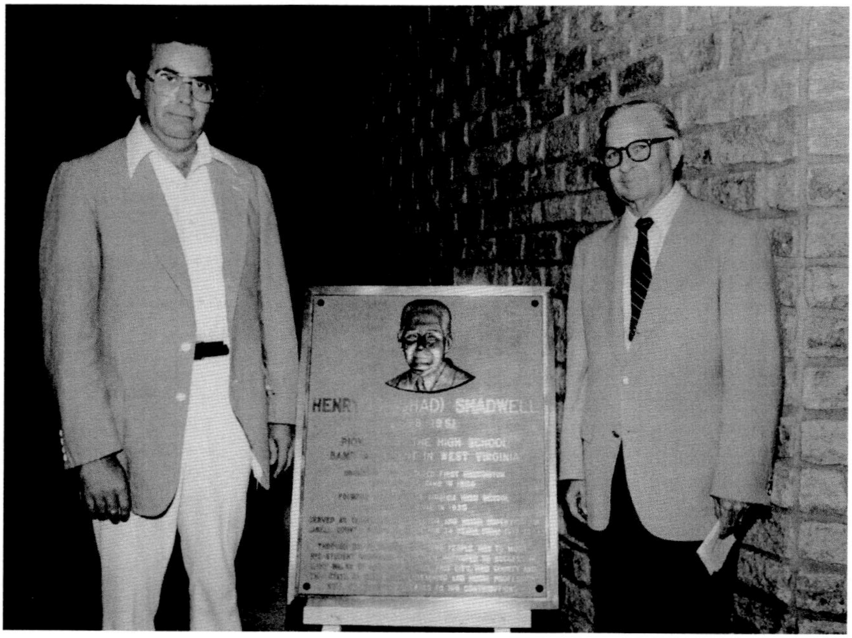

Henry C. Shadwell (1898–1951), who founded the West Virginia High School Band Festival in 1935, was a teacher, band director, and music supervisor in the Cabell County schools for 34 years. In the 1920s, he organized a band made up of local Boy Scouts that traveled the Chautauqua circuit playing concerts in dozens of cities. In 1924, he organized and directed the first Huntington High School Band. A plaque honoring Shadwell was installed in the music room at Huntington High in 1981. Pictured with the plaque are school superintendent Garth Errington (left) and Bob Dwight, who organized the memorial committee. (*H-D.*)

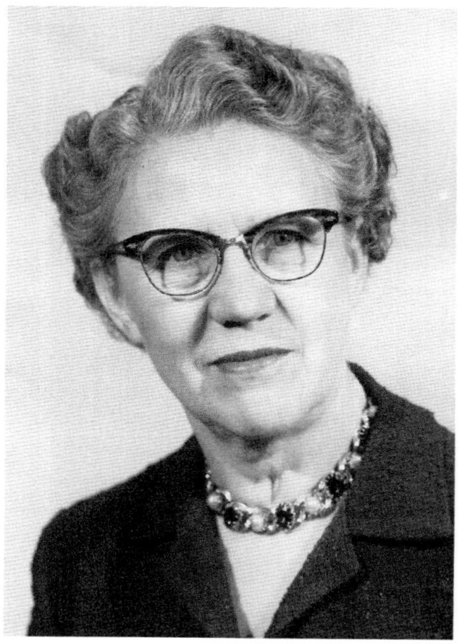

Named as principal at Huntington High School in 1955, Mae Newman was the school's first female principal since it opened in 1916. A native of Wayne County, she was a teacher and administrator in Cabell County schools for more than 40 years. She earned a bachelor's degree in physics and education at West Virginia University and a master's in mathematics and education at Columbia University in New York. She was a junior high school teacher, a math teacher at Huntington High, and the dean of girls at Huntington High from 1933 to 1955. She was principal at HHS for eight years, retiring in 1963. (*H-D.*)

Legends of the Game

Huntington residents love sports of all kinds, whether it is a big-time football game at Marshall University's Joan C. Edwards Stadium, a heated basketball contest at the Henderson Center, or a neighborhood little-league or soccer game. The city has spawned a truly amazing cadre of players and coaches, many of whom have gone onto national and even international prominence. Any list would start, of course, with Marshall coaches Bob Pruett, Cam Henderson, and Jule Rivlin. Then, a person might add stand-out Marshall players like Hal Greer and Mike D'Antoni, Chad Pennington, and Troy Brown, among others. And those people are just the beginning. At other levels, one needs to add legendary (the only word that does them justice) high school track coach Ray McCoy and Bill Archer, who almost single-handedly made Huntington the high school wrestling capital of West Virginia. Finally, there is amateur golf great William C. Campbell, the only man in golfing history to be president of the US Golf Association and captain of the Royal and Ancient Golf Club of St. Andrews. Is it any wonder why people in Huntington love sports so much?

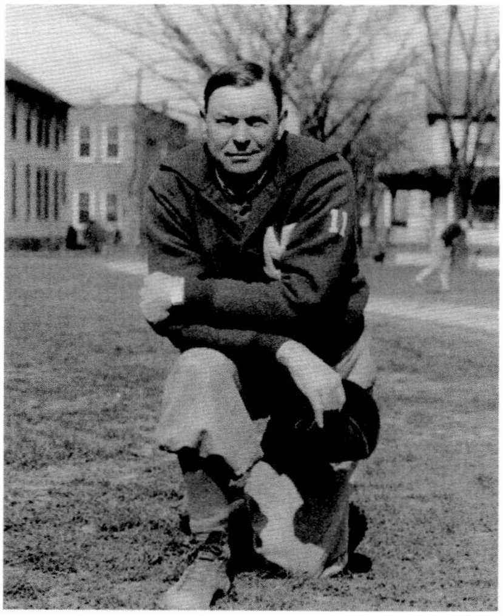

Eli Camden "Cam" Henderson (1890–1956) was a basketball innovator who is widely credited with originating the zone defense and the fast break, two staples of the modern game. Born at Joetown, West Virginia, he attended Glenville State Normal College, where he played football, basketball, and baseball. He joined Marshall in 1935 to coach both basketball and football. In 1947, he coached Marshall to victory in the NAIB national tournament in Kansas City. He resigned as football coach following the 1949 season but continued to coach basketball through the 1954–1955 season. He is Marshall's all-time winningest basketball coach, with a record of 362-16. The school's basketball arena, Cam Henderson Center, is named for him. (MU.)

Jule Rivlin (1917–2002) made his mark as both a basketball player and coach at Marshall. A Pennsylvania native, he played for three years under legendary coach Cam Henderson, graduating in 1940 after accumulating a total of 1,189 points and becoming Marshall's first basketball All-American. In 1955, "Riv" returned to campus, took over from Henderson as head coach, and guided the Big Green's 1955–1956 team to its first Mid-American Conference championship and NCAA tournament appearance. He held the job until 1963. (*H-D.*)

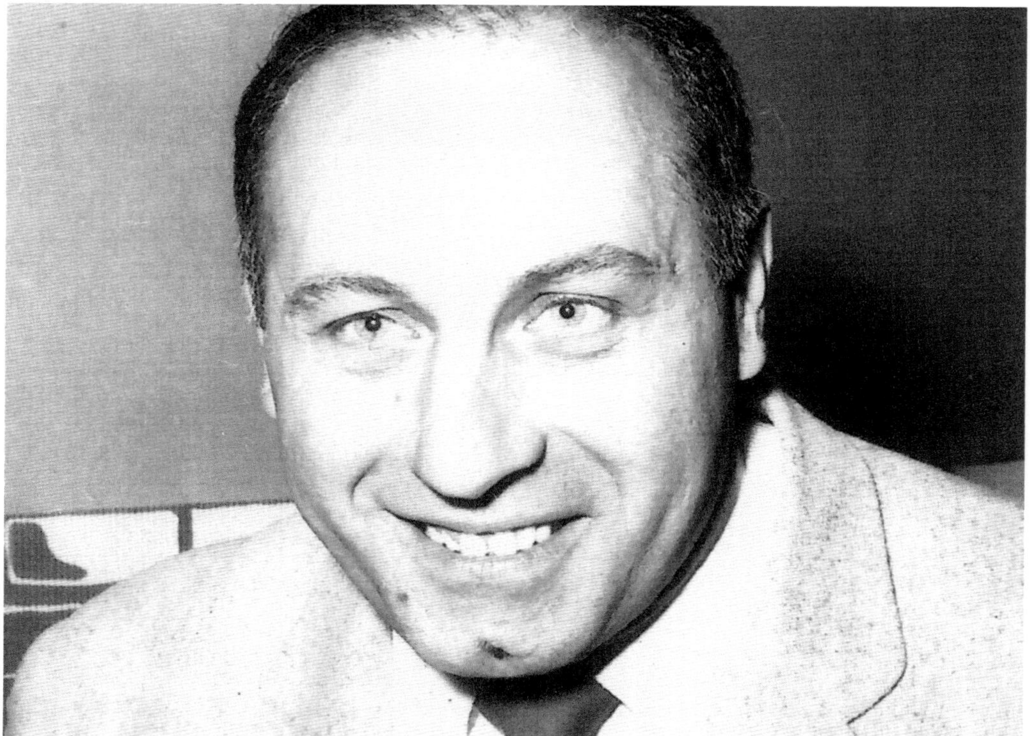

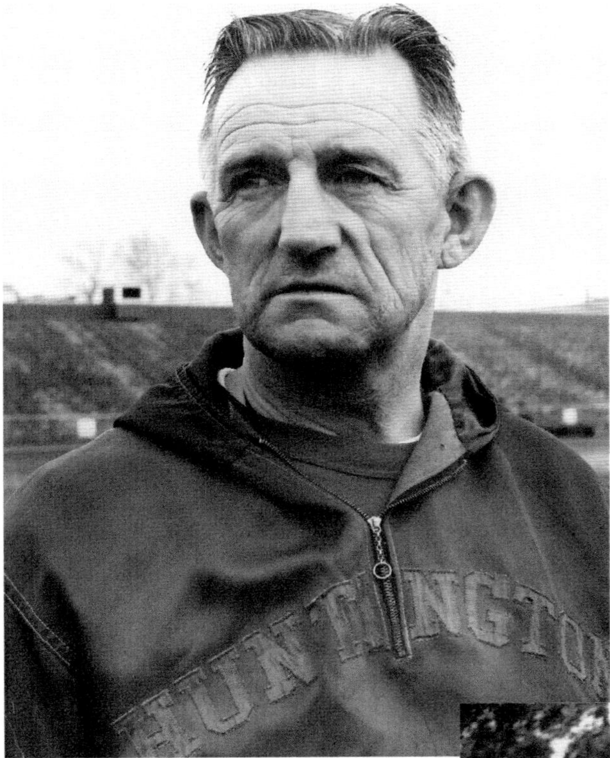

Ray McCoy (1908–1999) coached eight state championship track teams while at Huntington High School from 1944 through 1971. A demanding coach, McCoy was also a caring man who frequently bought track shoes for those who did not have them, as well as clothes and food for countless needy students. He was a graduate of Marshall College, where he played football from 1928 through 1931. The track at Huntington High is named in his honor, and each year the top track-and-field athlete in Cabell County is presented a trophy that is also named for him. After retiring as a coach, he served as a track official on the state and regional level. (*H-D.*)

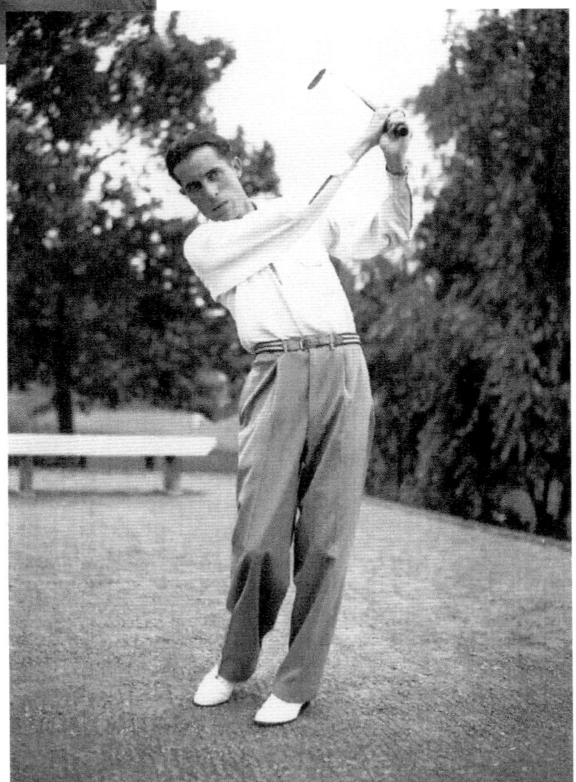

Arnold Browning (1914–1977) worked at Guyan Golf & Country Club for 50 years, 36 of those as club pro. Born in Logan County, he started at Guyan as a 12-year-old caddy. He went on to work as a club repairer and in the pro shop before moving onto the course as a teaching assistant and finally club pro. In an interview shortly before his death, he credited President Eisenhower for helping generate an upswing in the game's popularity. He said, "He was the only president we had in a long time who played it. When the people saw Ike, their old war hero, playing golf and loving it . . . he just helped the game grow." (*H-D.*)

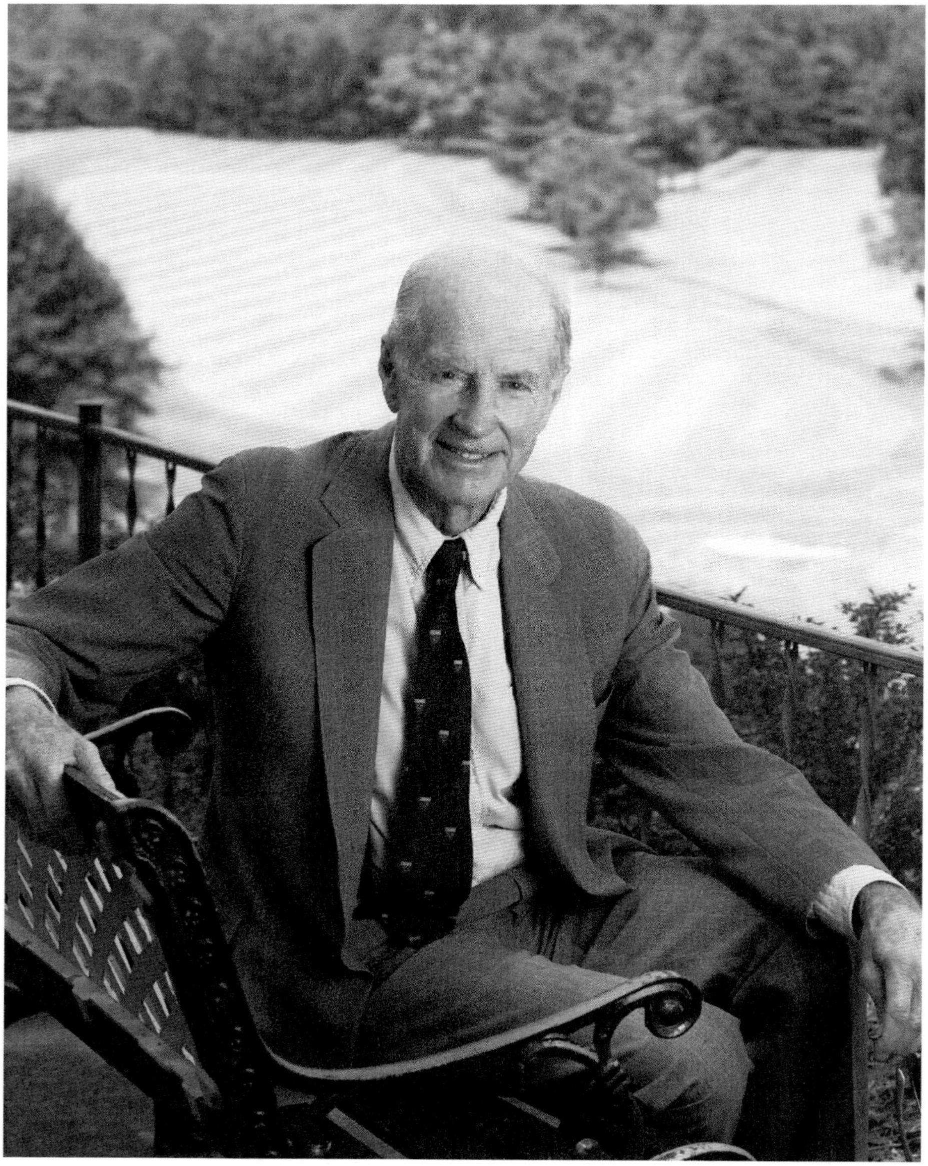

William "Bill" Cammack Campbell says he never wanted to be a professional golfer. Instead, he chose to enter the family insurance business; however, as an amateur, he compiled a golfing record destined to be unequaled. Born in Huntington in 1923, he was introduced to the game of golf by his father at the age of three. His game flourished even though he never took a lesson. In his long amateur career, Campbell played in 37 US Amateurs, winning the event in 1964. He played on eight Walker Cup teams, captaining the 1955 team. A runner-up in the 1954 British Amateur, he was a three-time runner-up in the Canadian Amateur championship. He won 15 West Virginia Amateur titles—and that is only a partial listing of his amazing record. He was president of the US Golf Association in 1982–1983, and when he captained the Royal and Ancient Golf Club of St. Andrews, he became the first individual to head both of golf's worldwide governing bodies. (*HQ.*)

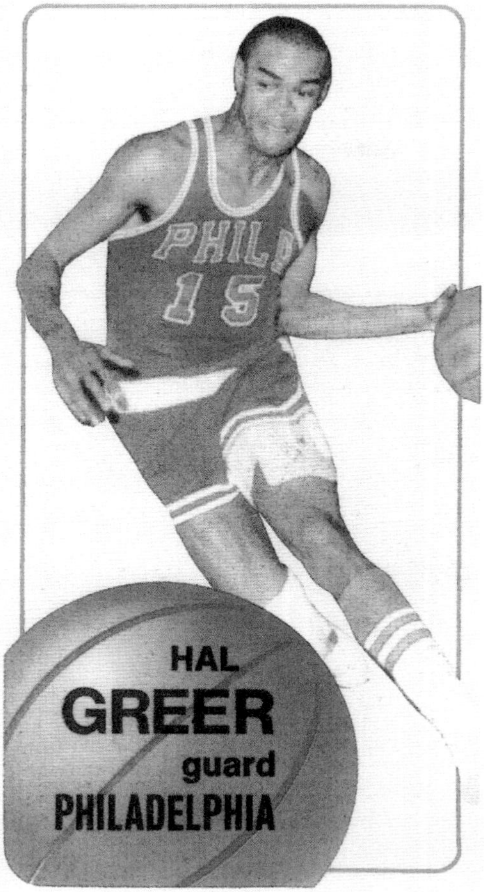

Born in 1936, Harold Everett "Hal" Greer grew up in Huntington and was a star player at the city's all-black Douglass High School. He broke the color barrier for African American college athletes in West Virginia in 1955 when he was awarded a basketball scholarship at Marshall College. He was picked by the Syracuse Nationals in the 1958 NBA draft and remained with the same franchise throughout his career, moving with the Nationals when they became the Philadelphia 76ers. Huntington City Council has honored him by renaming Sixteenth Street, which borders the MU campus, to Hal Greer Boulevard. He is shown here in an image from a vintage bubblegum card. (Author's.)

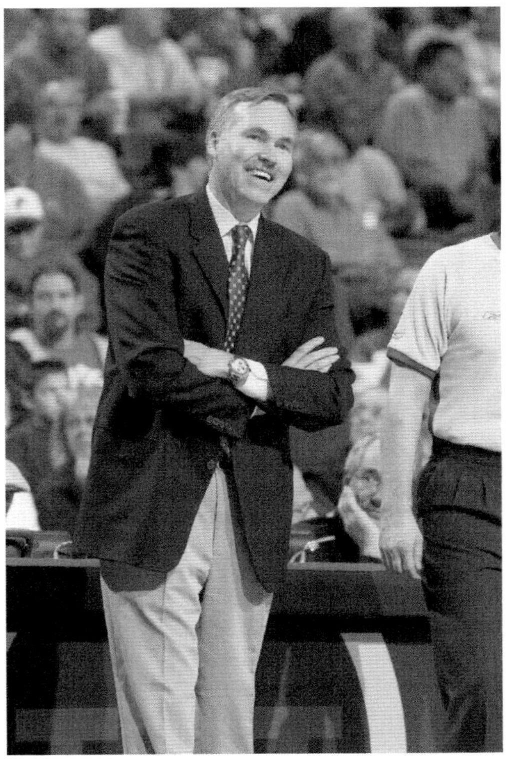

A member of the Marshall University Athletics Hall of Fame, Italian American Michael Anthony D'Antoni has made sports headlines both in this country and in Italy. Born in Mullens, West Virginia, he played high school basketball there before becoming a standout player at Marshall. Drafted by the Kansas City Kings, he played three seasons with them and then moved to Italy, where he quickly established a reputation as a talented player and later as a coach. Returning to this country, he became head coach of the Phoenix Suns. He was named NBA Coach of the Year in 2004–2005. In 2008, D'Antoni was hired to coach the New York Knicks, signing a four-year, $24 million contract. He resigned in March 2012, and the following November he was hired to coach the Los Angeles Lakers. (*HQ.*)

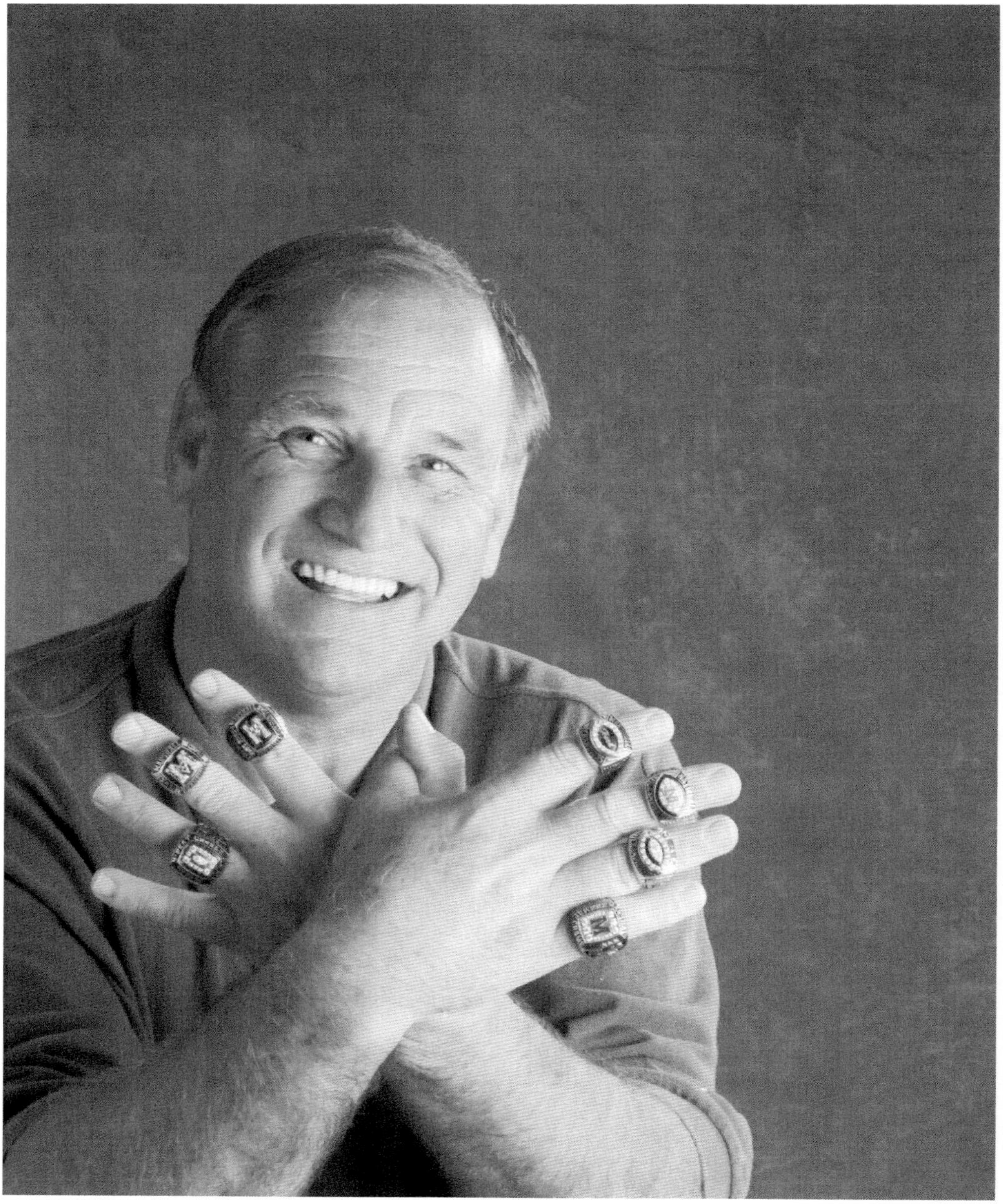

Bob Pruett was head football coach of the Marshall Thundering Herd for nine seasons, from 1996 to 2004, a tenure that can only be described as "spectacular." Not only did he take Marshall to an undefeated season and national championship during his first year as head coach, he went on to elevate Marshall from NCAA Division I-AA to the big-time ranks of Division I-A and, in the process, earned well-deserved recognition as "the winningest coach in college football." (*HQ.*)

Troy Brown retired from professional football in 2008 after playing his entire 15-season career with the New England Patriots. He earned three Super Bowl rings with the team and retired as the franchise leader in career receptions. Born in Barnwell, South Carolina, Brown played his college ball at Marshall University, where he was a standout wide receiver, punt returner, and kickoff returner. In his adopted hometown of Huntington, Brown is active in a number of charitable activities on behalf of Marshall, Hospice of Huntington, the A.D. Lewis Community Center, and other causes. (*HQ.*)

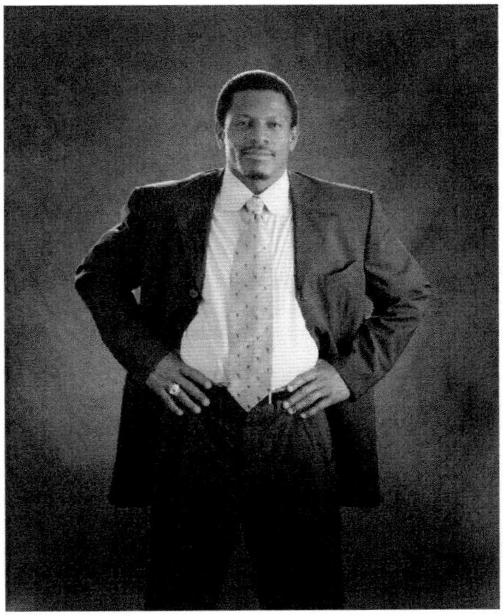

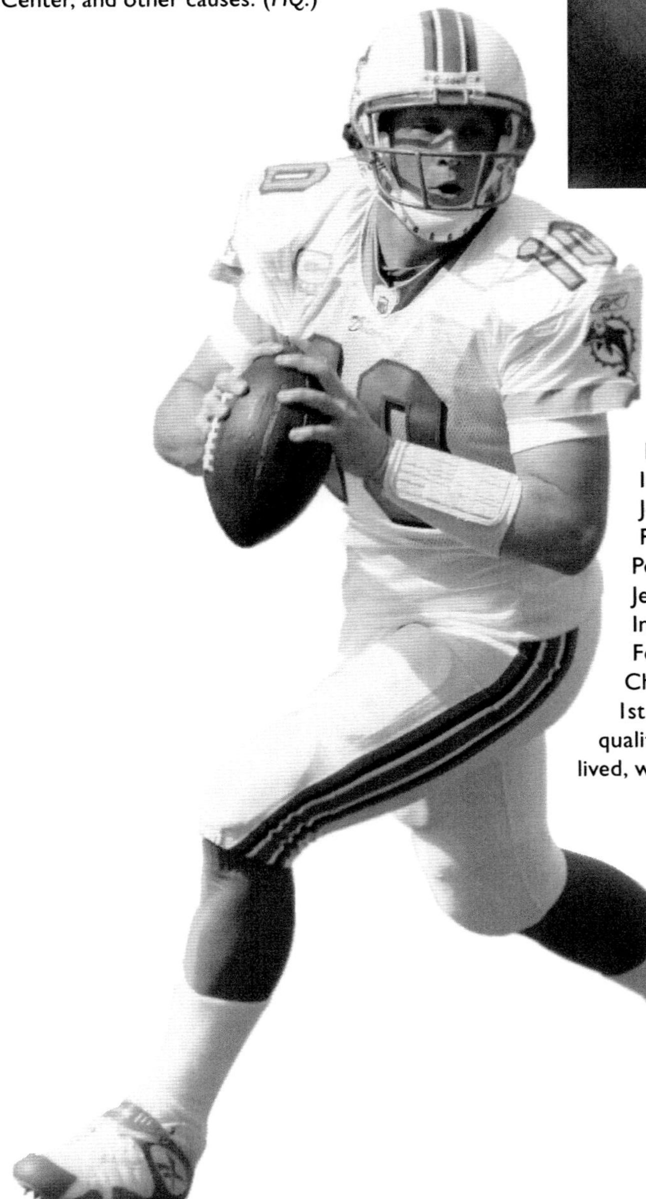

A standout quarterback at Marshall, Chad Pennington led the Thundering Herd to the school's first bowl victory in a 48-29 route of the University of Louisville in the 1998 Motor City Bowl. In 2000, he was picked by the New York Jets in the first round of the NFL draft. Plagued by injuries throughout his career, Pennington played eight seasons for the Jets and three for the Miami Dolphins. In 2011, he worked as a color analyst for Fox network's NFL telecasts. In 2003, Chad and his wife, Robin, established the 1st and 10 Foundation to help improve the quality of people's lives in areas they have lived, worked, and played. (*HQ.*)

As a student at Huntington High School and North College Hill High School in Cincinnati, Ovinton J'Anthony "O.J." Mayo was considered by many sportswriters to be the best high school basketball player in the nation. He went on to play college basketball for the University of Southern California and then turned pro after his first year. He was drafted by the Minnesota Timberwolves, which immediately traded him to the Memphis Grizzlies. Mayo played for Huntington High in 2006–2007 and helped lead the team to its third consecutive state Class AAA basketball championship. (*H-D.*)

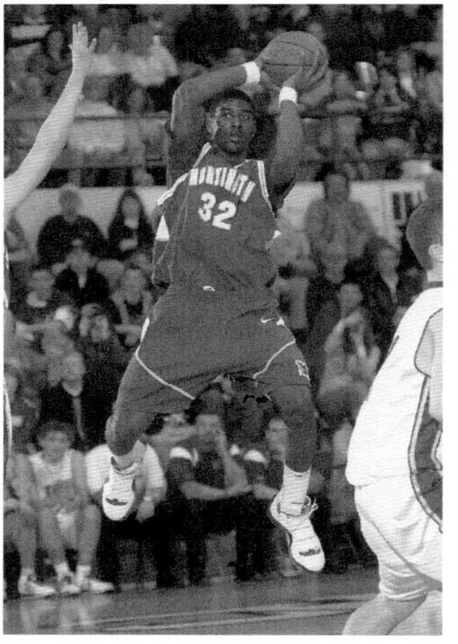

Honored as National High School Wrestling Coach of the Year in 1998, William "Bill" James Archer has dedicated his life to working with Cabell County students. During his 35 years as head wrestling coach at Huntington High School, he coached 26 individual state wrestling champions, four individual national champions, one Olympian, and 25 regional championship teams. It is largely due to his hard work that the state wrestling tournament and the WSAZ Wrestling Tournament have become annual events in Huntington. (*H-D.*)

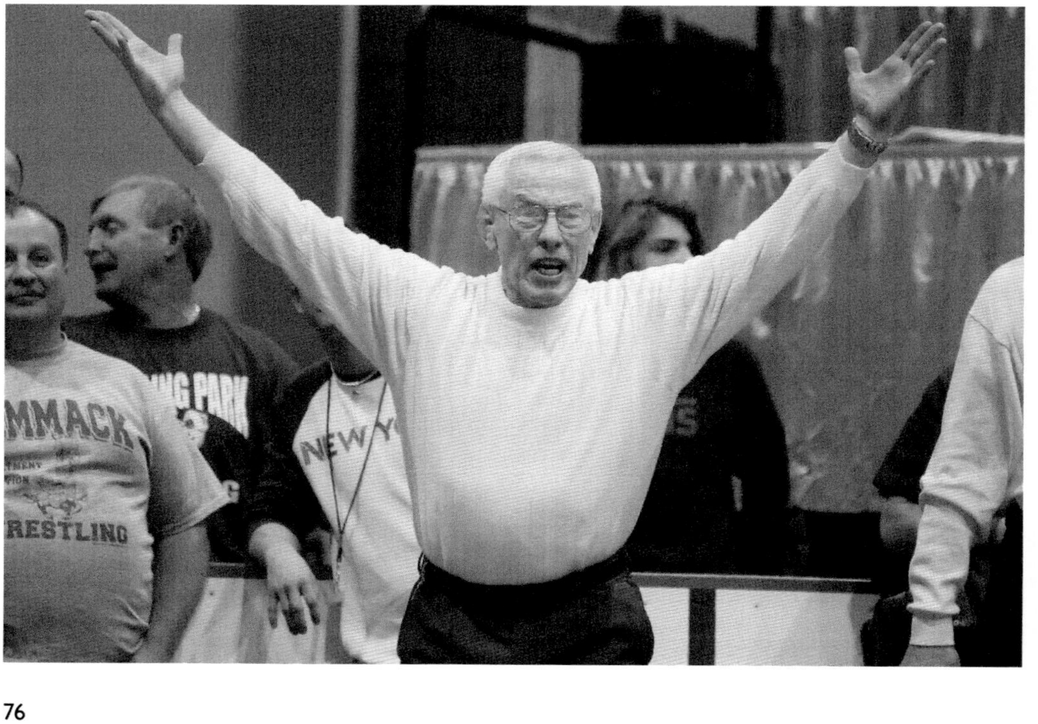

The Healers

From its earliest days, Huntington has been fortunate to have a contingent of physicians who represent the very best of their profession. A dozen of them are included in this chapter, and it would have been easy to include another dozen—or more. Each of those included has a fascinating story. Pharmacy's loss was urology's gain when Dr. Charles "Carl" Hoffman switched professions. He went on to earn one of the highest honors possible in medicine when he assumed the presidency of the American Medical Association. Dr. H. Darrel Darby invented an innovative postsurgical shoe that is in use worldwide. Dr. Jose Ricard fled his native Cuba and the repressive Castro regime and settled in West Virginia, where he became a nationally recognized expert in both family and sports medicine. Dr. Charles McKown has played a pivotal role in the growth and development of the Joan C. Edwards School of Medicine at Marshall University. And, finally, there is Dr. Paul Ambrose, whose young life was tragically cut short on 9/11. Had he lived, he surely would have brought even more deserved luster to the city's medical community.

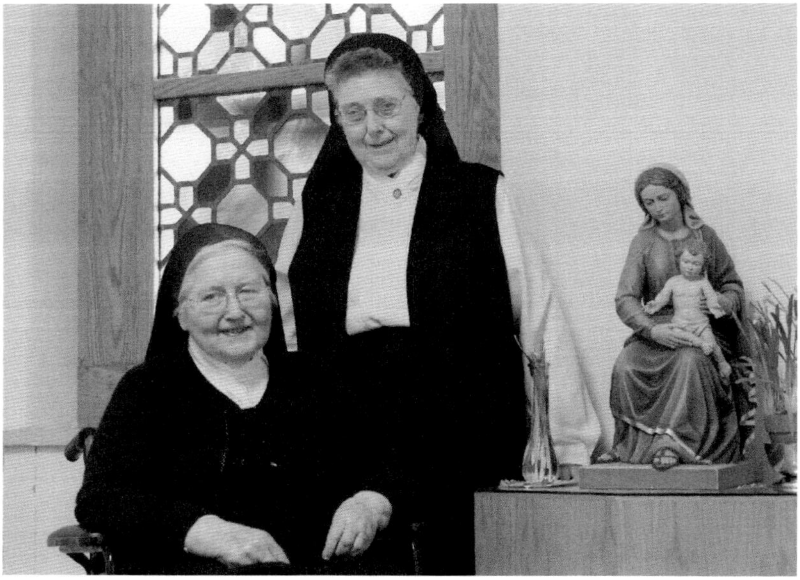

In 1912, a tiny band of Pallottine Missionary Sisters left their home in Bremerhaven, Germany, bound for America. Arriving in this country, they came to West Virginia and opened hospitals in Richwood and Buckhannon. In 1924, they came to Huntington and opened a 35-bed hospital. In the hospital's earliest years, the Sisters nursed the sick and injured, cooked, served, washed, ironed, cleaned, fired the clunky coal furnace, and even grew their own fruits and vegetables. Today, the tiny hospital they founded has evolved into St. Mary's Medical Center, a 440-bed, high-tech health-care facility. Over the years, the ranks of the Sisters at St. Mary's have thinned, but a dedicated handful of nuns still serve at the hospital. Among them are Sisters Celeste Lynch (left) and Diane Bushee. (*H-D.*)

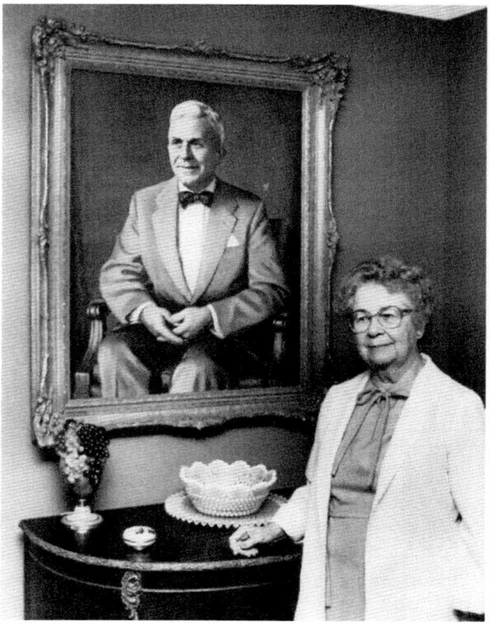

Born in Obids, North Carolina, Dr. Arthur Shad Jones (1885–1978) earned his medical degree at the University of Virginia Medical School in 1910 and served his orthopedic residency at Lakeside Hospital in Cleveland, Ohio. Moving to Huntington, he became the first orthopedic surgeon to practice in West Virginia. He opened the Huntington Children's Hospital in 1923, and it later became the Huntington Orthopedic Hospital and still later evolved into today's Huntington Hospital. Seeing a desperate need for medical care for crippled children, he regularly traveled throughout the state, holding free clinics. In this 1984 photograph, his widow, Fannie, poses with a portrait of her late husband. (*H-D.*)

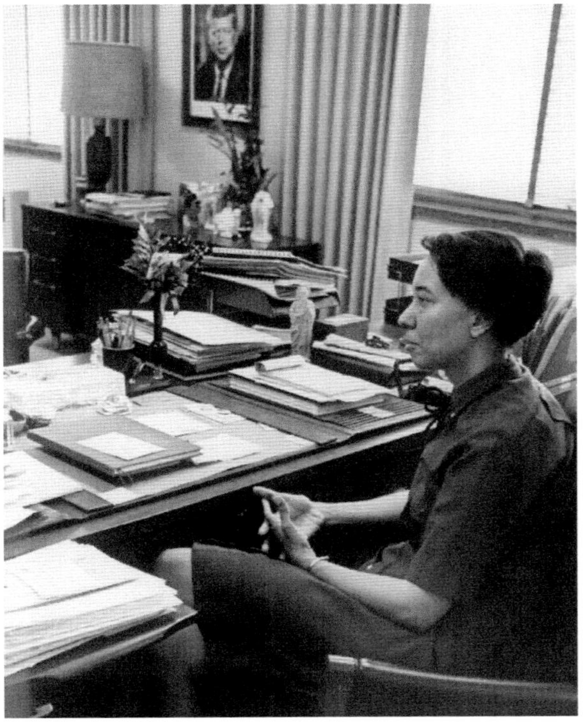

Dr. Mildred Mitchell-Bateman (1922–2012) made history in 1962 when she was named director of the West Virginia Department of Mental Health, making her the first African American woman to lead a West Virginia state agency. Born in Georgia, she came to West Virginia to work as a physician at Lakin State Hospital. After attending the Meninger School of Psychiatry in Topeka, Kansas, she returned to Lakin as the hospital's clinical director in 1955 and instituted a number of reforms in patient care. After she left her state post, she chaired the Department of Psychiatry at the Marshall University School of Medicine. From 1996 to 2000, she was clinical director at the Huntington State Hospital, which was renamed Mildred Mitchell-Bateman Hospital in her honor in 1999. (*H-D.*)

Ironton native Dr. Charles "Carl" Hoffman (1904–1981) was in his final year at the College of Medicine at the University of Cincinnati when he became ill and lost a kidney. The experience prompted him to specialize in urology. He completed his internship and residency at the Chesapeake & Ohio Railway Employees Hospital in Huntington and then went into private practice, dedicating the rest of his career to his profession and his community. Long active in the American Medical Association, he was elected its 127th president in 1972. Feeling it important that medical students and faculty at Marshall have access to texts on the history of medicine, he endowed the MU medical collection that bears his name. He is shown here with his portrait that hangs in the Hoffman Room at Marshall. (*H-D.*)

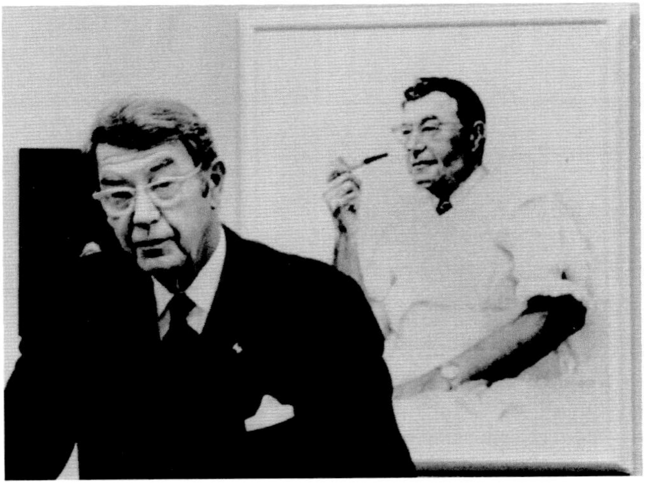

Dr. H. Darrel Darby (1928–2003) practiced podiatry in Huntington for 40 years, from 1956 until 1996. A member of the Trinity Church of God in Huntington, he was active in the community, aiding a long list of causes and organizations, from the Huntington City Mission to Marshall University. Frustrated with the design and performance of postsurgical shoes, he designed a new shoe and founded DARCO International, Inc., to manufacture and sell them. The Huntington-based company has grown to be a world leader in its field. In 2004, Dr. Darby was posthumously awarded the Distinguished Service Citation, the highest award given by the American Podiatric Medical Association. (*H-D.*)

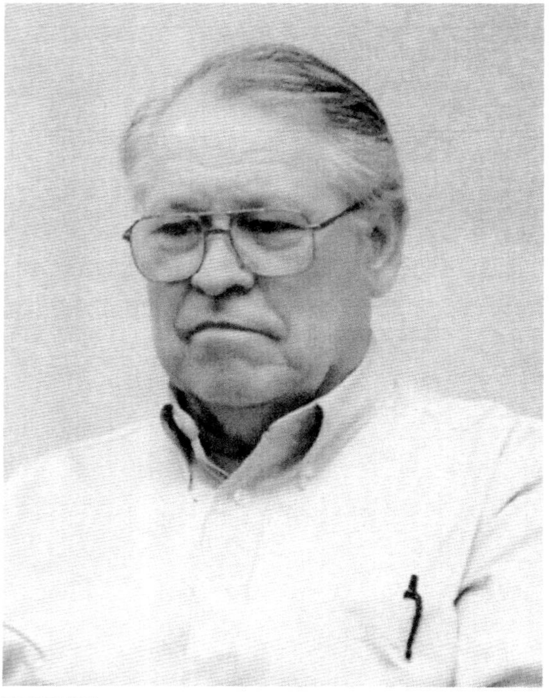

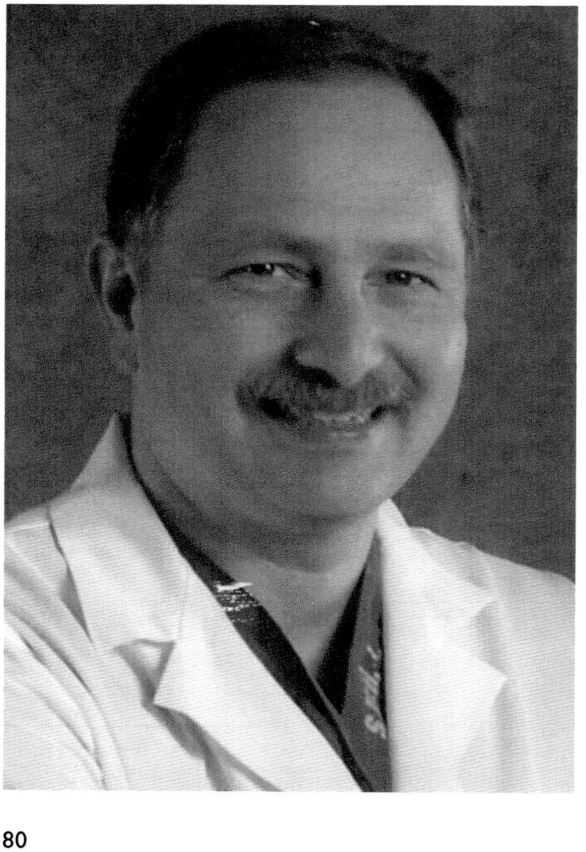

Dr. Jeffrey George and his 15-year-old daughter Hannah died in a Virginia traffic accident in 2008, but the former Huntington surgeon's memory lives on at the Jeffrey George Comfort House, which he worked to establish. The house provides shelter for the families of hospital patients. He envisioned the house, he said, because he was tired of seeing people "sleeping in chairs or on the floor." George graduated from Duke University and earned his medical degree at West Virginia University. He was gone from Huntington for nearly 20 years when his parents fell ill and he returned to care for them. Back in his hometown, he quickly became a key member of the medical staffs at Marshall University's Joan C. Edwards School of Medicine and St. Mary's Medical Center. He left Huntington to accept a new position in Roanoke in 2006. (*H-D.*)

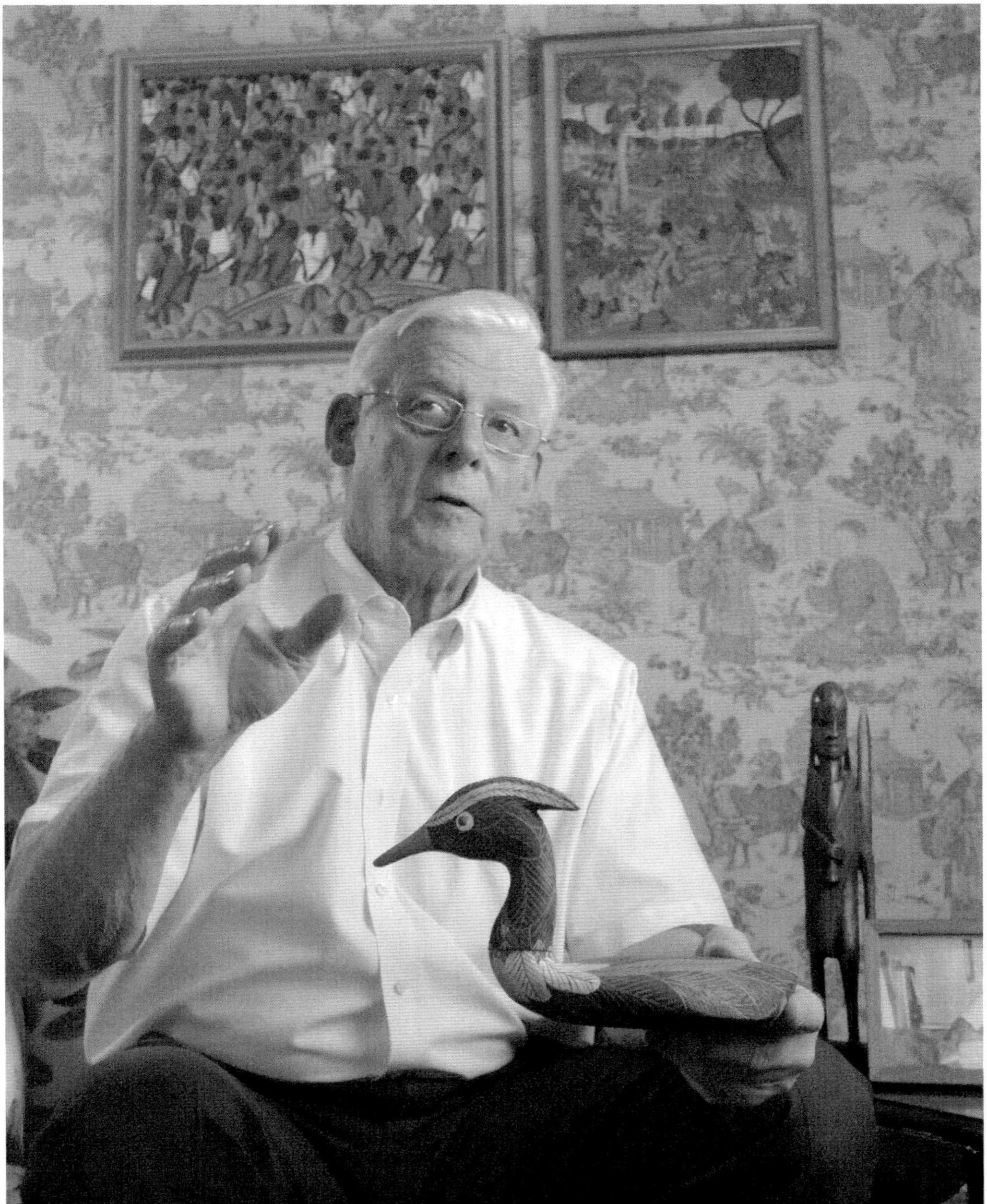

Huntington native Dr. Tom Scott followed in his father's footsteps when he entered medical school at the University of Michigan and, like his father, became an orthopedic surgeon. In 1963, he joined his father's practice. Founded in 1929, Scott Orthopedic Center is the oldest medical practice in Huntington. Now retired, Dr. Scott is a former member of the West Virginia State Senate. In 1980, he began making annual visits to Haiti, devoting his time and money to help provide medical care for the impoverished people there. His Huntington home is filled with artwork from that island nation. (*HQ*.)

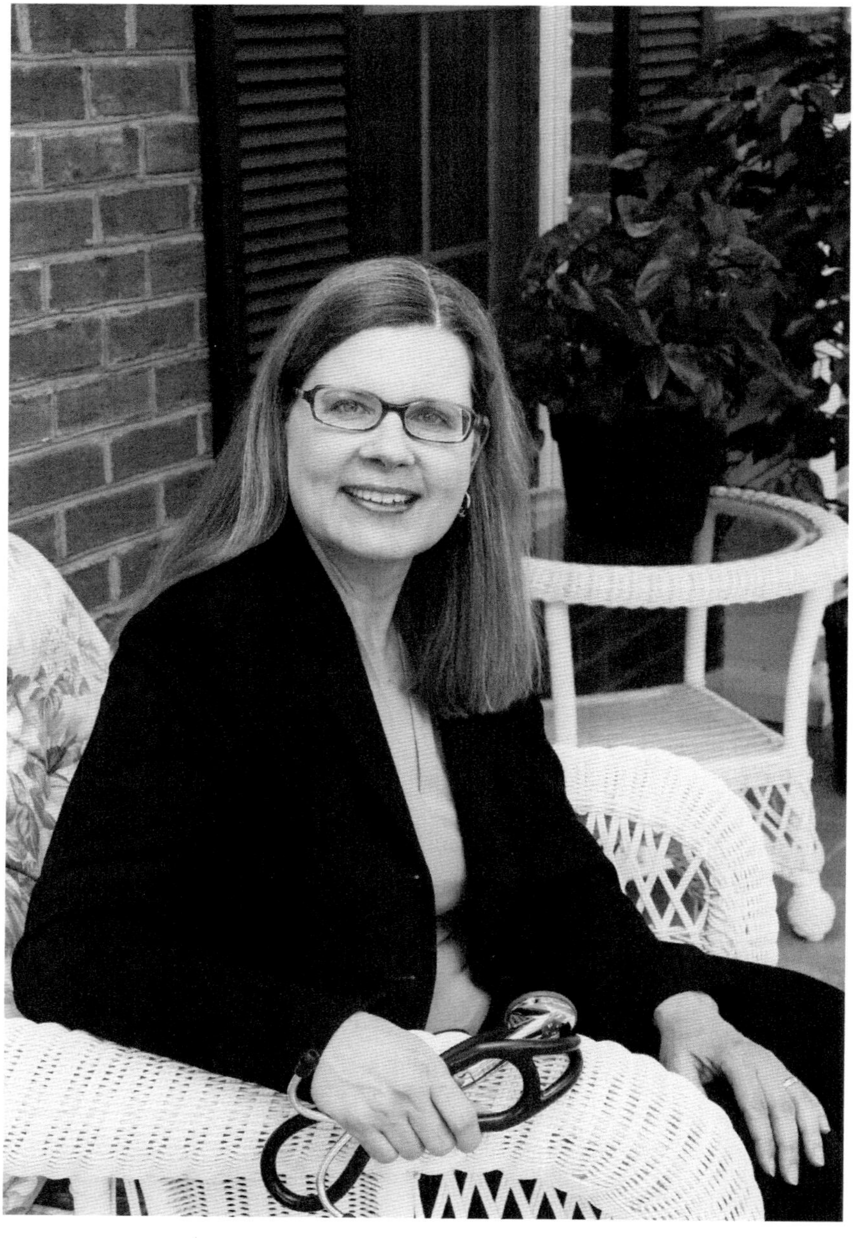

Dr. Ann Conjura, who died in 2011 at age 53, was the medical director of Hospice of Huntington, one of the many roles she filled in working for a healthier community. Born in Norfolk, Virginia, she was a graduate of the University of Virginia, the Johns Hopkins University School of Medicine, and the University of Maryland Medical System. When she and her radiologist husband, Dr. Rodger Blake, moved to Huntington, she began working as a volunteer with a number of organizations. Volunteering with hospice, she soon became the organization's medical director, a position from which she never stepped aside. After she became ill in 2008, a team of doctors worked to carry on until she could return; sadly, that day did not arrive. (*H-D.*)

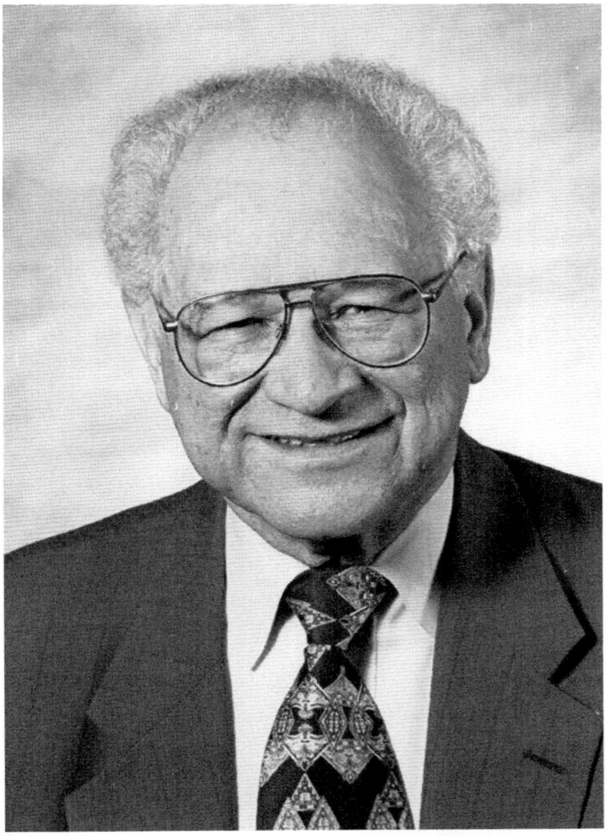

Dr. Jose Ricard (1928–2008) established the Sports Medicine Program at Marshall University, which was a statewide leader in sports medicine and family practice in West Virginia. Born in Havana, Cuba, he earned his medical degree at Havana University and served as director of sports medicine for the Cuban Olympic team. He fled his native Cuba and the repressive Castro regime in 1963 and later settled in Huntington. He was president of the West Virginia Academy of Family Physicians in 1990 and was awarded its Family Doc Award in 1994. He was instrumental in bringing the Annual Family Medicine Weekend and Sports Medicine Conference to Huntington each year for more than 20 years. (*H-D.*)

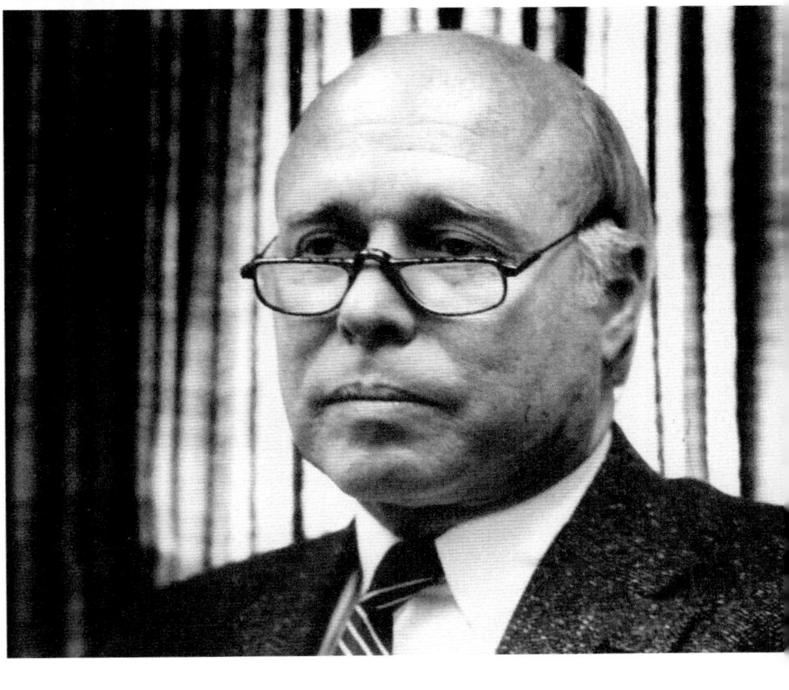

A Wayne County native, Dr. Charles McKown played a pivotal role in the growth and development of the Joan C. Edwards School of Medicine at Marshall University, stepping down in 2011 after 22 years as the school's dean. McKown earned his bachelor's degree at West Virginia University and his medical degree at the Medical College of Virginia. He joined the Marshall medical faculty in 1975 following an already impressive career at the McGuire VA Hospital in Richmond, Virginia, Walter Reed Army Medical Center in Washington, DC, and the National Institutes of Health in Bethesda, Maryland. (*H-D.*)

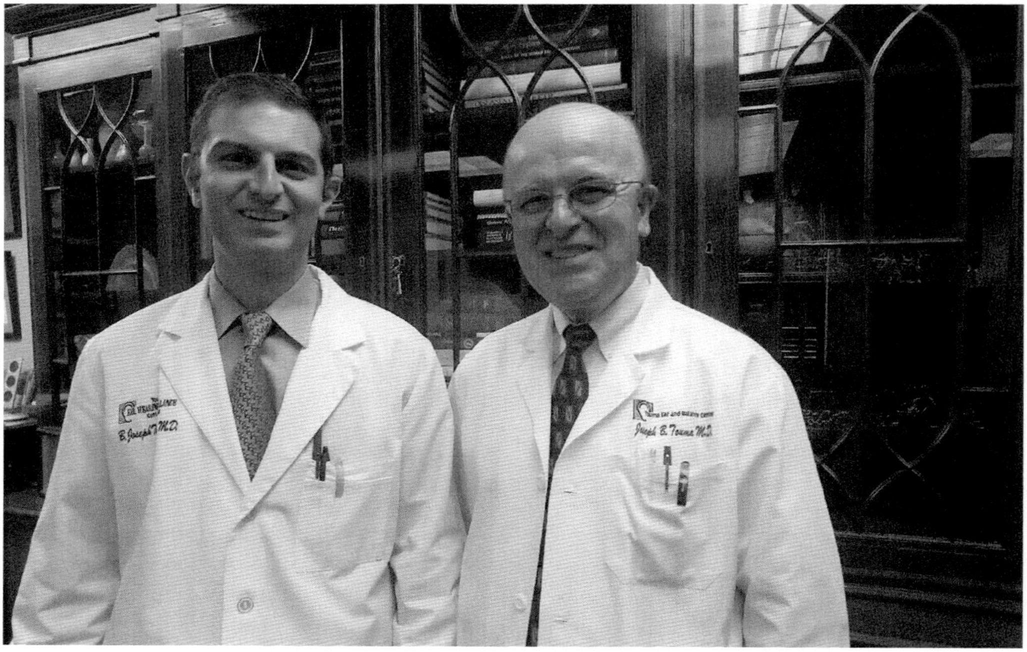

Dr. Joseph B. Touma is widely known for his medical expertise in otolaryngology, but in Huntington he is equally well known for much more: buying and painstakingly restoring a number of downtown retail buildings, his Touma Medical Museum with its unique collection of antique medical artifacts, and the generous gifts he and his wife, Omayma, have presented the Huntington Museum of Art, many of them housed in the Touma Near Eastern Gallery. A proud Dr. Touma is shown here with his son B. Joseph Touma, MD, who now practices with his father. (*H-D.*)

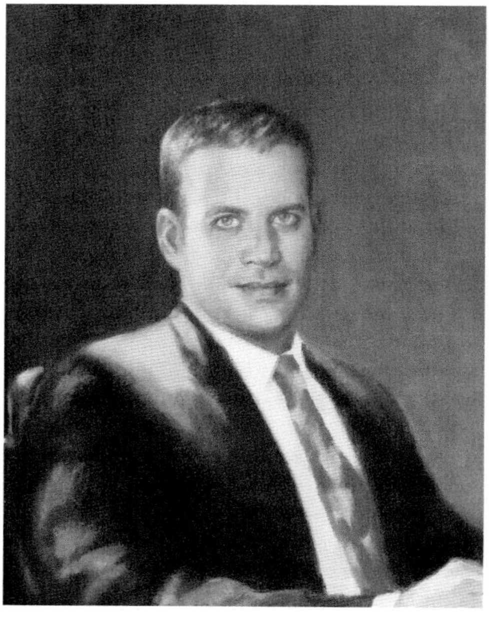

Dr. Paul Ambrose (1968–2001), a promising young physician, was a Huntington native and a graduate of Marshall University's Joan C. Edwards School of Medicine. After graduating from the Harvard School of Public Health, he earned a Luther Terry Fellowship and went on to become a senior clinical advisor with the Office of the Surgeon General, working closely with former Surgeon General C. Everett Koop. Many who knew him believed he was destined to become the next surgeon general. On September 11, 2001, he was aboard American Airlines Flight 77 on his way to a Los Angeles conference on adolescent obesity, when the plane was forced to crash into the Pentagon, killing all aboard. Huntington's Paul Ambrose Trail for Health is dedicated to his memory. (*HQ.*)

Marshall Memories

Marshall University is much older than the city of Huntington. Its roots stretch back to 1837, when residents of the village of Guyandotte and the surrounding area, then still a part of Virginia, determined that their sons and daughters needed a school. The new school first met at a log cabin, known as Mount Hebron Church. Tradition has it that local lawyer John Laidley convinced his neighbors to name the new school after his friend, Chief Justice John Marshall. In 1869, rail tycoon Collis P. Huntington arrived on the scene and set about building the new town of Huntington, chartered by the West Virginia Legislature in 1871. In the more than 140 years since, the histories of Huntington and Marshall have been inextricably intertwined. The school's presidents, from Lawrence J. Corbly to Stephen Kopp, have been influential community leaders, and longtime faculty members, such as Page Pitt, Simon Perry, and Charles Moffat, have molded generations of students. Meanwhile, continued growth in both programs and campus facilities is helping guarantee that Marshall, with its roots deep in the 19th century, is well prepared for the challenges of the 21st century.

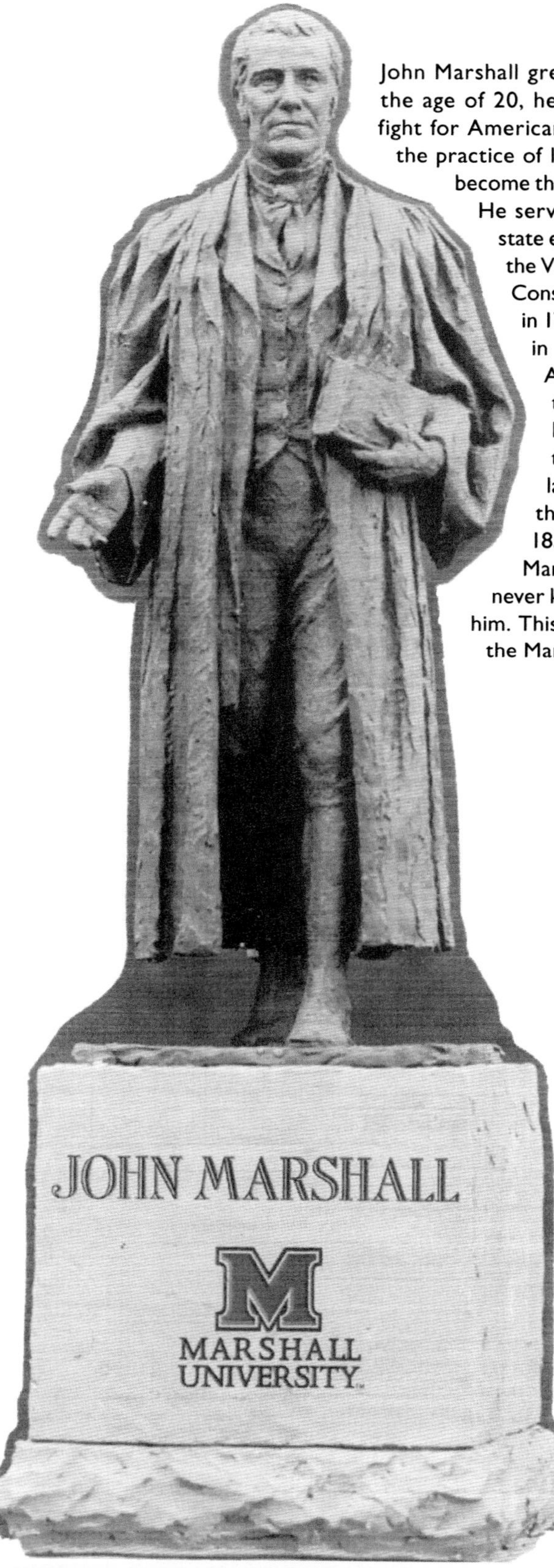

John Marshall grew up on the Virginia frontier. At the age of 20, he joined the Continental Army to fight for American independence. He later entered the practice of law in Richmond and, by 1790, had become the leading appellate lawyer in Virginia. He served in the House of Delegates, the state executive council, and as a delegate to the Virginia convention that ratified the US Constitution. He was elected to Congress in 1799 and appointed secretary of state in 1800. The following year, Pres. John Adams named him chief justice of the US Supreme Court. In that role, Marshall's great decisions shaped the basis of American constitutional law and established the authority of the Supreme Court. Marshall died in 1835, two years before the founding of Marshall Academy, thus the famed jurist never knew the school had been named for him. This statue of Marshall was erected on the Marshall campus in 1998. (MU.)

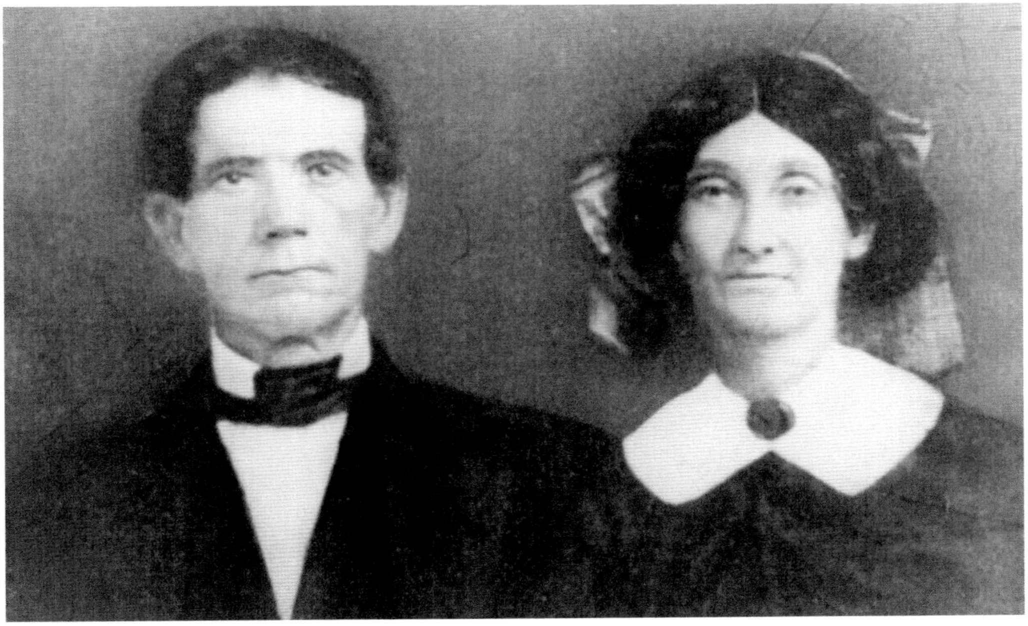

A number of Guyandotte citizens played roles in the founding of Marshall Academy. Chief among them was attorney John Laidley (1791–1863), shown here with his wife, Mary Scales Hite. Laidley was a friend and admirer of Chief Justice Marshall, with whom he had served in the Virginia Constitutional Convention of 1829–1830, and it was at Laidley's behest that the new school was named for the famed jurist. Born in Morgantown, Laidley read law with his brother James in Parkersburg and served in the War of 1812. After the war, he made his home in Guyandotte, where he practiced law until his death. In 1937, Marshall named Laidley Hall, a dormitory, in his honor. (MU.)

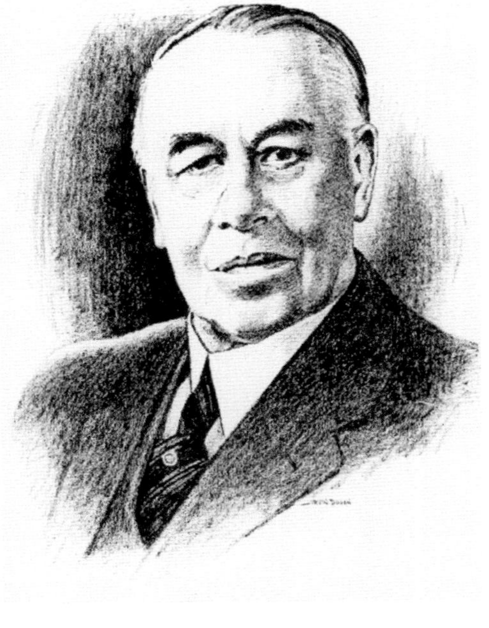

Marshall was still basically a secondary school when Lawrence J. Corbly became its principal in 1896. He immediately set about expanding the curriculum, and in 1907 his title was changed from principal to president in keeping with the new curriculum. He would serve as president until 1915. During his administration, intercollegiate athletics was established, and the student newspaper and yearbook, the *Parthenon* and *Mirabilia*, began publication. Old Main acquired its towered western addition so familiar to generations of alumni, and College Hall, a dormitory for women, was established in the easternmost portion of Old Main. Under Corbly, legislative appropriations for Marshall went from $20,000 in 1897 to $158,000 in 1915, including $45,000 for construction of a science building and a gymnasium. Marshall's Corbly Hall is named in his honor. (MU.)

Born in Pennsylvania, Morris P. Shawkey earned a teaching certificate at Oberlin College in Ohio and came to West Virginia to teach in 1895. He served in the West Virginia Legislature and as superintendent of schools in Kanawha County before becoming state superintendent of schools in 1909, a post he held until 1921. He became president at Marshall in 1923. Under him, Marshall doubled its enrollment and won accreditation for both its teachers college and College of Arts and Sciences. Shawkey resigned in 1935 under political pressure. (MU.)

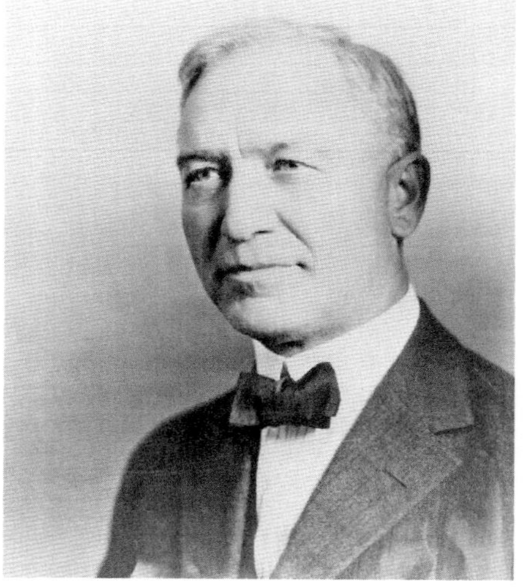

As Marshall president, Shawkey envisioned a building "where students and faculty might meet on common ground." Dedicated in 1933 and financed through a combination of student fees and public donations, the building was fittingly named the Shawkey Student Union. A popular hangout for Marshall students for 40 years, it was replaced in 1973 by the university's Memorial Student Center. (MU.)

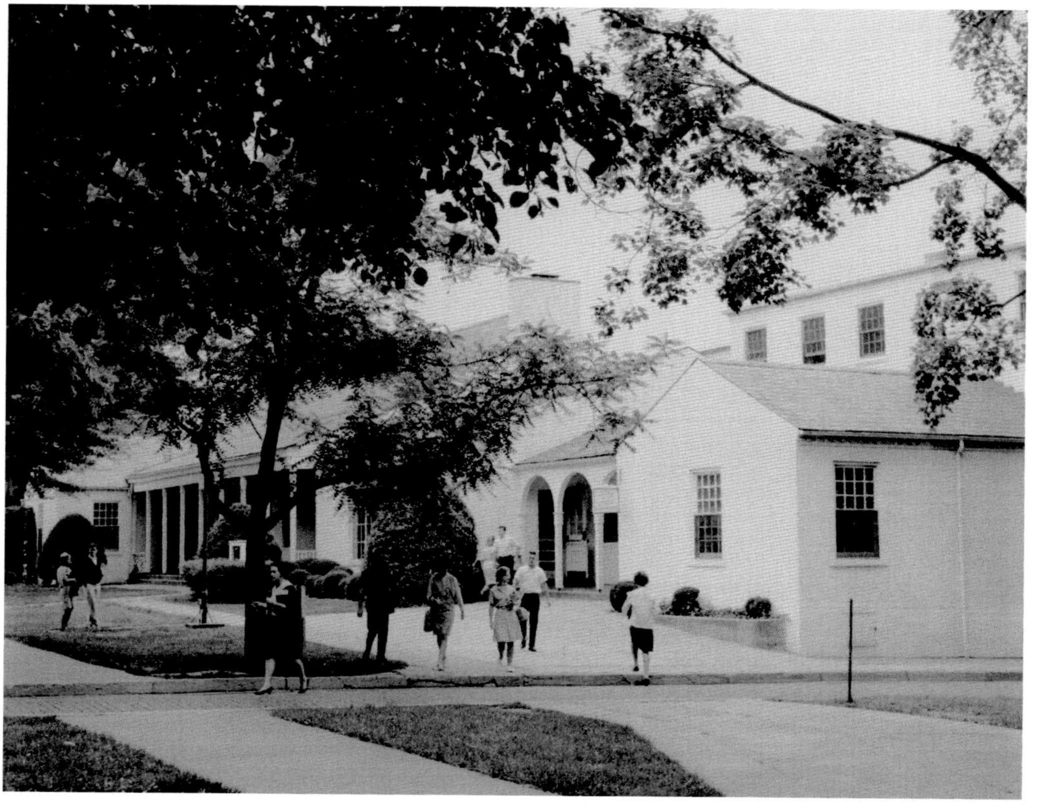

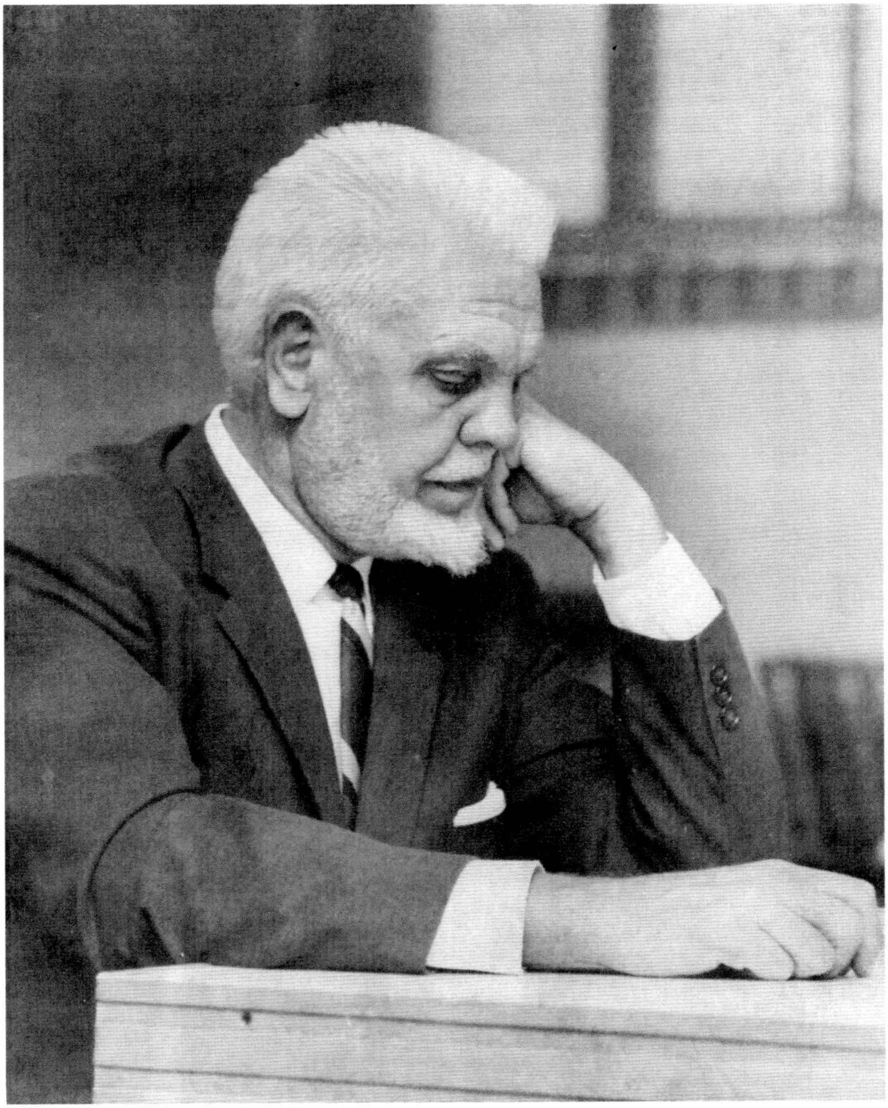

In 1926, when William Page Pitt (1900–1980) arrived in Huntington to join the faculty of what was then Marshall College, he found one journalism class with five students. In his 45-year career at Marshall, he built its journalism program into one with dozens of classes, hundreds of students, and a reputation for excellence. Today, Marshall University's W. Page Pitt School of Journalism and Mass Communications is named in his honor. Born in New York City, Pitt moved with his family to Shinnston, West Virginia, when he was 12. He graduated from Ohio's Muskingum College in 1925 and taught for a year at Glendale College, also in Ohio. Later, he earned a master's degree at Columbia University in New York. After the age of five, Pitt was sightless in one eye and had only three-percent vision in the other; nonetheless, he refused to let himself be handicapped by his vision problem. Not only a legendary professor, he was a prolific writer whose byline frequently appeared in national magazines and newspapers. He also was an expert bridge player and shot a mean game of pool. Retiring in 1971, he moved to Stuart, Florida, where he died. (MU.)

Lillian Helms Buskirk, a 1928 Marshall graduate, retired in 1970 after serving at the school for 33 years, most of that time as dean of women. A native of Hinton, West Virginia, she earned a master's degree in student personnel administration from Columbia University in 1945. She was faculty advisor to Marshall's Panhellenic Council for 30 years. In 1976, Marshall named Buskirk Hall, a dormitory, in her honor. (*H-D.*)

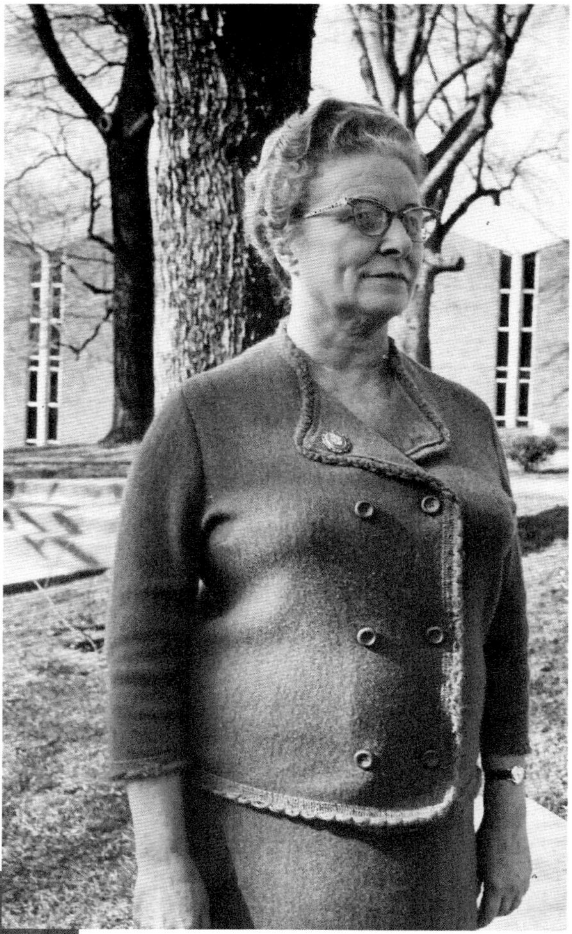

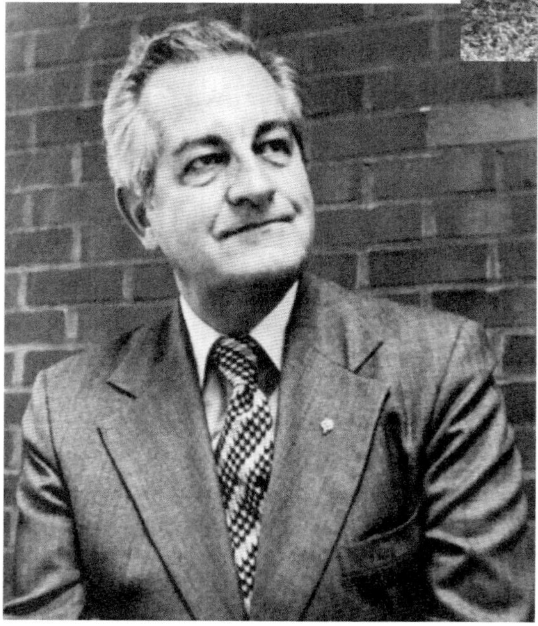

Joining Marshall in 1959 as an English professor, Dr. A. Mervin Tyson (1911–1998) became chairman of the English department, then dean of arts and sciences, and later university vice president. A native of Red Lion, Pennsylvania, he received his bachelor of arts at Gettysburg College, his master's at the University of Michigan, and his doctorate at the University of Pennsylvania. During World War II, he was a staff sergeant cryptographer with the Army Air Force, stationed in Great Britain. He retired from Marshall in 1977 and moved to Florida in 1990. (*H-D.*)

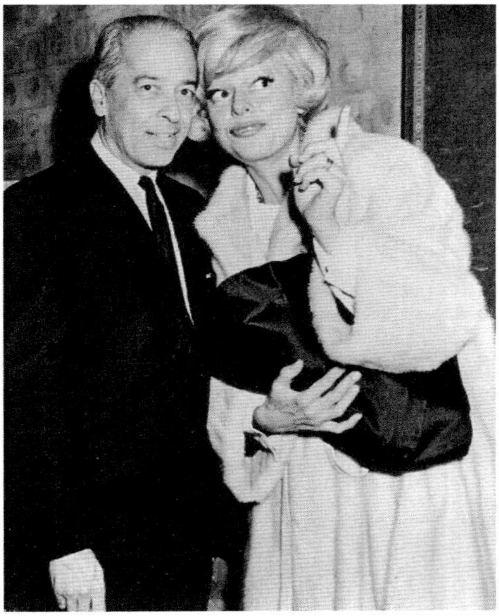

In 1936, as Marshall was planning its 100th anniversary celebration, Dr. Curtis Baxter (1908–1983), a professor in the school's English department, convinced the administration to schedule a year-long series of cultural attractions as part of the celebration. The first event was an appearance by polar explorer Richard E. Byrd. From that modest beginning grew the Marshall Artists Series, which continues to bring world-class entertainment to the campus and community each year. A native of Ravenswood, West Virginia, Baxter graduated from Marshall and earned his master's degree at Washington and Jefferson College. He taught at Glenville State College before joining the Marshall faculty. Shown here with Broadway star Carol Channing, Baxter managed the Marshall Artists Series for 36 years before retiring in 1972. (*H-D.*)

When state lawmakers designated Marshall a university in 1961, it was largely a result of the efforts of one man, Marshall president Stewart H. Smith (1904–1982), who worked tirelessly to make it happen. A Pennsylvania native, he was a graduate of Gettysburg College, later earning a master's degree from Columbia University and a doctorate at Syracuse University. Dr. Smith was dean of the Marshall Teachers College when he became president in 1946. Popular with faculty, students, and the community, he went on to serve 22 years, longer than any Marshall president before or since. He and his wife, Evelyn, are shown here greeting students at a reception. (MU.)

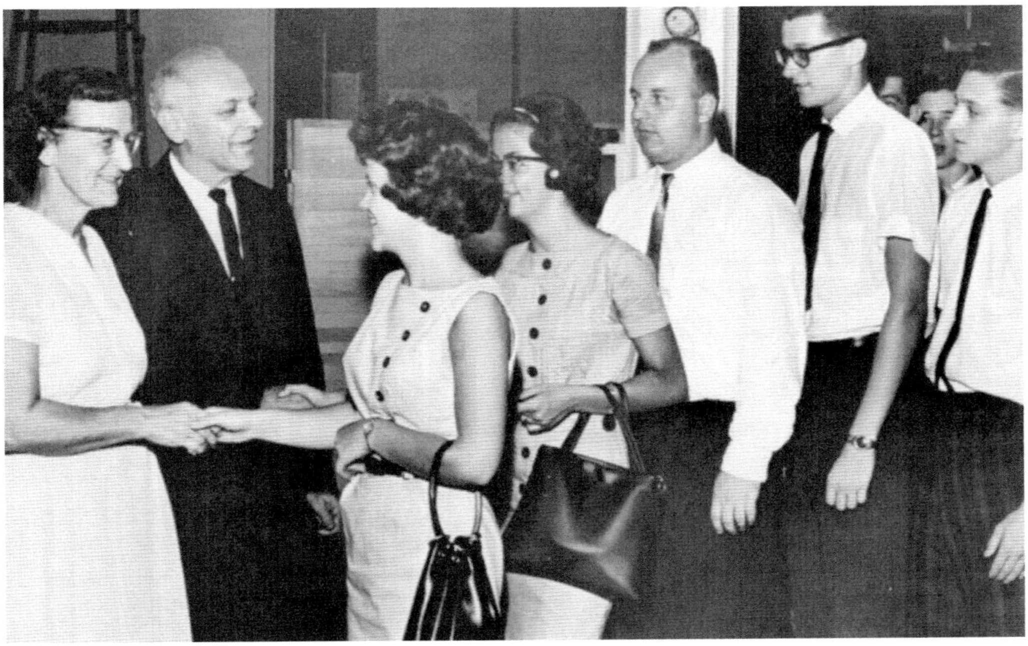

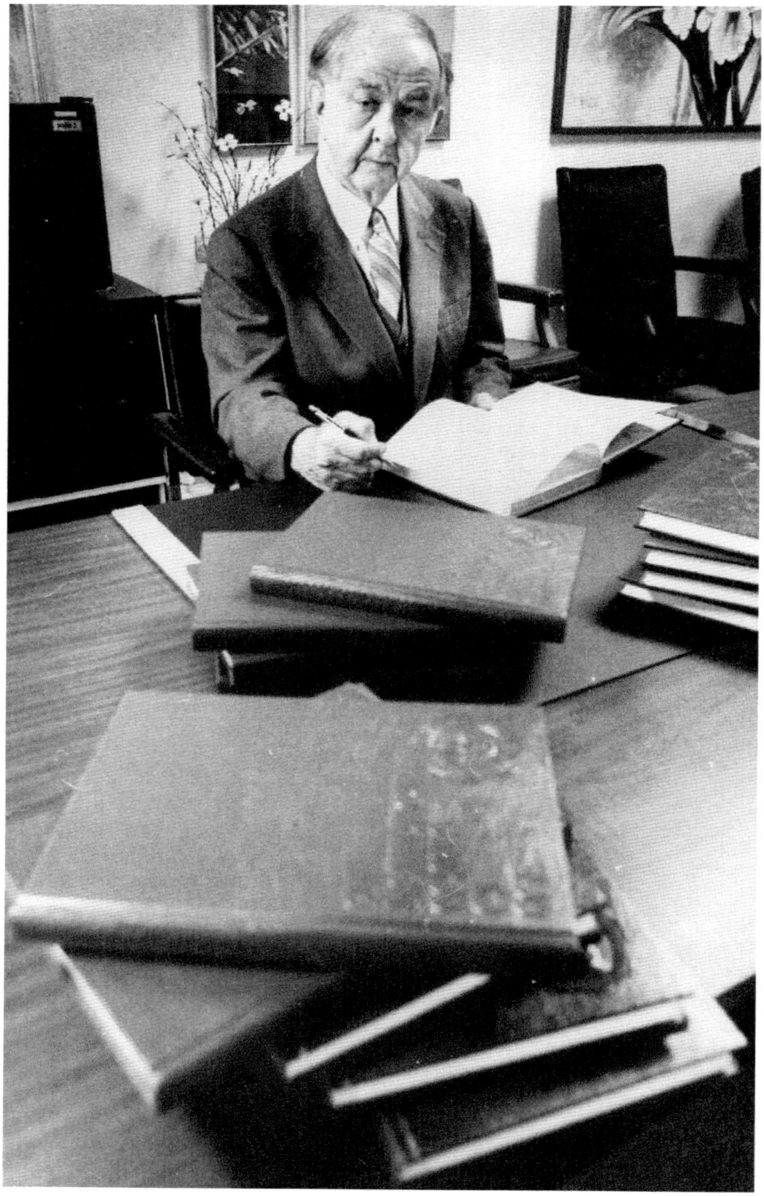

As a boy, Charles Hill Moffat (1912–2001) dreamed of becoming a lawyer, but money was tight in those Depression years, so he opted for a career with a steady paycheck: teaching. And what a teacher he was. For more than three decades, from 1946 to 1977, he brought history alive for thousands of Marshall University students. A native of Mississippi, he never lost his Southern drawl, a fact that added a dramatic ring of authenticity when he lectured on his favorite subjects, the Civil War and the history of the South. As one former student recalled, "When Dr. Moffat described the Battle of Gettysburg, you could smell the gunpowder." He earned his bachelor's and master's degrees at the University of Mississippi and his doctorate from Vanderbilt University. A talented author, he wrote a number of books, including a lively history of Marshall. This 1981 photograph shows him autographing copies of that history. (*H-D.*)

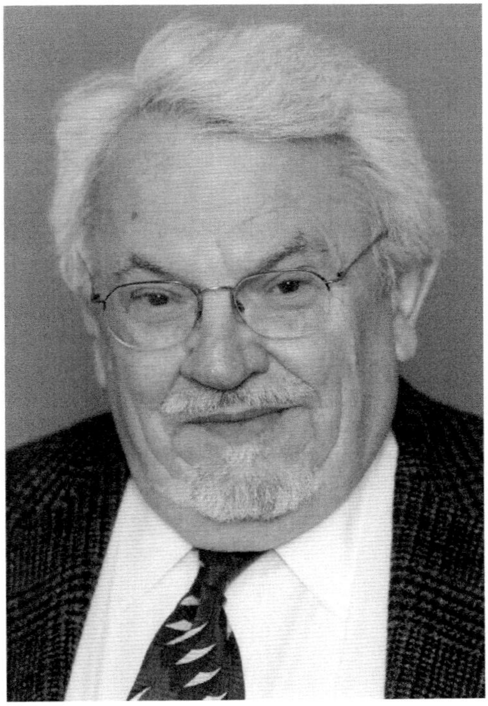

Passionate about politics, Dr. Simon Perry shared that passion with more than 20,000 political science students during his long career at Marshall. He began teaching at the university in 1962 and retired in 2010. A native of Gilbert, West Virginia, he attended public school in Mingo County and earned undergraduate degrees in political science and history from Berea College, a master's degree from the University of Tennessee, and a doctorate from Michigan State University. Upon his retirement, Marshall honored him by creating the Simon Perry Center for Constitutional Democracy, an academic program designed to promote the study of the history and contemporary significance of the US Constitution. (MU.)

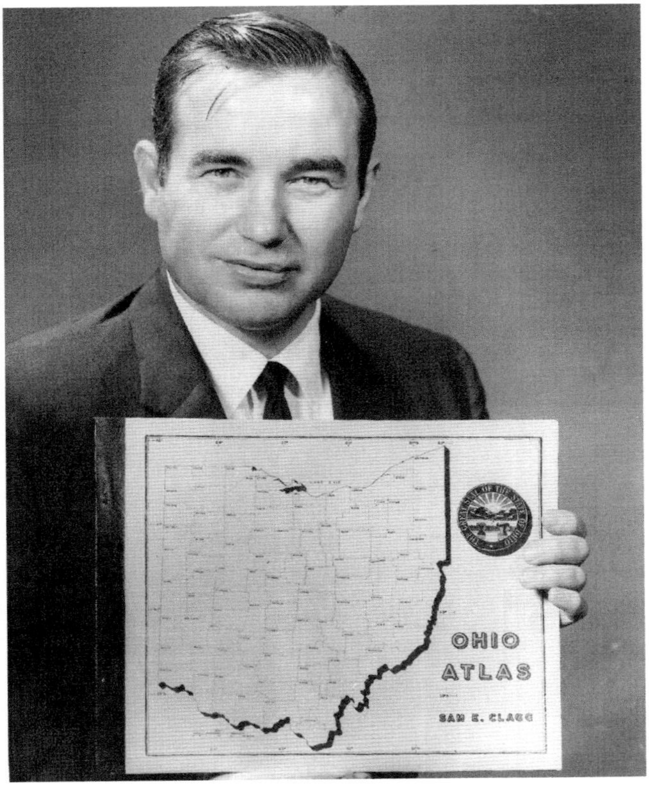

Veteran Marshall geography professor Sam Clagg has published a dozen books, including a biography of legendary Marshall coach Cam Henderson. In this 1959 photograph, he proudly displays a copy of one of his first books, a state atlas for Ohio. Dr. Clagg earned his bachelor's and master's degrees at Marshall and his doctorate degree in education at the University of Kentucky. A retired lieutenant colonel with the US Marine Corps, he was a member of the Department of Geography faculty from 1948 until his retirement in 1986. He also was Marshall's acting president from 1983 to 1985 and served as a coach on both the Marshall football and wrestling teams. (*H-D.*)

The Marshall career of Dr. Robert B. Hayes spans more than 40 years and a long list of posts, including the school's presidency. A native of Clarksburg, West Virginia, he earned degrees from Asbury College and the University of Kansas following service in the US Marine Corps during World War II. In 1965, he was named dean of MU's College of Education, a post he held until becoming president in 1974. His nine years as president saw MU establish a School of Medicine and erect two new classroom buildings, a basketball arena, and a major addition to the Science Building. After his tenure as president, Dr. Hayes was a professor until 1991. Since 1992, he has filled several posts, including dean of the College of Business and interim president of the former Marshall Community and Technical College. He is shown here at the dedication of MU's Harris Hall in 1976. (*H-D.*)

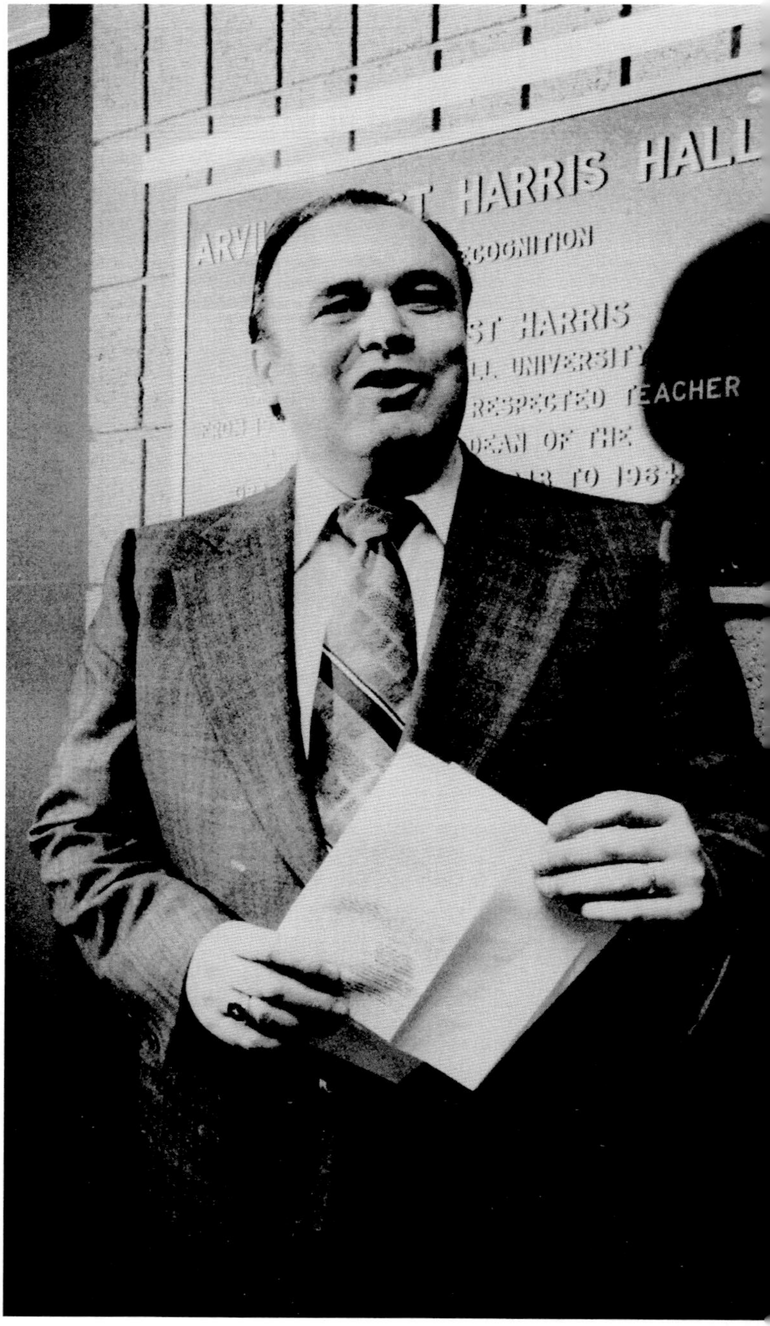

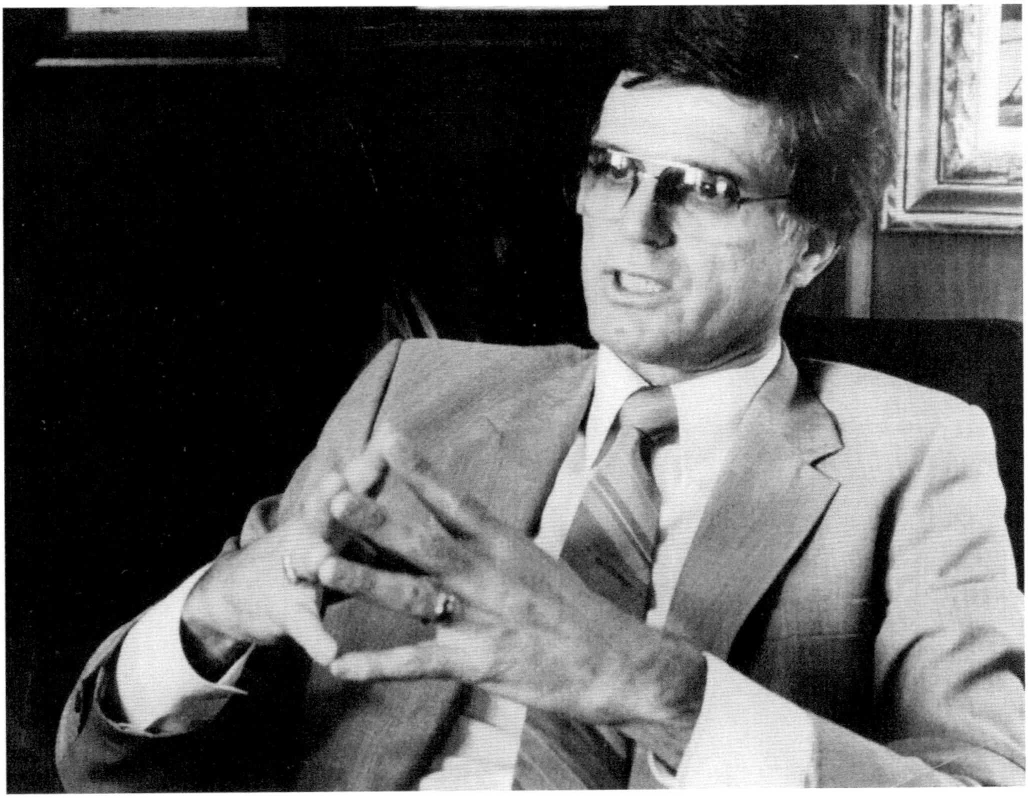

Dr. Dale F. Nitzschke arrived on the campus of Marshall in 1984 from Nevada to become the school's 11th president, succeeding President Hayes. A graduate of Loras College, where he earned a bachelor of arts degree with honors in education, he received his master's in education and doctorate degrees in guidance and counseling from Ohio University. As Marshall president, he conducted a highly successful campaign to elevate the school's profile at the state and national levels. He left MU in 1990 to become president of the University of New Hampshire. (*H-D.*)

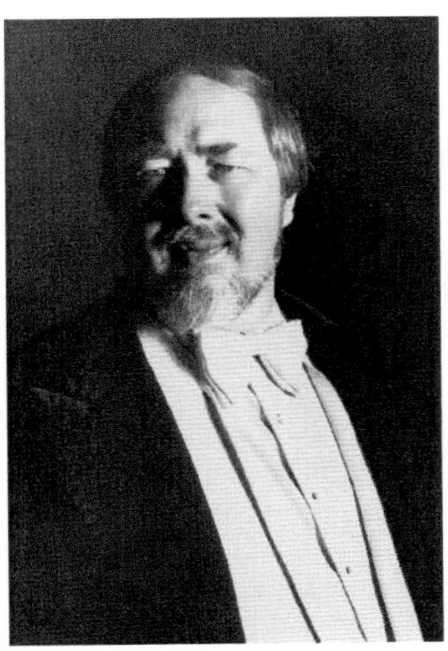

A legendary voice was stilled with the 2005 death of Dr. Paul Balshaw, a longtime professor of music at Marshall. Balshaw's memorable renditions of the "Marshall Alma Mater" and the "National Anthem" were part of Marshall commencement ceremonies for many years. A graduate of the Eastman School of Music, where he earned a doctor of musical arts degree, he joined the Marshall faculty in 1965 and would serve the university in a number of roles over the next 40 years. He was founding dean of the school's College of Fine Arts but returned to teaching after serving in that post for a decade. (*H-D.*)

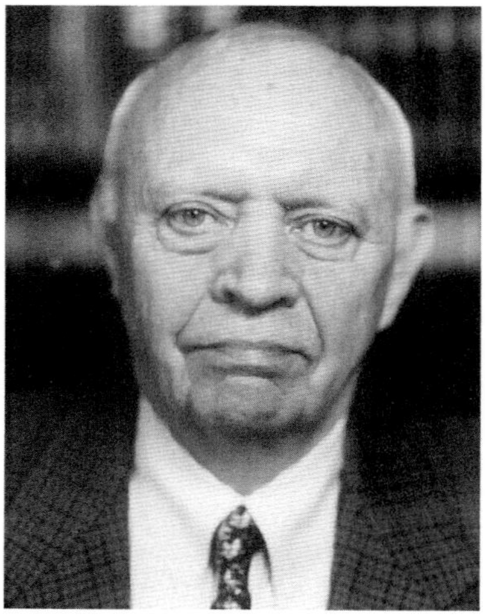

Political columnist George Will has called Jean Edward Smith "today's foremost biographer of formidable figures in American history." Smith graduated from high school in Washington, DC, earned a bachelor of arts from Princeton University and, after a stint in the US Army, received his doctorate from Columbia University. His many books include widely acclaimed biographies of Dwight Eisenhower, Franklin D. Roosevelt, Gen. Ulysses S. Grant, and Chief Justice John Marshall. He taught at the University of Toronto for 35 years. Today, he is the John Marshall Professor of Political Science at Marshall. (MU.)

Terry W. Fenger was born and raised in northern Illinois, attended Northern Illinois University at Dekalb and Southern Illinois University in Carbondale, where he received his doctorate in microbiology in 1976. He conducted postdoctoral research at Louisiana State University in New Orleans, studying the replication of the measles virus and the herpes virus infection of the eye. When that work was complete, he joined the Marshall faculty. At Marshall, he has built the Forensic Science Center into one of the school's most successful programs. He has served as the center's director since 1994 and oversees its nationally accredited Forensic Science Master of Science Degree Program, DNA laboratory, and digital forensics section. In 2011, he was inducted into the Greater Huntington Wall of Fame. (*H-D.*)

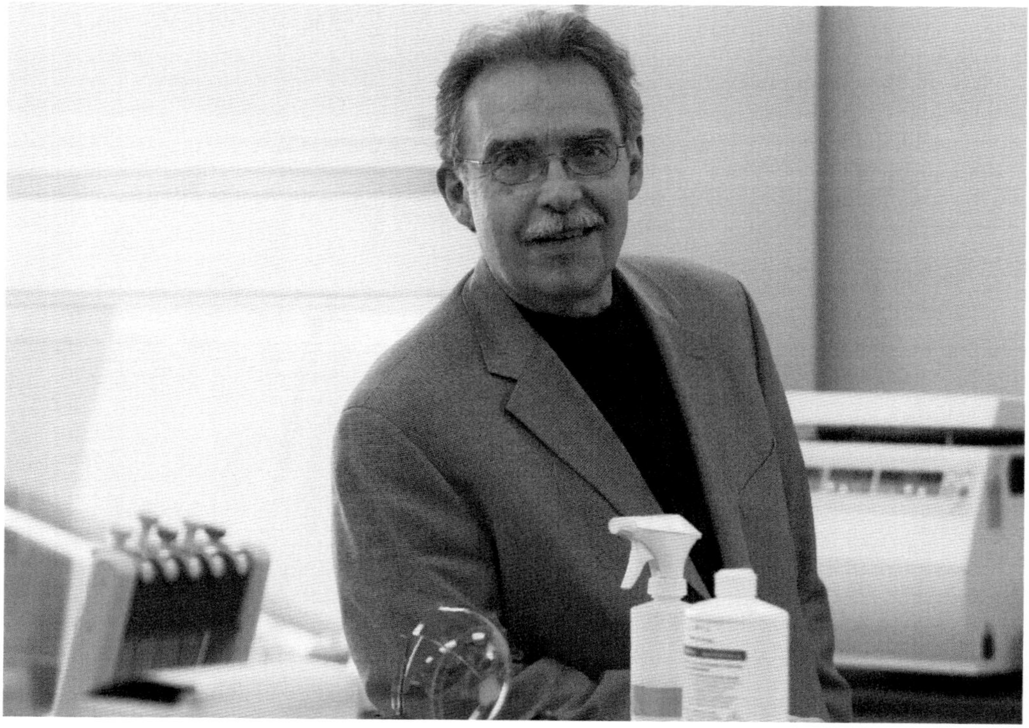

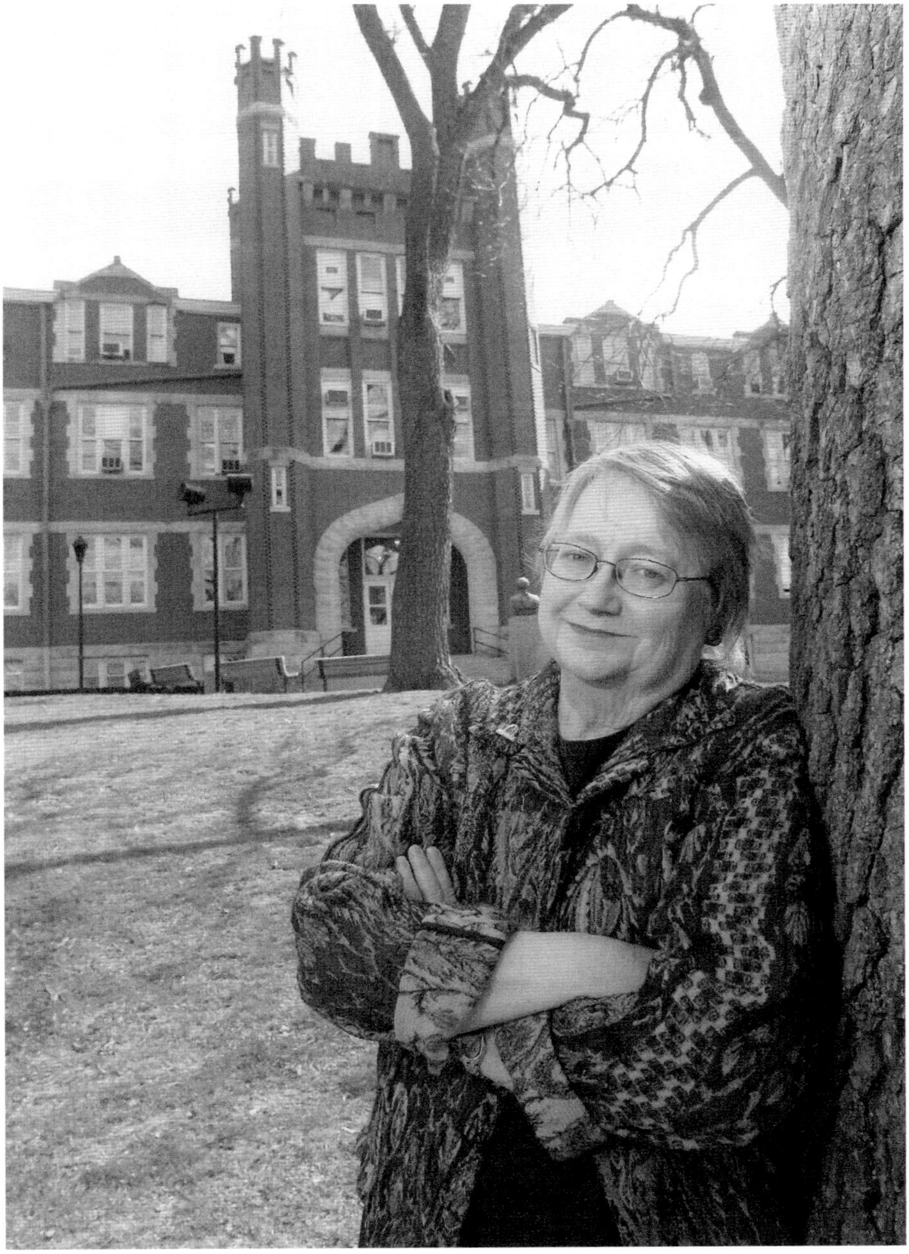

Dr. Sarah Denman retired in 2008 after 39 years in education, including 33 at Marshall. She had been with the university since 1975, when she was hired as part of the team that helped establish the former Marshall Community and Technical College. She steadily rose through the university's ranks, retiring as provost and senior vice president for academic affairs. A native of Kenova, she earned her bachelor's at Marshall and then taught at Ceredo-Kenova High School while completing her master's. She received her doctorate in higher education administration from West Virginia University in 1986. Upon her retirement, she noted she had served with nine presidents during her years at Marshall. (*H-D.*)

Dr. J. Wade Gilley was appointed Marshall president in 1991, succeeding President Nitzschke. Gilley came to Marshall from George Mason University in Fairfax, Virginia, where he was senior vice president. A native of Fries, a small mill town in Virginia, he earned three degrees in engineering from Virginia Tech. During his presidency, Marshall grew from 12,000 students to 16,000, invested $250 million in campus renewal, and saw its football program become the "winningest" in the nation. He left Marshall in 1999 to become president of the University of Tennessee. (*HQ.*)

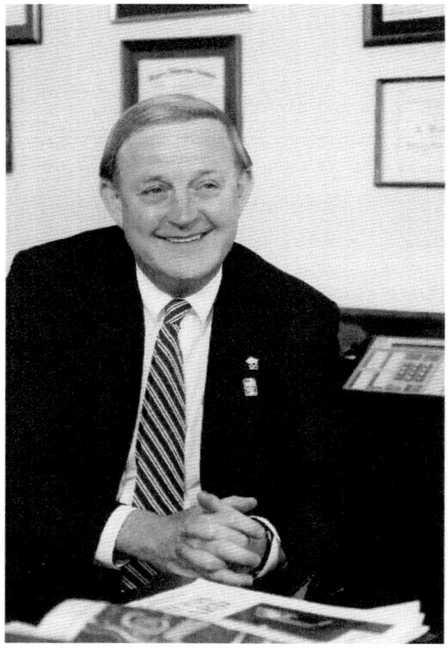

Dr. Stephen J. Kopp assumed the presidency at Marshall in 2005. He joined Marshall following leadership positions with Midwestern University, Central Michigan University, and Ohio University. He received a bachelor of science degree in biology in 1973 from the University of Notre Dame and his doctorate in physiology and biophysics in 1976 from the University of Illinois at Chicago. During his tenure, Marshall has thrived, experiencing unprecedented growth in enrollment and development of its infrastructure and academic programs. (MU.)

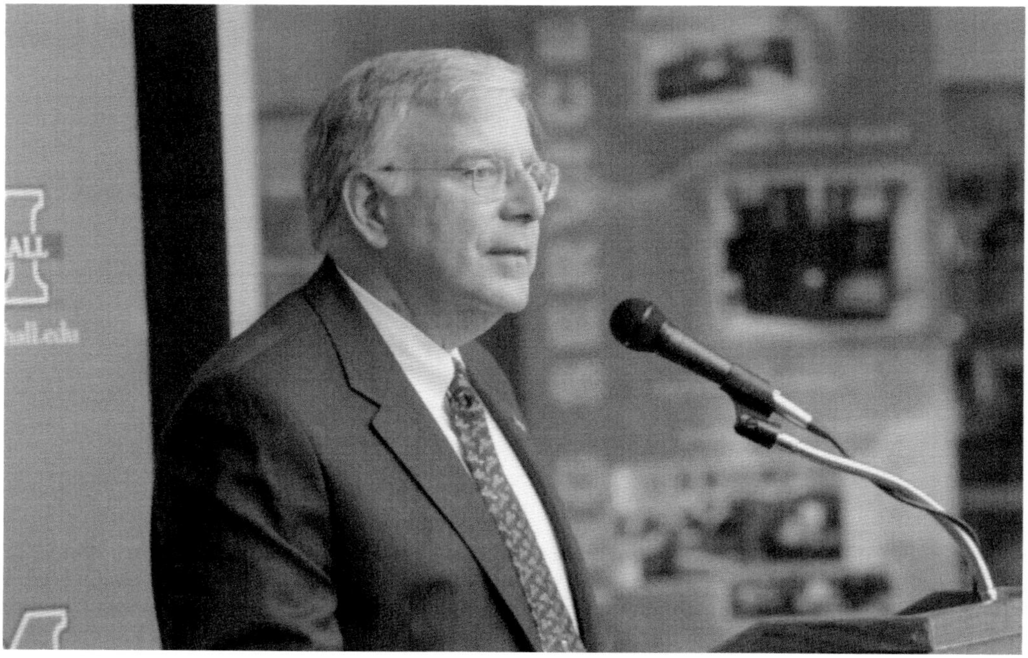

Entertainment and the Arts

Huntington has given entertainment and the arts a remarkable mix of talented personalities, from blonde bombshell Dagmar and pie-throwing comic Soupy Sales to gospel singer Michael W. Smith and Broadway star J. Mark McVey, from horror filmdom's Brad Dourif and game-show host Peter Marshall to television's Conchata Ferrell and *Today* host Matt Lauer. No, Matt Lauer was not born in Huntington and in fact his stay at the city's WOWK-TV was brief, but his job there was his first in broadcasting, so it surely seems fair to count him. Hawkshaw Hawkins was killed in a 1963 plane crash, but country music fans are still listening to his records. The art world has been enriched by Chuck Ripper and his remarkable wildlife paintings. Local art fans surely owe a debt of gratitude to director Roberta Emerson, who transformed the once-sleepy Huntington Galleries into today's Huntington Museum of Art. And, finally, there are the writers: Jesse Stuart, Breece D'J Pancake, Julia Keller, Craig Johnson, Lee Maynard, and Nelson Bond. All of their wonderful books are at the nearest library or bookstore, waiting to be discovered.

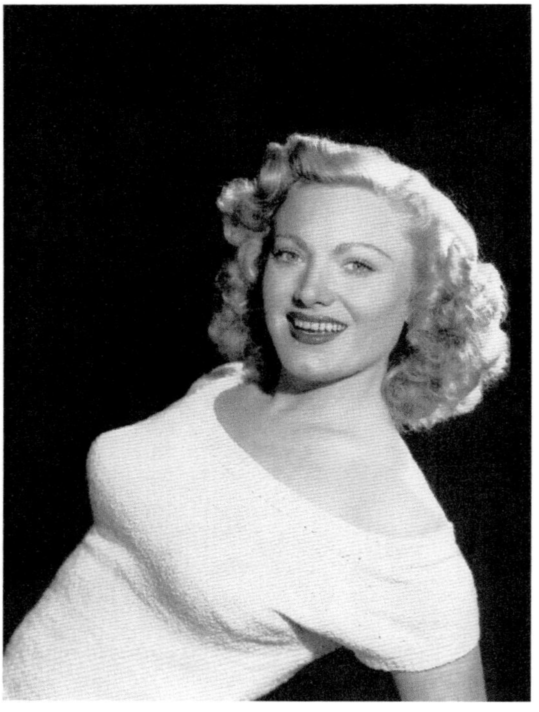

A star of early television, Dagmar (born Virginia Ruth Egnor, 1921–2001) was a dumb-as-a-fox blonde who at the height of her popularity received thousands of fan letters a week. Born Virginia Ruth Egnor, she was a waitress at Walgreen's in Huntington before she moved to New York, where she worked as a model and actress. Her big break came when she was picked for the cast of *Broadway Open House*, a vaudeville-style mix of music and jokes that ran on NBC in 1950–1951 and was a forerunner of the *Tonight Show.* The program's producers christened her "Dagmar" and the name stuck. She was told to wear a low-cut gown, sit on a stool, and act dumb when host Jerry Lester talked with her. The studio audience loved it, as did the viewers at home. Over the show's brief run, her neckline plunged and her salary soared, from $75 a week to $3,000. She went on to perform in the theater, summer stock, and Las Vegas and was a regular on television's *Hollywood Squares.* (*HQ.*)

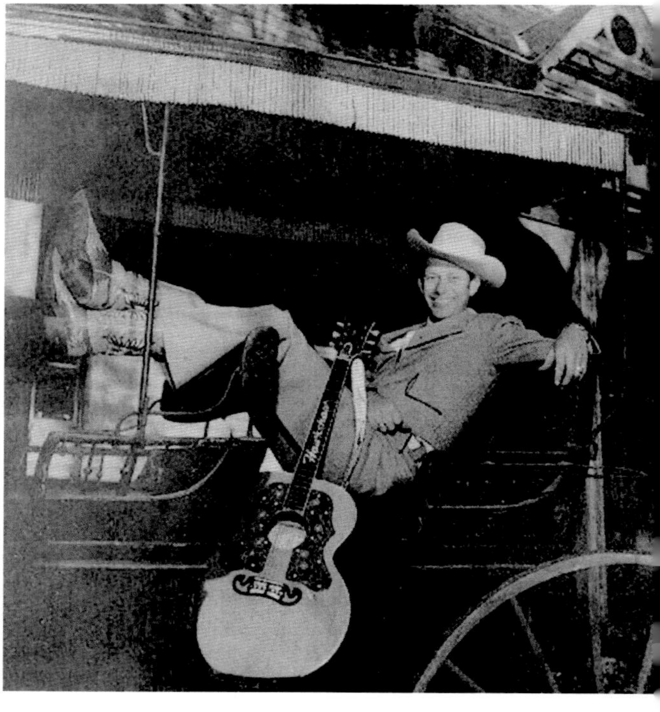

Before his life was cut short in a 1963 plane crash, Hawkshaw Hawkins was one of West Virginia's best-known country musicians. Born Harold Franklin Hawkins in Huntington in 1921, he got his start in music when he traded five trapped rabbits for his first guitar. His first appearances were with small traveling shows and on radio stations WSAZ in Huntington and WCHS in Charleston. From 1946 to 1954, he worked on the *Wheeling Jamboree*, a WWVA broadcast. He then went to Nashville and the famed Grand Ole Opry. Hawkins, Patsy Cline, Cowboy Copas, and Randy Hughes died in a plane crash returning from a benefit concert. In 2009, Hawkins was inducted into the West Virginia Music Hall of Fame. (*H-D.*)

When Chuck Ripper was going to art school, his instructors warned him he would never make a living painting birds and bugs. And they told him he would have to move to New York or some other big city if he ever hoped to be successful as an artist. Ripper proved them wrong on both counts. Today, he is one of the best-known wildlife artists in the country. His work has appeared in dozens of books and on countless magazine covers, greeting cards, playing cards, jigsaw puzzles, and even US postage stamps. Moreover, he has achieved that kind of success while working in a studio fashioned from the garage at his West Huntington home rather than in a big city. Born in 1929 in the Pittsburgh area, Ripper studied at the Art Institute of Pittsburgh. He came to Huntington in 1953 to work as art director at the former Standard Printing & Publishing Company. In 1965, he left the company to become a full-time artist. (*HQ*.)

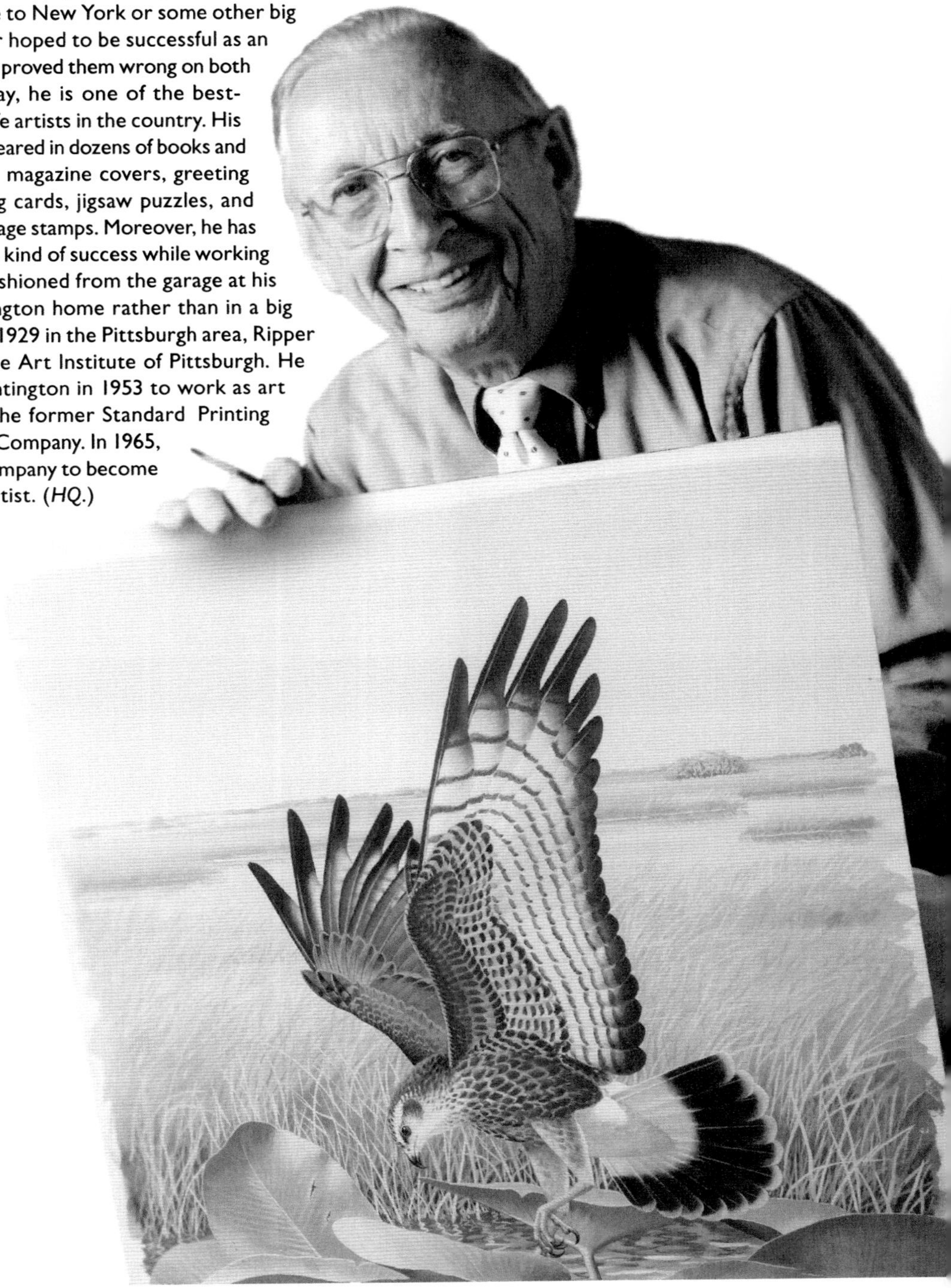

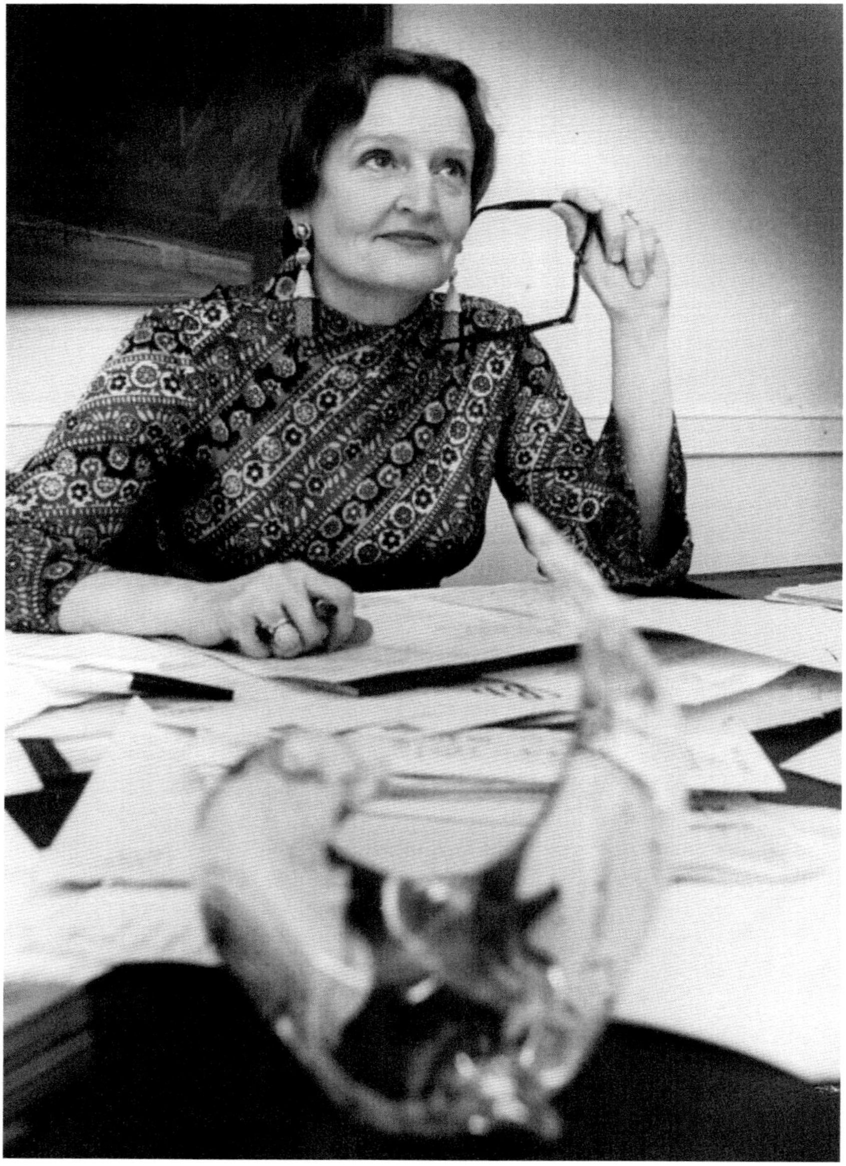

Director Roberta Shinn Emerson (1922–1998) was instrumental in transforming the Huntington Galleries into the Huntington Museum of Art, a transition that meant far more than a change in name. Under her leadership, the museum grew from a staff of five and an annual budget of $125,000 to a staff of 30 and a budget of $1.25 million. As a girl, she lived in a number of towns because her father was an engineer who took long assignments with different companies. She studied art history at Northwestern University and the University of Chicago but left one semester shy of graduating to marry Robert K. Emerson in 1943. While he was serving in the Navy, she lived with her parents in Huntington, where her father was on assignment to the International Nickel Company. She took classes at Marshall University, finishing her degree. First involved with the museum as a trustee, she was named director in 1972 and held that post until her retirement in 1988. (*H-D.*)

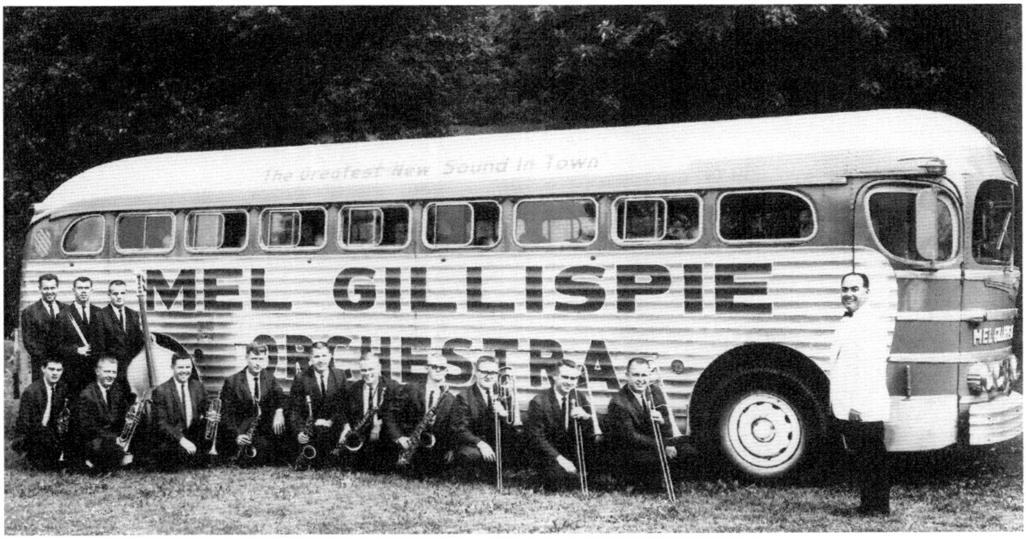

Mel Gillispie was "Mr. Music" in Huntington from the 1960s until his death in 2004. When he graduated from Marshall College, he headed for New York City, where he earned a master's degree in music at Columbia University. Returning home, he immediately organized a band. The Mel Gillispie Orchestra played its first engagement in 1960 and went on to become perhaps the best-known musical aggregation in the region. Gillispie bought a used Greyhound bus, which took the band far and wide—to every state east of the Mississippi—until the gasoline crisis of the 1970s forced him to sell it. Closer to home, he taught music for 25 years at West Virginia State College in Institute and offered frequent free concerts at Ritter Park. (*H-D.*)

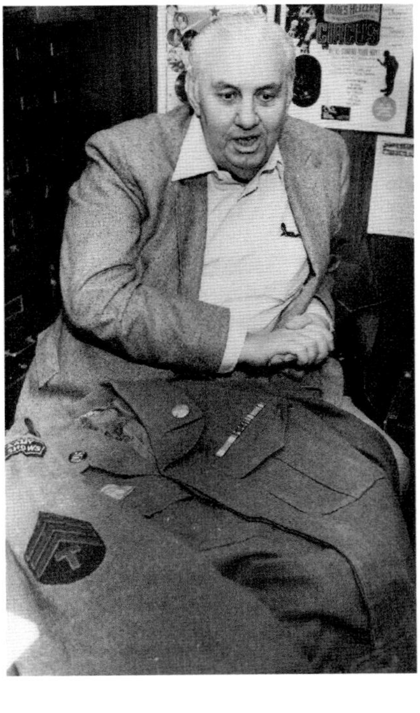

James Thomas Hetzer, who died in 1987 at the age of 71, loved entertaining from his earliest years. A promising career as a tap dancer was cut short by World War II, when he traveled by jeep to entertain troops at the front lines. He is shown here with the uniform he wore while overseas. Back home after the war, he abandoned the stage for a behind-the-scenes role. He launched Hetzer Theatrical Productions and from his office in the Huntington Arcade on Fourth Avenue produced a nearly continuous series of touring shows, large and small, for nearly 40 years. (*H-D.*)

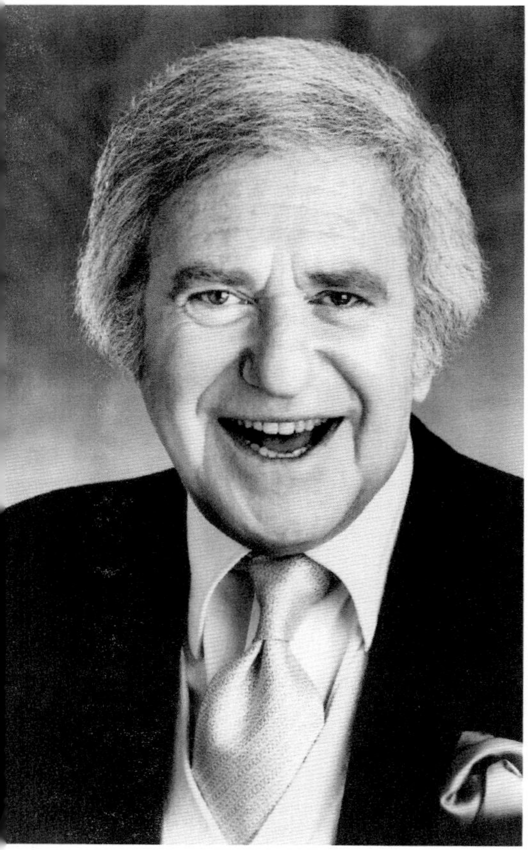

Although born in North Carolina, pie-throwing comic Soupy Sales (1926–2009) grew up in Huntington and looked at it as his hometown. He earned a journalism degree at Marshall University, worked as a radio deejay at Huntington's WHTN, and started doing stand-up comedy at area clubs. Later, he hosted a television dance party in Cincinnati, but his career really took off in 1953, when he moved to Detroit and began doing a children's show that became a huge hit on ABC-TV. Over the years, there is hardly a show-business venue he did not tackle. Radio and television, dinner theater, comedy clubs, recordings, and movies—Soupy did it all. In 1968, he joined the panel on television's *What's My Line?* and went on to do 1,500 shows during a seven-year run. (*H-D.*)

Janet Bromley was six years old when her parents looked out the window and saw her in the yard with one stick under her chin and another as her violin bow. She then received a violin for her seventh birthday. By the time she was in the ninth grade, she was playing second violin in the Huntington Symphony Orchestra. She earned two bachelor's degrees at Oberlin College in Ohio in arts and in music education, taught at Berea College from 1947 to 1949, and, back home, was one of the founders of the Huntington Chamber Orchestra. She is shown receiving a plaque from the Reverend Timothy Dixon for her many years of dedication and service to Huntington's First Congregational United Church of Christ. (H-D)

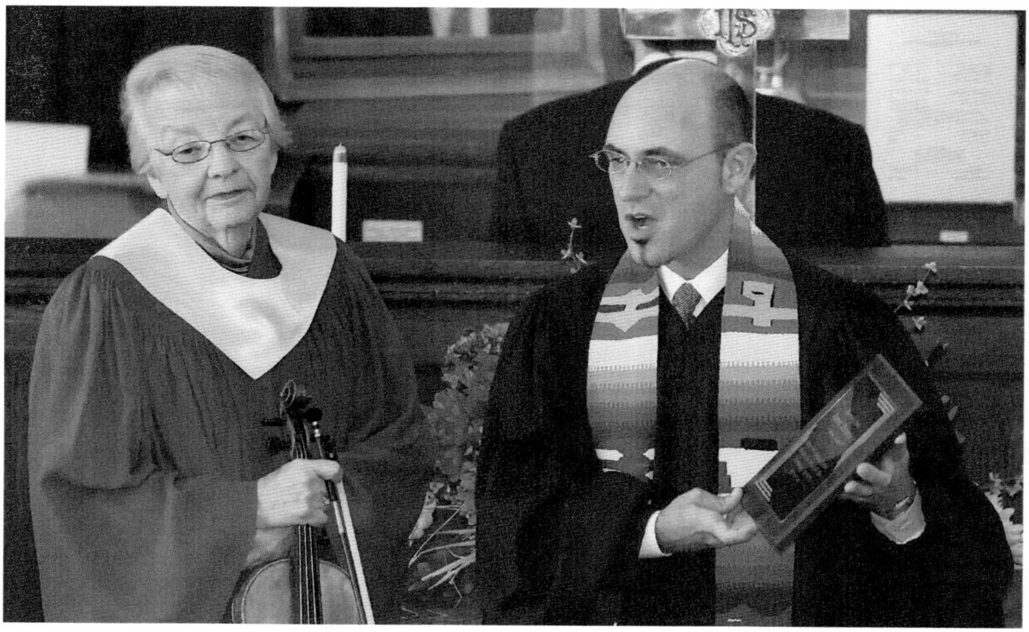

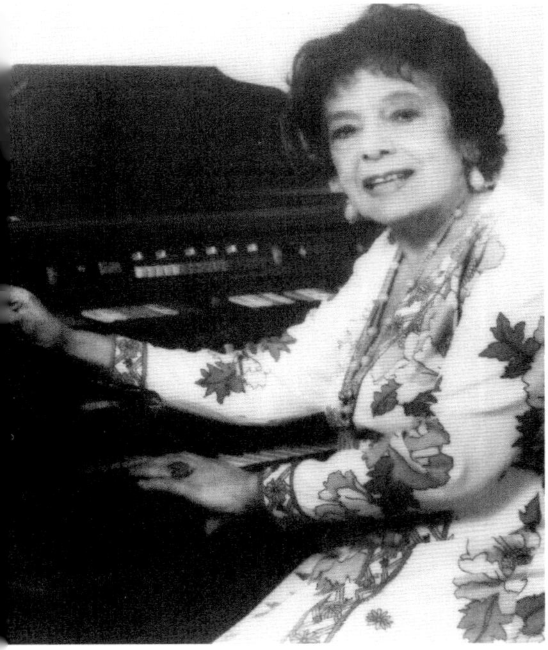

Revella Hughes (1895–1987) began playing piano at age 5 and violin at age 10. She studied music at Hartshorn Memorial College, in Richmond, Virginia, Oberlin Conservatory in Oberlin, Ohio, and Howard University in Washington, DC. By 1920, she was in New York, where she recorded on W.C. Handy's Black Swan record label. In the 1920s, she was choral director for *Shuffle Along* and the female lead in *Runnin' Wild*, two Broadway musicals with all-black casts. In 1932, she returned to Huntington to care for her mother. As supervisor of music in the community's African American schools, she created the band at Douglass High School. When her mother died, Hughes returned to New York and her performing career. She retired in 1955 but staged a final round of concerts, including an appearance at Radio City Music Hall, 25 years later. (*H-D.*)

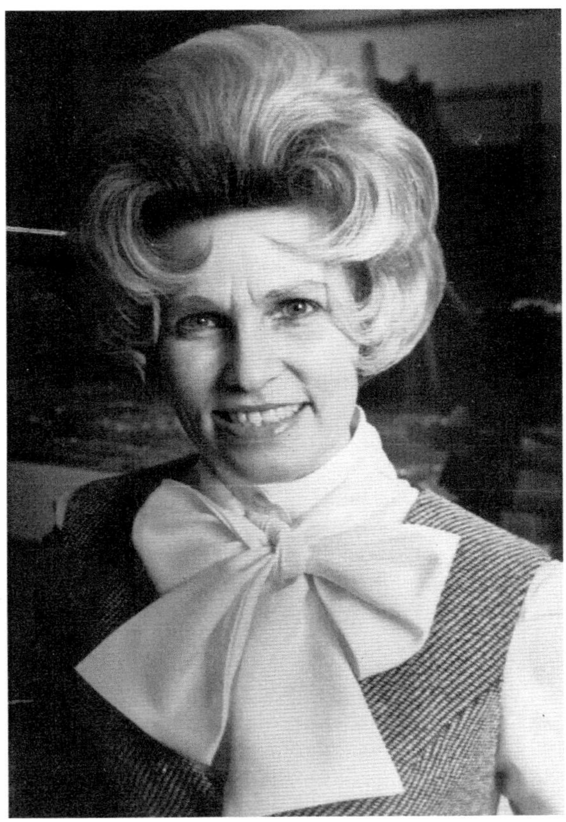

Janice Chandler Gold has been a professional singer, director of choral music, composer, arranger, organist, and pianist. Director of choral music at the former Huntington East High School for 27 years and director of music at Beverly Hills United Methodist Church for more than 50 years, she has also directed the Renaissance A Capella Choir and the Gold 'n Girls and served as music director at the Woodland Retirement Community. In 2000, the auditorium at the former East High was named in her honor. (*H-D.*)

Like many young boys, Michael W. Smith, born in the Huntington suburb of Kenova, loved to play baseball. Unlike other boys, though, he wrote his first song at age five; he has been writing songs ever since. He attended Marshall University for one semester before heading for Nashville and a music career. Success did not happen overnight, but in 1982 he landed a spot backing up gospel singer Amy Grant, and the next year he cut his first album. Since then, he has made nearly two dozen albums, written 10 books, performed in a multitude of settings, and won a flock of music awards. Despite his success, he states on his website that his wish is "to be remembered as a God-fearing man who loved his wife and kids well." (*HQ*.)

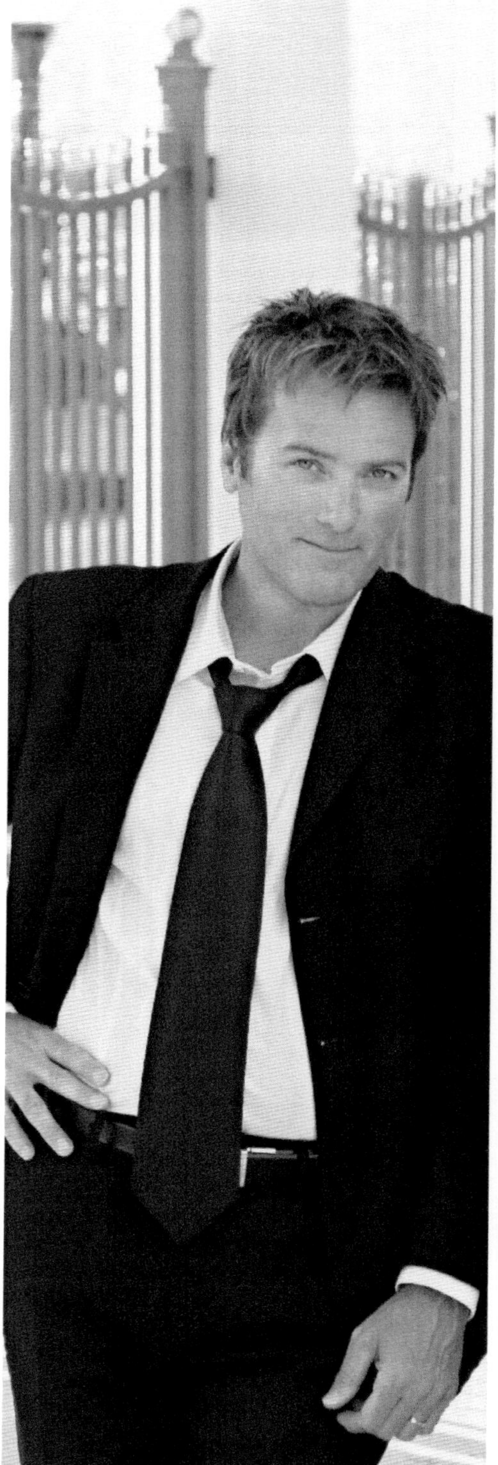

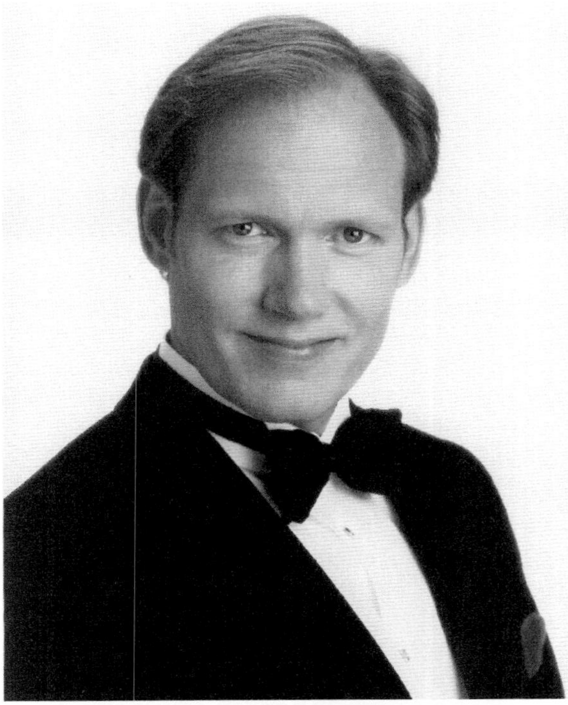

Huntington-born singer J. Mark McVey has performed as Jean Valjean, the valiant hero of *Les Miserables*, nearly 3,000 times in productions on Broadway, in London, the Hollywood Bowl, and elsewhere. McVey graduated from Huntington High School and went on to Marshall University, where, at his father's urging, he majored in marketing, not music. But music has been at the center of his life ever since. His early stage career had its ups and downs until he landed a spot as an understudy to the lead in the first national tour of *Les Miz*. It was not long before he moved up to the lead role, and he has never looked back. (*H-D.*)

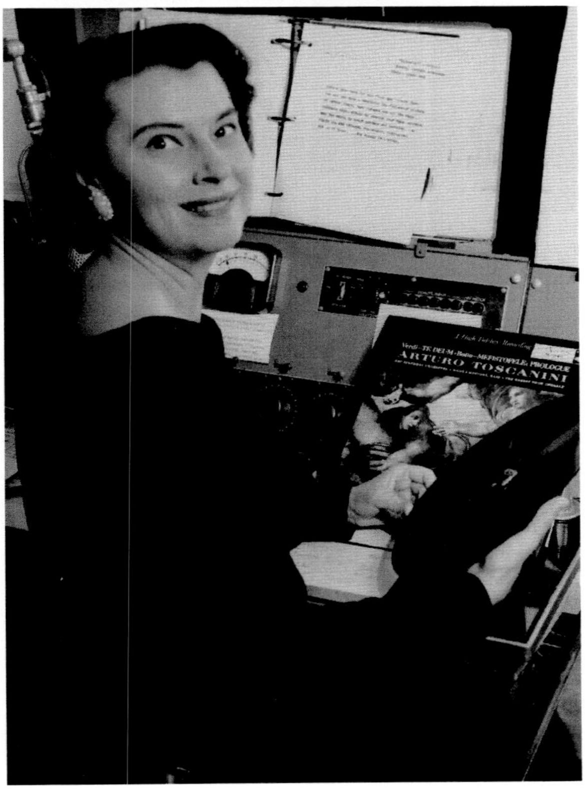

Born Flora Jane Boewdeker in Nebraska, Jane Shepherd (1918–1984) began piano training at age seven, which would carry her to an associate degree from William Woods College in Fulton, Missouri, a diplome d'execution in Piano from the American Conservatory in Fontainebleau, France, and bachelor's and master's degrees from the Cincinnati Conservatory of Music. Encouraged to begin voice training, she completed four years at the Juilliard School of Music in New York, culminating with a concert at Town Hall in New York in 1946. With her career as a mezzo-soprano launched, she took the stage name of Jane Hobson, her grandmother's name, and performed with many of the nation's major orchestras. After her marriage to Robert Shepherd in 1950, she made her home in Huntington, where she taught privately, hosted a local classical music radio show, and, in 1958, joined the faculty of Marshall College. (*H-D.*)

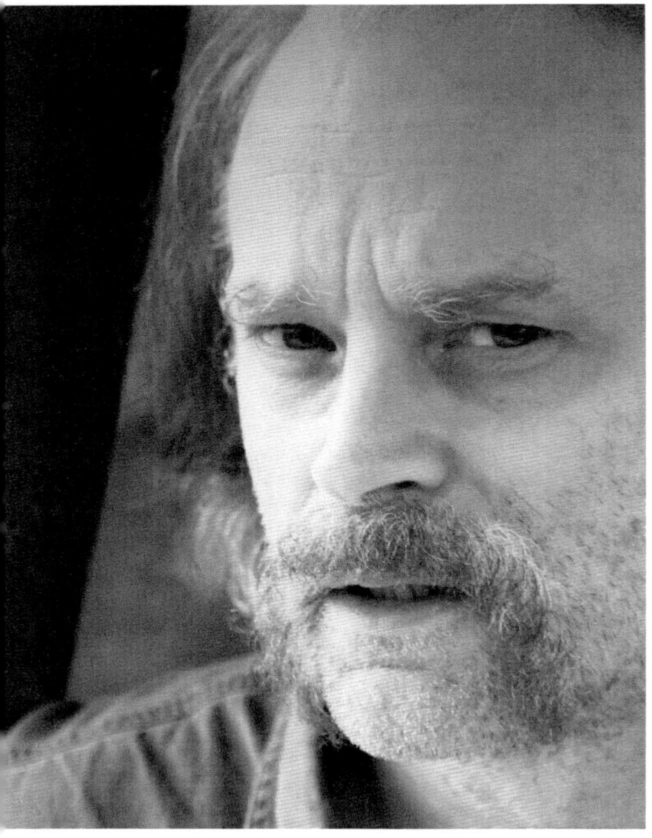

Actor Brad Dourif drew rave reviews for his portrayal of Bill Bibbit in *One Flew Over the Cuckoo's Nest* (1975) and has since appeared in many memorable roles. He is the voice of Chucky in the *Child's Play* horror films, was Grima Wormtongue in *The Lord of the Rings*, and Doc Cochran in the hit HBO television series *Deadwood*. He has appeared in 150 movie and television roles, often playing twisted or eccentric characters. Dourif was born in Huntington in 1950. His father died when he was only three, and he and siblings were raised by his mother Joan and stepfather, famed amateur golfer William C. Campbell. (*HQ*.)

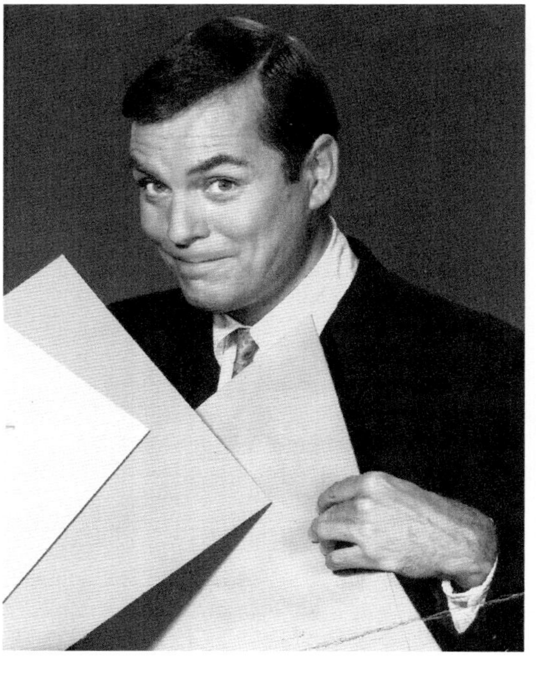

Peter Marshall was born Ralph Pierre LaCock in 1926 in Huntington. Following his father's death, he lived in New York with his mother and his older sister, actress Joanne Dru. In the 1950s, he worked in nightclubs, television, and films, adopting a stage name derived from Marshall College. He was unable to find steady work in the industry until becoming the easy-going host of the show *Hollywood Squares*, a fabulously successful game show that ran from 1966 to 1981. After *Hollywood Squares*, he continued working as a game-show host and playing character roles on television and the stage. (*H-D.*)

Today, Conchata Ferrell is instantly recognizable to the millions of television fans who enjoy her as housekeeper Berta on the hit series *Two and a Half Men*. But it took her more than 30 years of hard work to achieve that coveted status. Born in Loudendale, near Charleston, West Virginia, Ferrell grew up in Circleville, Ohio, and graduated from Marshall University. Bitten by the theater bug, she headed for New York City. In 1973, she was cast as prostitute April Green in an off-Broadway production of Lanford Wilson's *The Hot L Baltimore*. She later reprised the role for a short-lived television series. (*HQ*.)

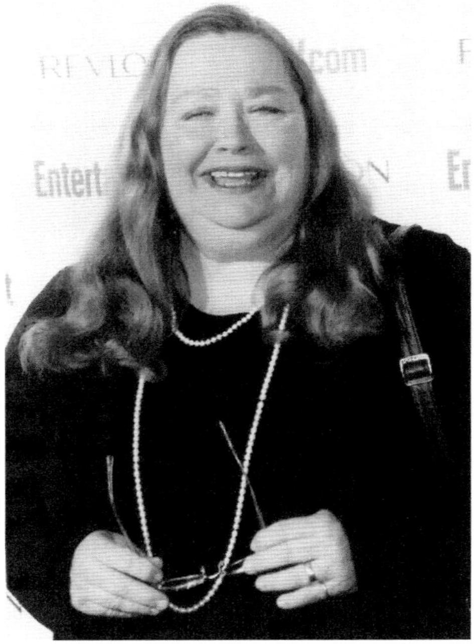

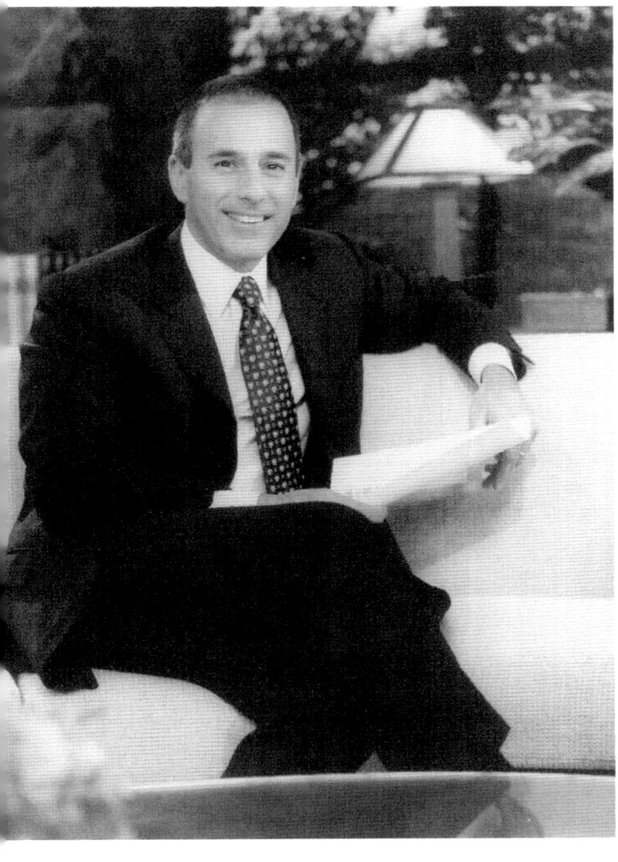

Matt Lauer has been coanchor of NBC's *Today* show since 1997. Before that, he frequently moved around the country to further his television career, working in a number of cities. It was in Huntington, though, that his broadcasting career began. "I had an internship at WOWK my senior year," Lauer told *Huntington Quarterly* in a 2007 interview. "When the summer ended they offered me a job. I left college needing four credits, and to be honest, the credits I needed were in a classic literature course, so I thought I'd find time to do that later"—and that he did. He worked with Ohio University to complete his bachelor's degree in 1997, the same year he returned to the school as commencement speaker. (*HQ*.)

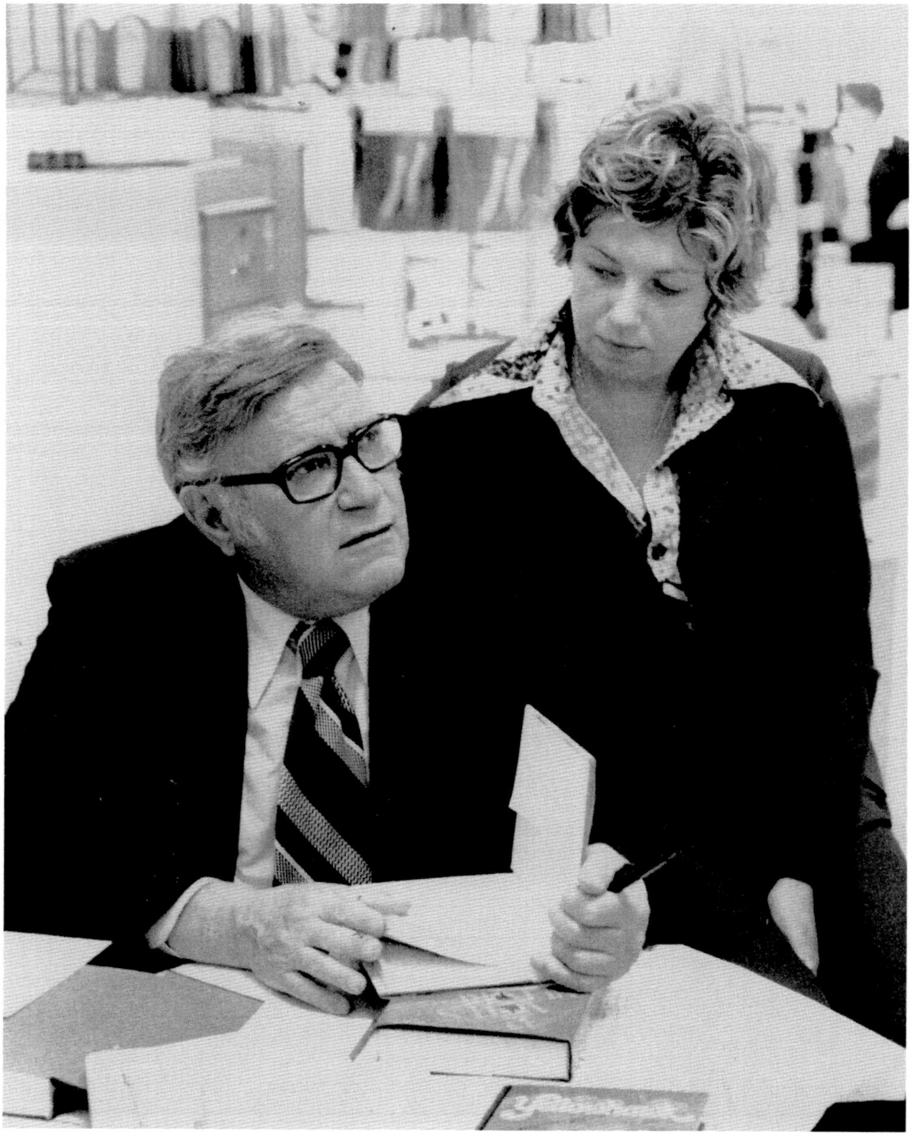

Author Jesse Hilton Stuart (1906–1984) was born in W-Hollow, Kentucky, and lived there his whole life except for his college years and later when he was traveling abroad. But his visits to Huntington and the Marshall University campus were so frequent that many in the community looked on him as one of their own. Graduating from Peabody University in 1929, he went on attend graduate school at Vanderbilt University and Peabody College and became a teacher before leaving the classroom to work full-time as a writer. While still in college, he began writing stories and poems about the hill people in his section of Kentucky. His poetry collection, *Man with a Bull-Tongue Plow*, was published in 1934 and was widely praised. He would go on to publish dozens of books and hundreds of poems and short stories. Today, Marshall has an extensive collection of his papers and books. He is shown here with his daughter Jane, also a writer, during one of his many autograph sessions at the former Anderson-Newcomb department store in downtown Huntington. (*H-D.*)

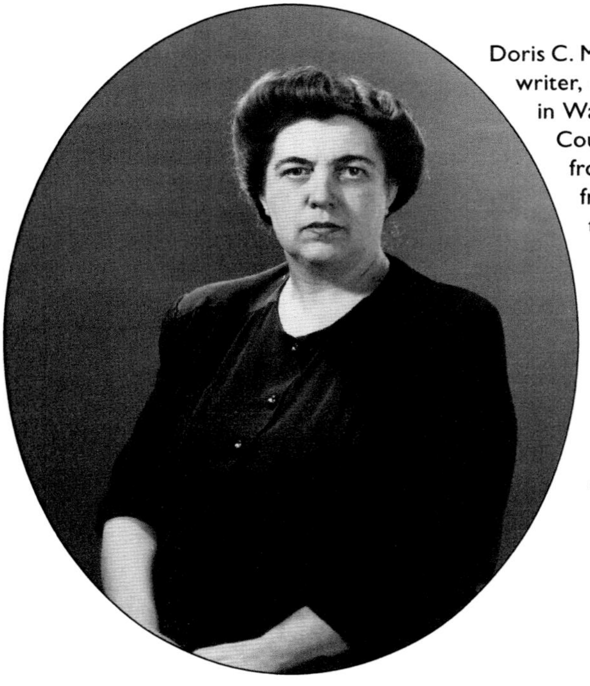

Doris C. Miller (1903–1993) was a teacher, newspaper writer, church secretary, and poet. Born at Shoals in Wayne County, she was proud of her Wayne County roots. She earned a bachelor's degree from Marshall College in 1933 and a master's from Marshall in 1943. At age 18, she began teaching at a country school in Wayne County. She later wrote for Huntington newspapers and was secretary at Central Christian Church. Her column, "Poetry Today," was a Sunday feature in the papers for more than 15 years. She coedited *Echoes of West Virginia*, a poetry magazine, and published two volumes of her poetry. She also wrote the *Centennial History of Huntington, W.Va., 1871–1971*. (H-D.)

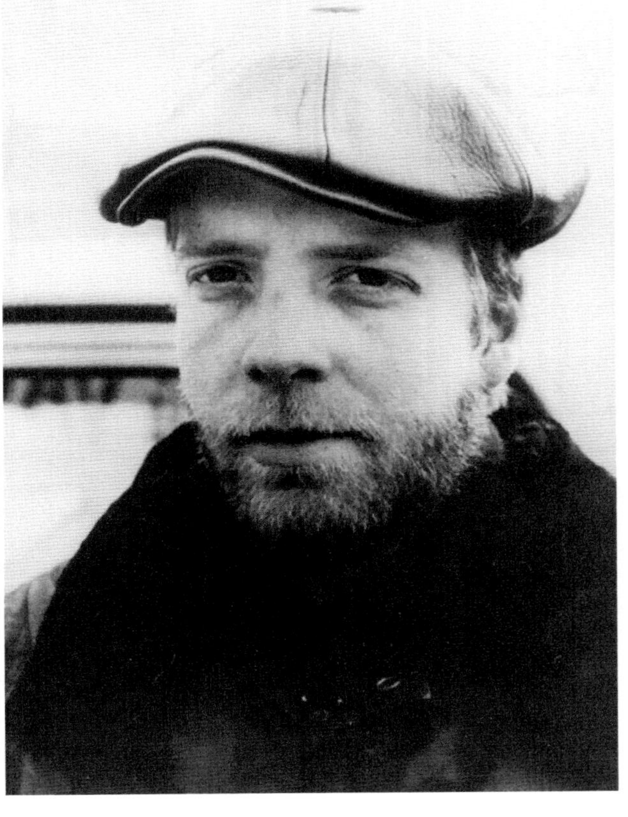

In his brief life, Breece D'J Pancake (1952–1979) wrote only a dozen short stories: six were published during his lifetime and another six after his death by a self-inflicted gunshot wound. His stories have gained a cult-like following and seem destined to be read for decades to come. Raised in Milton, West Virginia, just outside Huntington, Pancake graduated from Marshall University and studied at the University of Virginia's Creative Writing Program. His unusual middle name of "D'J" originated when *The Atlantic Monthly* misprinted his middle initials in the byline of a story; Pancake decided not to correct it. (Milton Branch, Cabell County Public Library.)

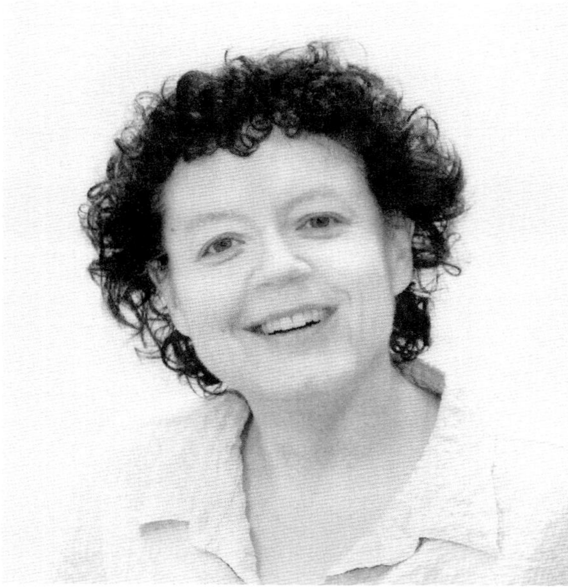

Pulitzer Prize–winner Julia Keller, the cultural critic for the *Chicago Tribune*, is a two-time graduate of Marshall University. Keller was born and raised in Huntington, receiving her bachelor's degree in English in 1976 and a master's degree in English in 1981. She earned her doctoral degree in English from Ohio State University in 1996. In 2005, she won a Pulitzer for a three-part series on a tornado that ripped through Utica, Illinois. (*Chicago Tribune*.)

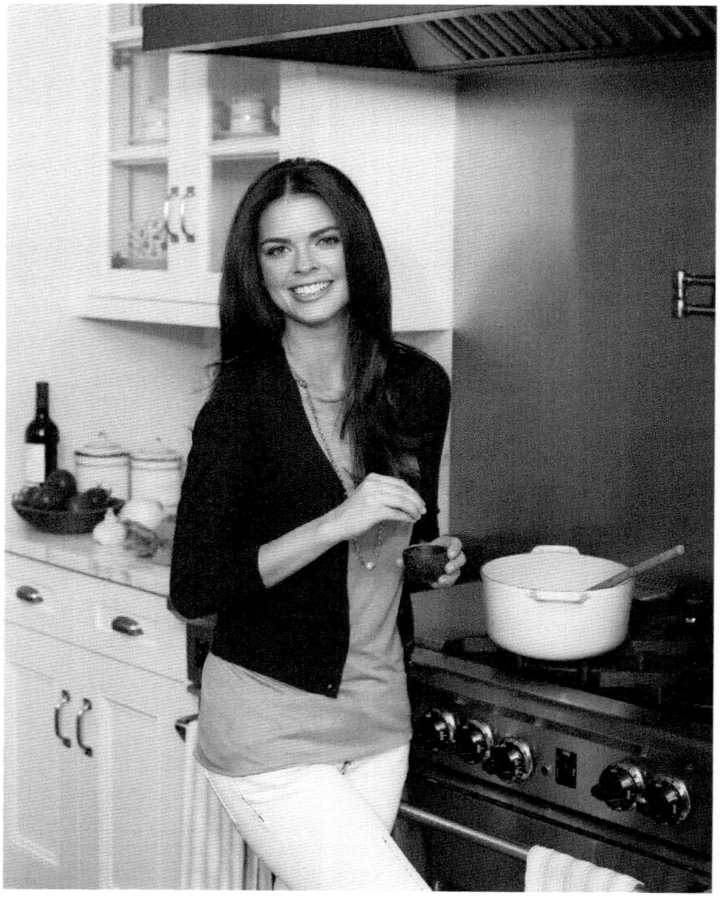

Today, Katie Lee is a famous chef and cookbook author who makes her home in the Hamptons, the posh enclave in New York, but no matter where her career takes her she says she will always consider West Virginia home. Milton native Lee began cooking at age four under the careful eye of her grandmother Dora and gave her first recorded cooking demonstration at 12, proudly videotaped by her mother. She graduated from Cabell Midland High School and Miami University at Oxford, Ohio. An assignment to write a cooking column for *Hamptons* magazine launched her writing career, which includes a long list of national magazines. She has become a familiar face on television and published her first novel, *Groundswell*, in 2011. (*HQ*.)

Craig Johnson grew up in Huntington but created a mystery series that is set a long, long way from his boyhood home. Johnson graduated from the former Huntington East High School (class of 1979) and Marshall University. Today, he is a Wyoming rancher and has used his adopted state as the setting for a stack of modern-day Western novels (eight so far) featuring Walt Longmire, the sheriff of fictional Absaroka County. Johnson's novels long have been a favorite of critics and fans alike and, in the summer of 2012, gained a whole new audience with the debut of a television series, *Longmire*, on A&E. (Craig Johnson.)

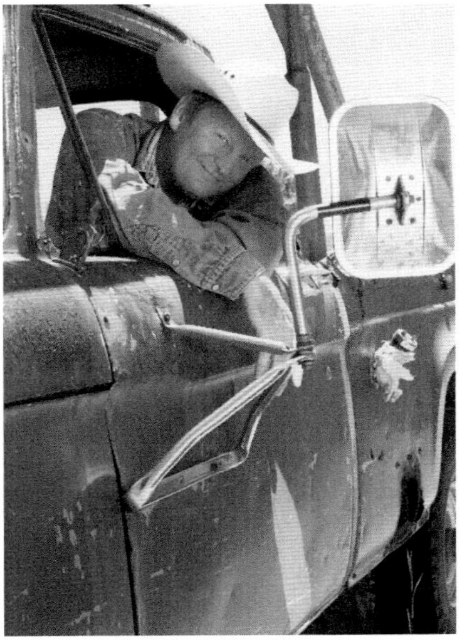

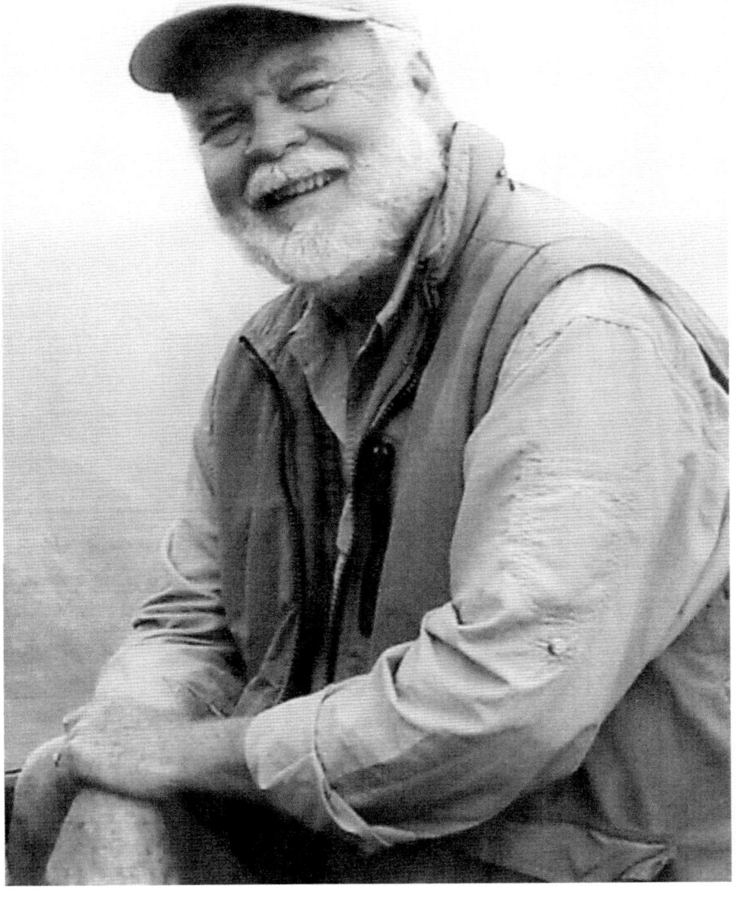

Lee Maynard was born and raised in the tiny Wayne County community of Crum. Today, he lives in New Mexico. For 20 years, Maynard regularly wrote articles for the *Reader's Digest* and other magazines. When he turned his hand to fiction, his first novel, titled *Crum*, a fictionalized account of his boyhood, was so filled with four-letter words and references to bodily functions that Tamarack, the state's official arts and crafts marketplace, refused to stock it. Two sequels have proved equally outrageous, leaving some readers shaking their heads but delighting his many loyal fans. And that, Maynard insists, is just fine by him. (Lee Maynard.)

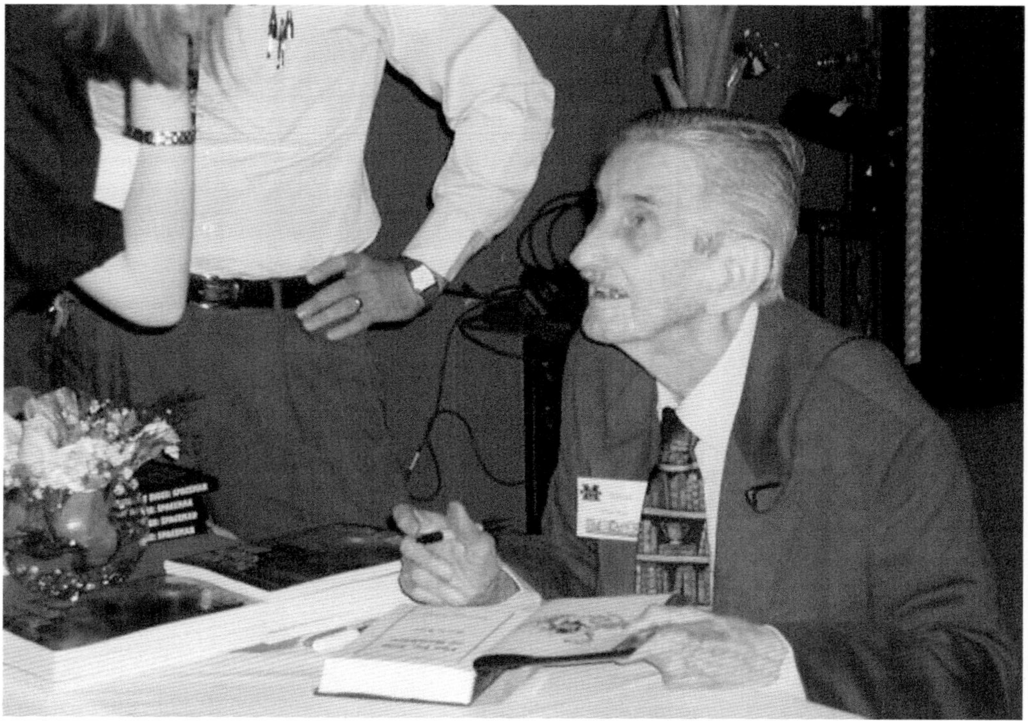

Nelson Bond, a pioneer writer in fantasy and science fiction, grew up in Philadelphia and then attended Marshall College from 1932 to 1934. He worked briefly in public relations before becoming a full-time writer. Bond wrote for the pulp magazines of the 1930s and 1940s and literally cranked out hundreds of stories. Later, he wrote for radio and, with the arrival of television, scripted for it as well. Late in his career, he renewed his ties with Marshall and, in 2003, donated his papers and files to the school's library. He is shown during a visit to the campus. He died in 2006, just 19 days short of his 98th birthday. (MU.)

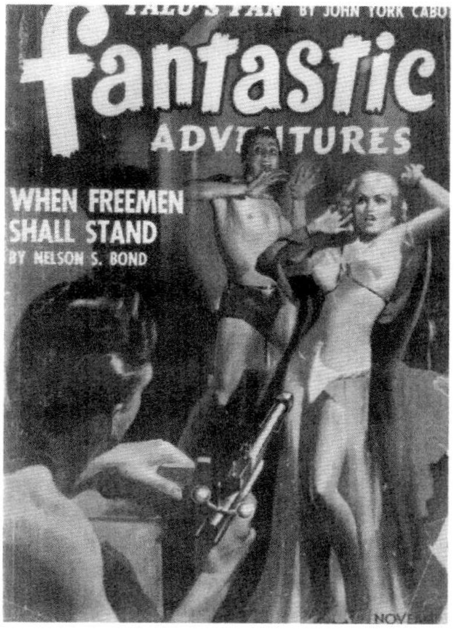

Marshall's collection of Bond memorabilia contains many copies of vintage magazines where his stories appeared. This 1942 issue of *Fantastic Adventures* is a typical example. Many of the magazines may seem almost laughable today, but Bond's stories have retained their appeal to fantasy and science-fiction fans, and collections of them are still in print. (MU.)

Heroes

Virtually every chapter in this book includes its share of heroes. What else can one call it when a judge such as John W. Hereford devotes his time off the bench to founding a club for the city's disadvantaged boys and girls? Water utility executive Max Jones did not have to devote much of his life to helping create Cabell Huntington Hospital and the Veterans Memorial Field House; his willingness to do so surely marks him as a hero. And what about coach Ray McCoy's generosity to young student athletes who could not afford track shoes or, in some cases, even food? That, too, is heroic. Drs. Jeffrey George and Ann Conjura demonstrated real heroism in their efforts on behalf of the Jeffrey George Comfort House and Hospice of Huntington. Now, in this final chapter are stories of people who have exhibited such a special brand of heroism that it merits them this place of honor. Some displayed their heroism on the battlefield, some in the struggle for civil rights, and some in championing other important causes. Each has a story that is very different, but each is a Huntington hero.

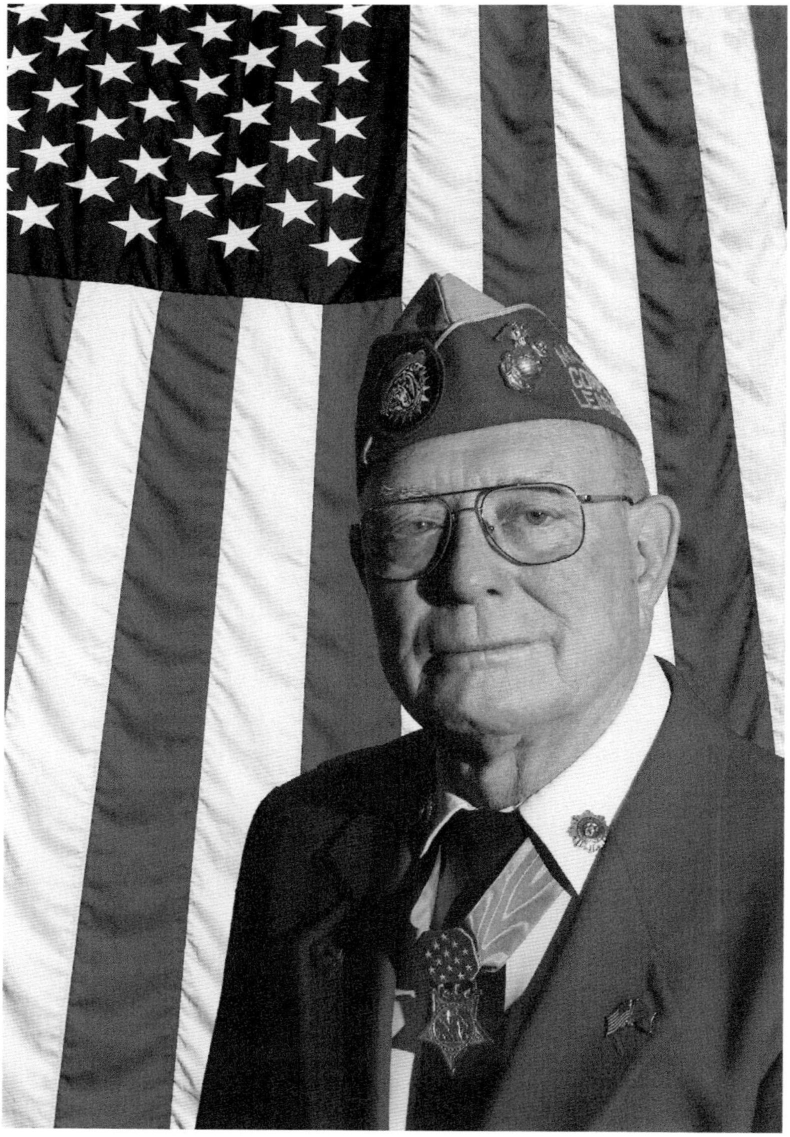

In 1945, the American military was determined to capture Iwo Jima. In US hands, the island would be the perfect spot to launch bomber attacks on the Japanese homeland. The Japanese were equally determined to hold onto the island. When the invading US Marines stormed ashore, they were pinned down by withering fire from a network of Japanese pillboxes. An officer asked for a volunteer to try and take out the pillboxes. "I'll see what I can do," said Hershel Woodrow "Woody" Williams, a scrawny young Marine from West Virginia. Using a series of flamethrowers, Williams repeatedly risked his life to take out seven pillboxes that day—an incredible feat that soon would have him standing stiffly at attention in the White House Rose Garden as President Truman presented him the Medal of Honor. After the war, Williams returned to West Virginia, making his home in Ona, just outside Huntington, working as an official with the Veterans Administration. He resists being called a hero, saying, "The Marines who were killed in that battle and never got to come home . . . are the true heroes." (*HQ.*)

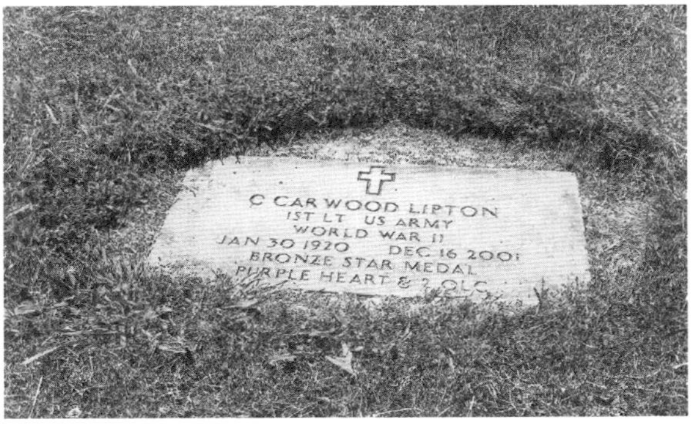

In World War II, Huntington native Carwood Lipton (1920–2001) parachuted into France as a member of E Company of the Army's 101st Airborne, a fighting unit whose exploits were chronicled first by author Stephen Ambrose in his book *Band of Brothers* and later in an HBO miniseries of the same name. Actor Donnie Wahlberg portrayed Lipton in the series. Lipton earned a Bronze State and a battlefield commission to second lieutenant in the fighting. After the war, he returned to Huntington, graduated from Marshall College, and went to work for the Owens-Illinois Glass Company. Steadily rising through the company's ranks, he retired in 1983 as its director of international development. He is buried in Huntington's Woodmere Cemetery. (Author's.)

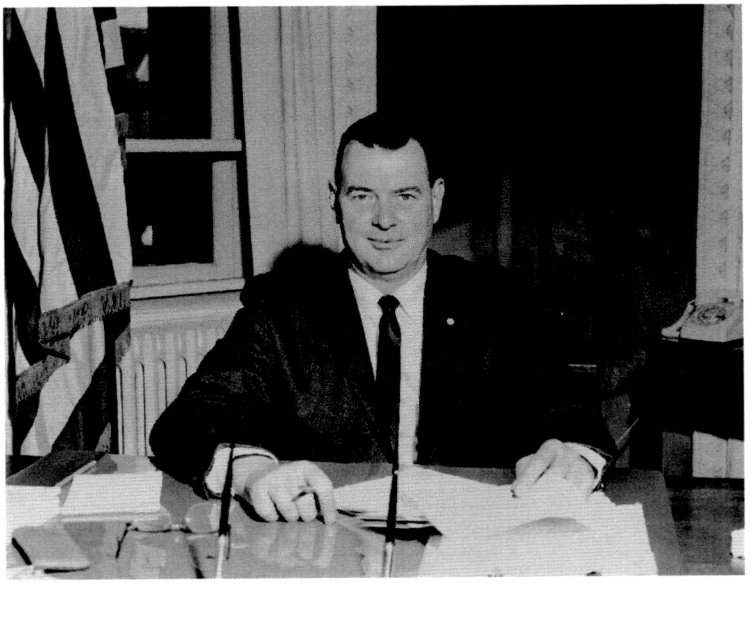

Maj. Justice Chambers (1908–1982) was at summer camp with his US Marine Corps Reserve unit when it was called up to active duty in 1940. Chambers answered that call and went on to serve with valor on the bloody island battlefields of the Pacific. He was wounded three times; the last time came on Iwo Jima, where he was critically wounded while rallying his fellow Marines to capture a key enemy ridge. His actions that day were honored with the Medal of Honor. A Huntington native, he was educated at Marshall College and earned a law degree in 1931. Prior to and after World War II, he served in a number of posts with the federal government. From 1962 to 1964, he was deputy director of the Office of Emergency Planning. (*H-D.*)

A native of Lincoln County, just a short drive from Huntington, Charles E. "Chuck" Yeager made aviation history on October 14, 1947, when he became the first man to fly faster than the speed of sound. Although he has never lived in Huntington, Yeager has always had close ties to the community and to Marshall University. In 1969, Marshall presented him with an honorary degree. Later, he agreed to have his name used for Marshall's Society of Yeager Scholars, a scholarship program for talented youngsters. Over the years, the famed flyer has frequently returned to meet with young members of the society. Many of Yeager's trophies, awards, and other mementos from his long career are housed in the Marshall Library's Yeager Room. (*H-D.*)

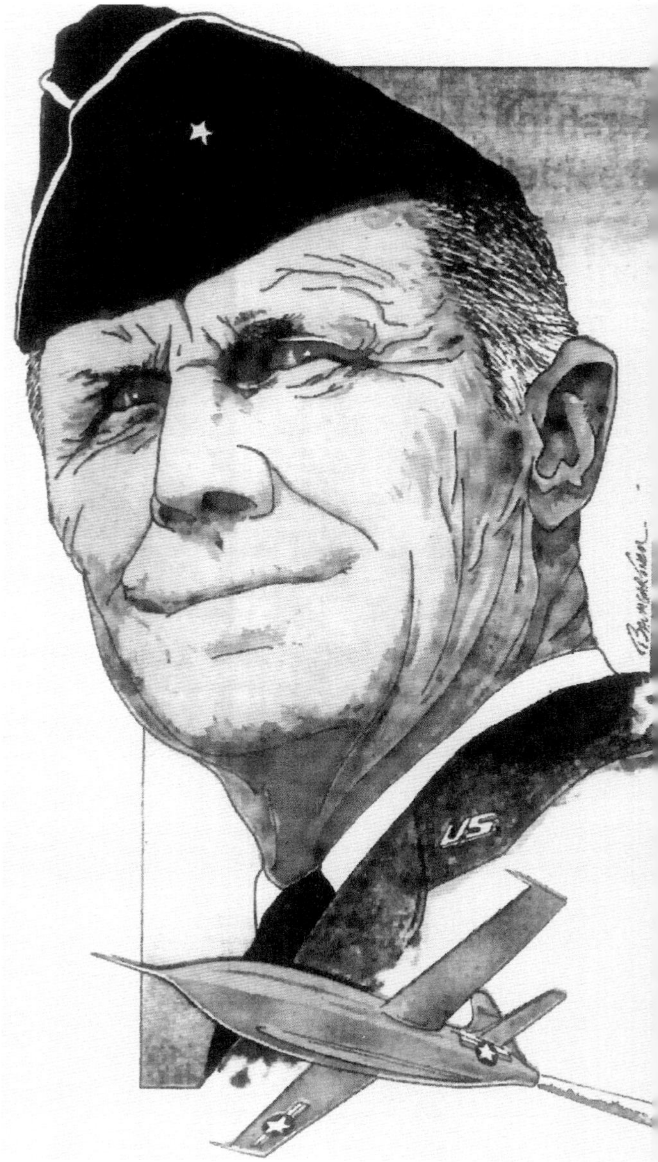

(OPPOSITE PAGE)

Herman Williams (1897–1988) proudly donned his World War I uniform each Veterans Day for decades. On his chest, he wore a half-dozen medals. In his elbow, he wore several pieces of shrapnel. Born in Crockett, Virginia, Williams was a motorcycle dispatch rider for Gen. John J. "Blackjack" Pershing during the war. He came to Huntington in 1927 to establish a White motor truck equipment business. When he retired in 1960, he started a second career of service to the community's veterans. He logged nearly 3,000 hours as a volunteer at the Huntington VA Medical Center and turned up, wearing his original "doughboy" uniform, at countless veterans events. At the time of his death, he was the last surviving charter member of Huntington's Veterans of Foreign Wars Post No. 1064. (*H-D.*)

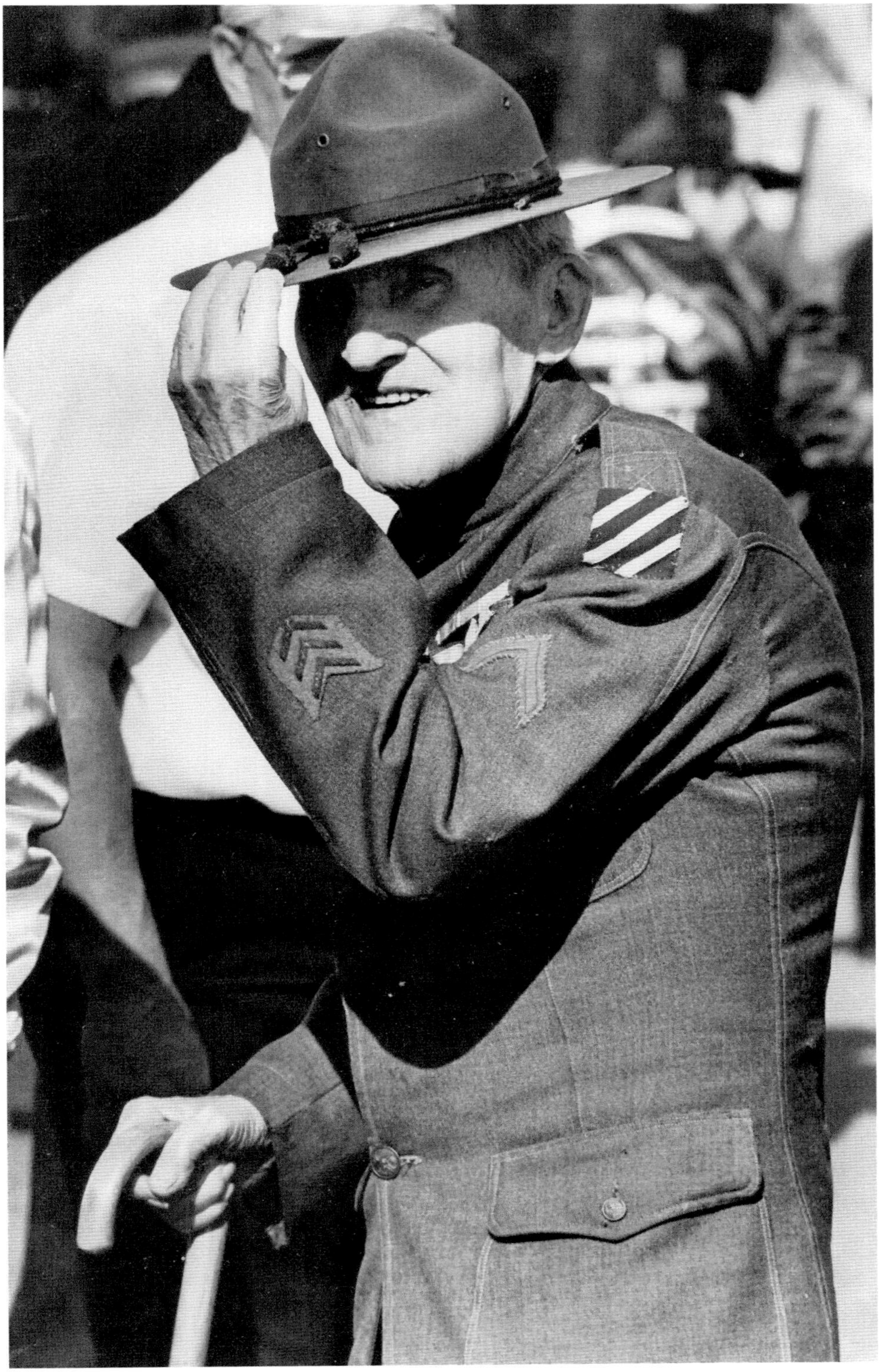

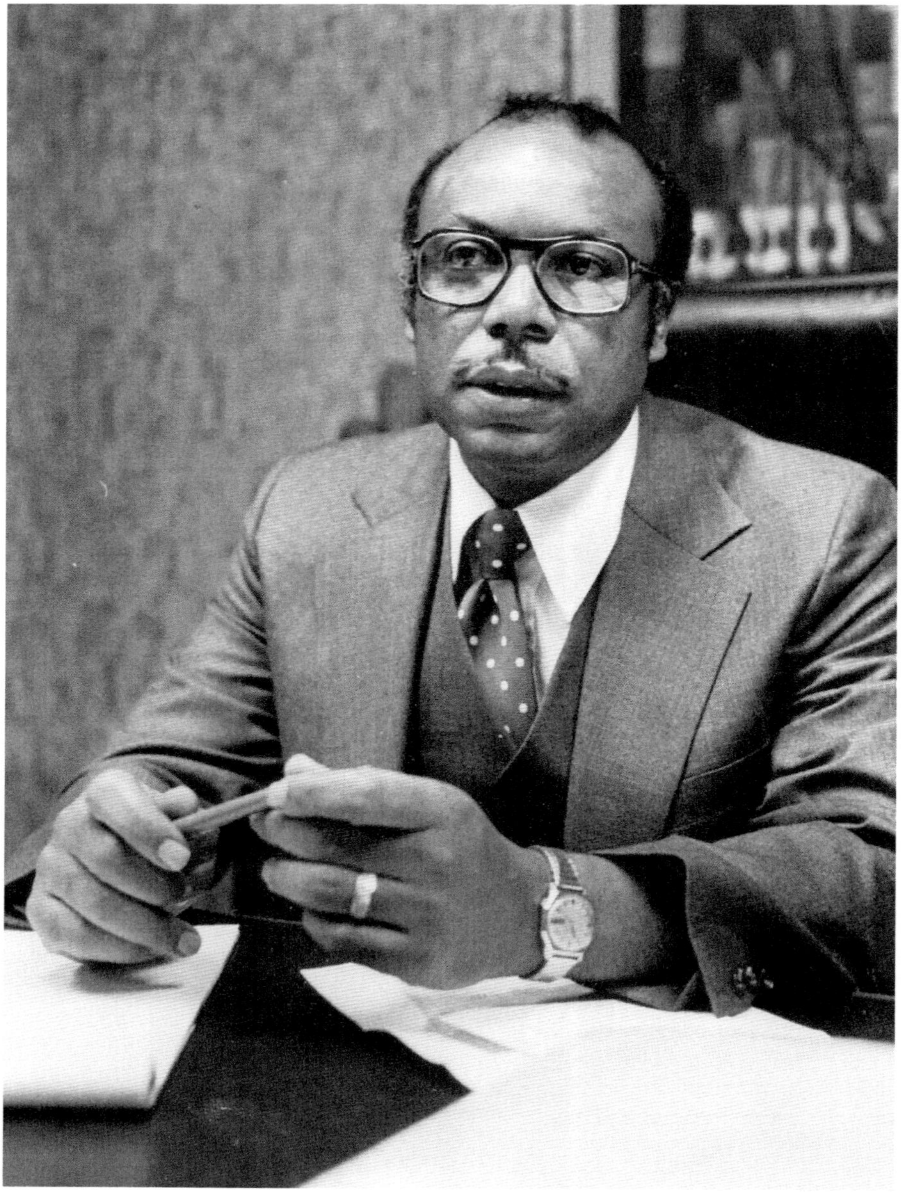

In the history of civil rights in West Virginia, few if any names are written larger than that of Huntington attorney Herbert H. Henderson (1929–2007). Henderson graduated from West Virginia State College (now University), where he captained the football team. He went on to become the first African American student to graduate from the George Washington University Law School. He completed law school in less than three years while working at the post office and driving a taxi to support his family. He was president of the West Virginia NAACP for 20 years and was an advisor and counsel to the organization at the national level. A respected friend of Benjamin Hooks, Julian Bond, and other nationally known black leaders, he was lead attorney in the successful lawsuit that saw the ironically named White Pantry and other segregated Huntington restaurants opened to members of all races. (*H-D.*)

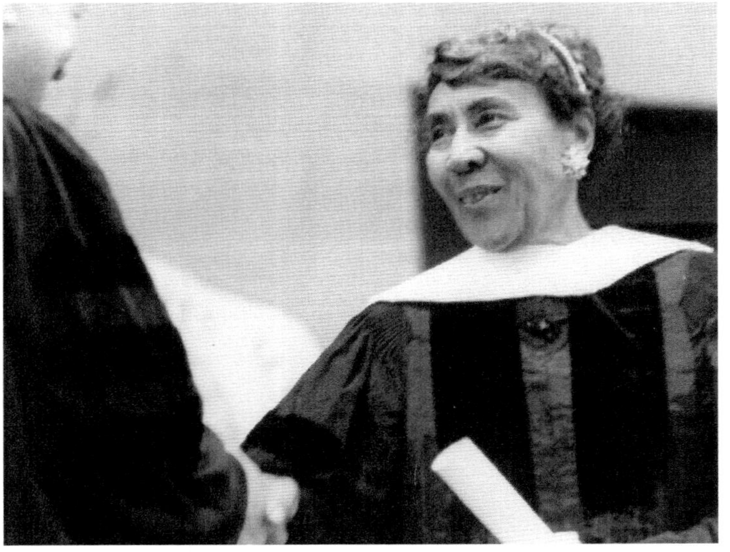

As a young Memphis Tennessee Garrison sat in the unheated Jim Crow car of a train in the early 1900s, she vowed to become a lawyer and do something about the law that had barred her from sitting in a heated car with the train's white passengers. She did not become a lawyer ("my mother couldn't wash enough clothes to send me to law school"); instead, she became a teacher and nationally recognized civil rights worker. She taught school in the McDowell County coalfields for 40 years before retiring and moving to Huntington. Over the years, she helped organize NAACP chapters throughout West Virginia and rose in the NAACP ranks to become a national vice president. She is pictured here as she received an honorary doctorate from Marshall University in 1970. She died in 1988 at age 98. (*H-D.*)

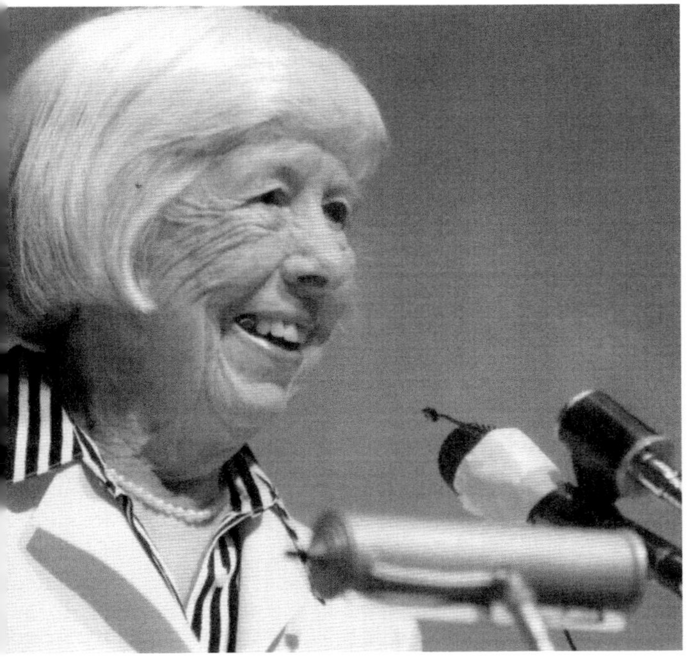

In 1963, when told her three-year-old son Joseph was autistic, Ruth Christ Sullivan knew nothing about autism. What started as a personal quest to help her son has become a decades-long crusade on behalf of autistic children everywhere. She founded the Autism Society of West Virginia and was the first president of the Autism Society of America. She prompted the opening of the Autism Training Center at Marshall University, established an autism hotline in Huntington, and in 1979 started her own Autism Services Center. She retired from the center in 2007 at age 83. (*H-D.*)

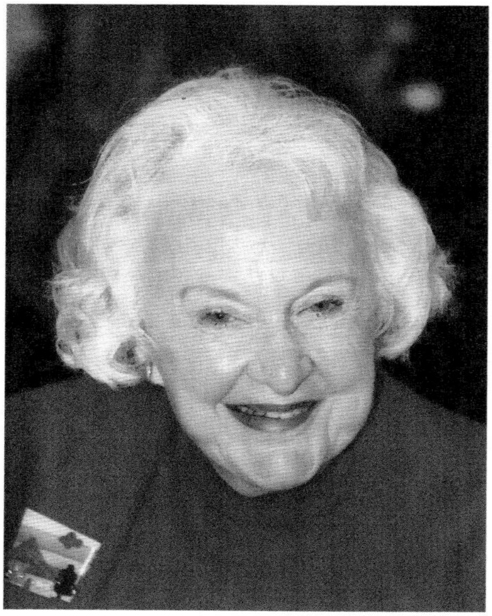

A native of Chicago who adopted Huntington as her home, Betty Barrett, a former member of Huntington City Council, has been an outspoken advocate for the less fortunate. The Cabell-Huntington Coalition for the Homeless and the Information and Referral Service are just two of the many groups that have benefited from her hard work. Under her leadership, local and state organizations came together to create Huntington's Vanity Fair, a housing project that provides single-occupancy apartments and advisory services for the homeless. (*H-D.*)

Hospice of Huntington began in 1978 when 49-year-old Laura Darby, wife of Dr. Darrel Darby, returned to Marshall University to fulfill her dream of becoming a nurse. In her final semester, she envisioned a hospice program that would provide end-of-life care for Huntington-area patients. She was told the project was too big for someone who had not even graduated from nursing school. Undaunted, she assembled a training class, recruited a physician to serve as medical director, and gathered community leaders to serve on a board of trustees. A makeshift office was set up in a hotel room, with donated medical supplies stacked in the bathtub. Today, Hospice of Huntington boasts a $12 million budget, a modern facility, and 50 employees, who over the years have cared for nearly 15,000 patients. All of it was made possible because Laura Darby refused to take "no" for an answer. (*H-D.*)

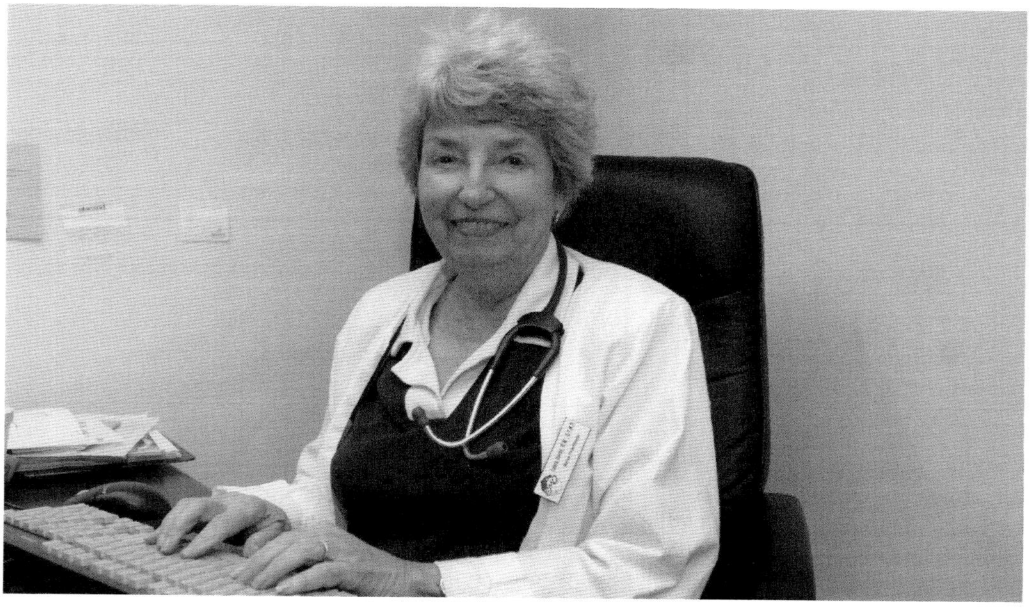

The life of Callie Barnett (1871–1980) spanned 109 years and paralleled the history of Huntington. Her grandmother was a former slave, her husband was one of the first African American men to graduate from Denison University, and her father-in-law came to Huntington to work for the Chesapeake & Ohio Railway in the city's earliest years. "He walked out here from Buckingham, Virginia, and saw how badly the railroad needed workers," she recalled. "He returned to Buckingham and encouraged others to follow him to Huntington." Her father-in-law, the Rev. Nelson Barnett, was one of the first pastors of the city's First Baptist Church, a historically black congregation. Her husband, Carter Harrison Barnett, was principal at Douglass High School, which served Huntington's African American students. For a time, she also taught there. She was one of the first members of the Huntington NAACP, when it was organized in the 1920s. "They always said separate but equal, but you know that was never true," she said in a 1974 interview. (*H-D.*)

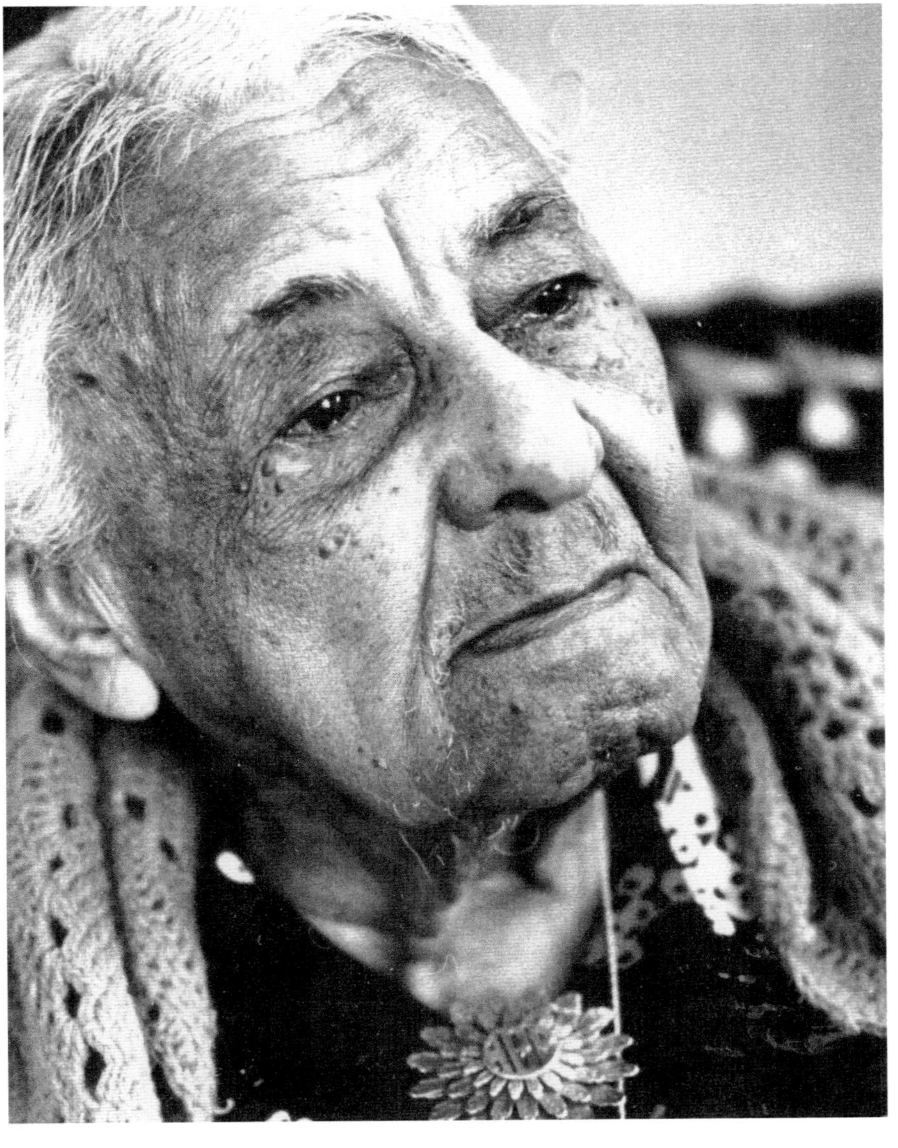

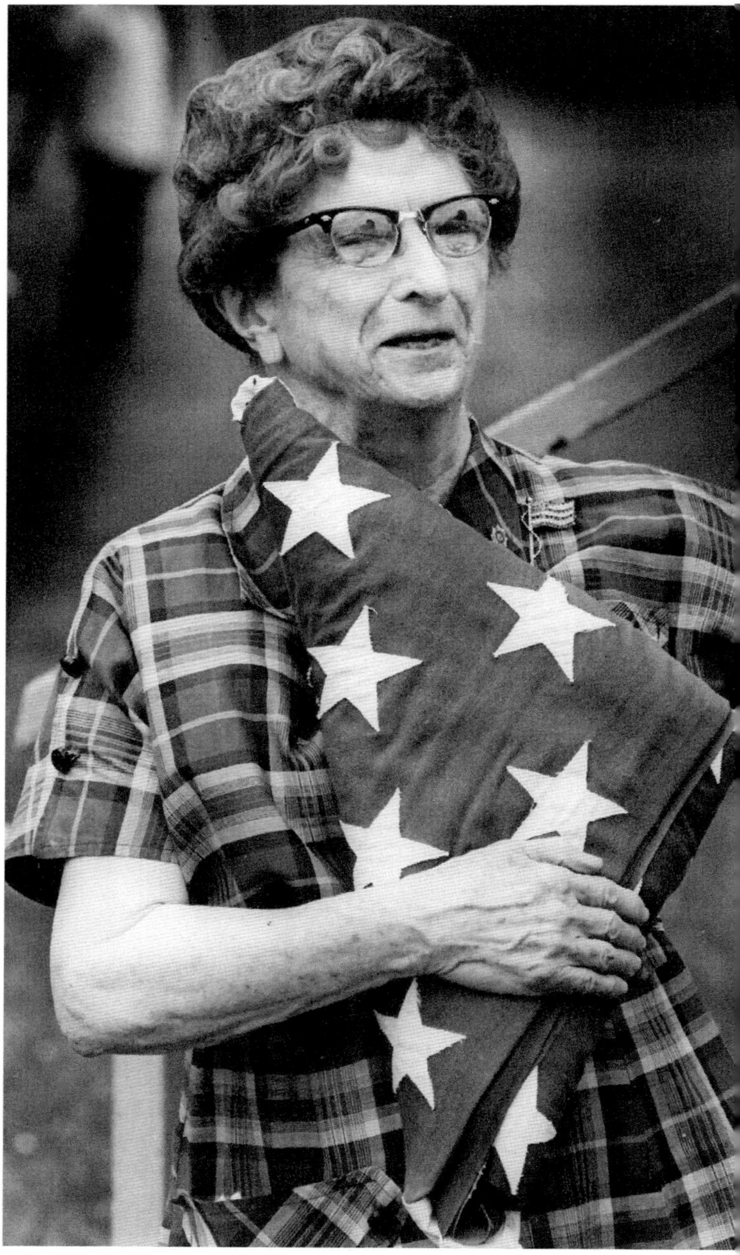

Stella Fuller (1883–1981) ministered to the needy of Huntington for more than 60 years, first as a member of the Salvation Army, then as head of her own Stella Fuller Settlement. Born in Point Pleasant, West Virginia, she grew up in rural Mason County. At age 19, she moved to Huntington, where she attended business school. After graduation, she moved to Welch, West Virginia, to work for a law firm. She returned to Huntington after marrying Elmer Fuller in 1907. She joined the Salvation Army in 1916 and served for 25 years. In January 1943, long-simmering problems between Fuller and the Army came to a head, and she left to found her own settlement house, located at 128 Washington Avenue in one of Huntington's poorest neighborhoods. In her final years before her death at age 97, ill health forced her to turn over operation of the settlement to her son Robert Fuller Jr. In 2008, she was posthumously inducted into the Greater Huntington Wall of Fame in recognition of her lifelong efforts in helping the community's poor and disadvantaged. (*H-D.*)

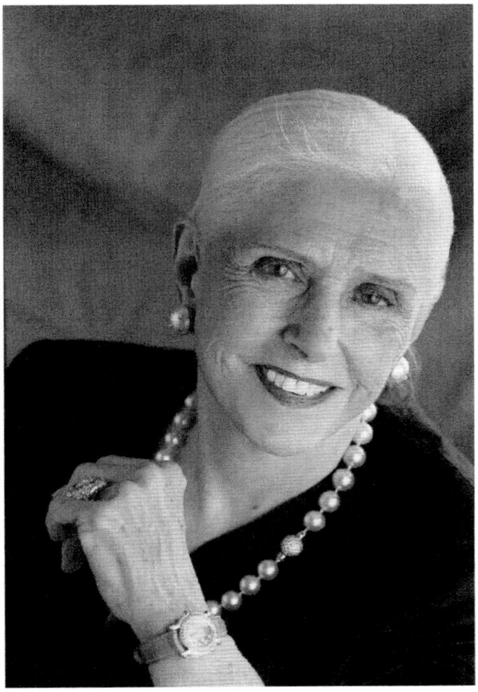

Joan Edwards (1918–2006) was born in London and arrived in New Orleans at the age of four. By age 11, she was singing on a New Orleans radio station, the start of a promising musical career. While singing at Pittsburgh's William Penn Hotel, she met James F. Edwards of Huntington, owner of the National Mattress Company, whom she married in 1937. When he died in 1991, his will called for multimillion-dollar bequests to a number of community projects. She not only carried out those bequests but went on to donate millions more of her own money. Overall, Joan and James Edwards donated more than $65 million to Marshall University and the Huntington community. Marshall's Joan C. Edwards Stadium is the only NCAA Division I stadium named after a woman. Marshall's medical school and performing-arts center also are named in her honor. She spent the last few days of her life receiving treatment and care in the Edwards Comprehensive Cancer Center she helped to create at Cabell Huntington Hospital. (*HQ*.)

The victims of the 1970 Marshall University plane crash are heroes who will never be forgotten. On the west wall of Joan C. Edwards Stadium is this impressive 17-foot-by-23-foot bronze sculpture memorializing the football players who died in the crash. The sculpture, by artist Burl Jones, cost $150,000, all of which was contributed by generous Marshall fans. (Author's.)

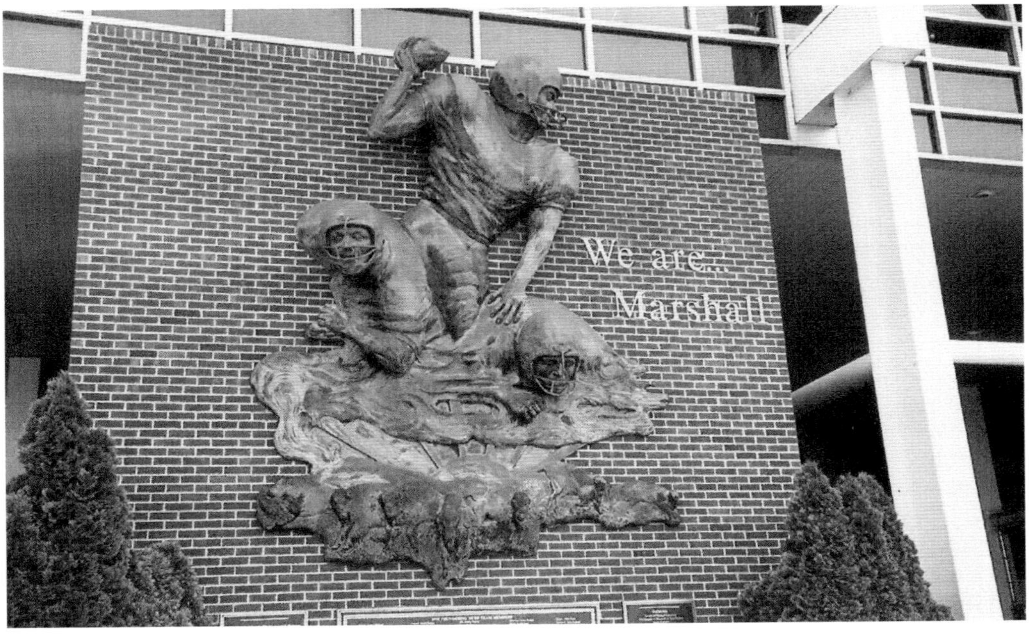

Casto, James E. *Cabell County.* Charleston, SC: Arcadia Publishing, 2001.

———. *Huntington: An Illustrated History.* Northridge, CA: Windsor Publications, 1985.

———. *Marshall University.* Charleston, SC: Arcadia Publishing, 2005.

Miller, Doris C. *Centennial History of Huntington, West Virginia, 1871–1971.* Huntington, WV: Huntington Centennial Commission, 1971.

Moffat, Charles H. *A History of the Cabell County Medical Society, 1890–1985.* Parsons, WV: McClain Printing Company, 1986

———. *Marshall University: An Institution Comes of Age, 1837–1980.* Huntington, WV: Marshall University Alumni Association, 1980.

Wallace, George Selden. *Cabell County Annals and Families.* Richmond, VA: Garrett and Massie, 1935.

———. *Huntington through Seventy-Five Years.* Huntington, WV: self-published, 1947.